AF529486

DALITS IN INDIA

Mahender Singh

4831/24, Ansari Road
Darya Ganj
New Delhi-110 002
Phone: 3260807
Fax: 3274173
E-mail: essess@del3.vsnl.net.in

DALITS IN INDIA

First Published, 2003

ISBN 81-88583-08-01

Price Rs.800/-

Published by:
Reference Press
4831/24, Ansari Road,
Darya Ganj,
New Delhi - 110002.
Phone: 3260807
Fax: 3274173
E-mail: essess@del3.vsnl.net.in

Printed in India at:
Mehra Offset Press, Delhi.

Contents

Preface (vii)

Introduction 1

PART ONE: BACKDROP

1. **Origin and Roots** 13
Pre-historic Period •Stages of Development •Dravidians •The Aryan Race •Rig Veda •The Brahmins •The Upanishads •Kalpa Sutras •The Epic Age •Social Deterioration of Vaishyas •The Shudras •Chandalas •Trade Guilds •Caste Definition •Mixed Union of the Four Castes •The Tribe, Class and Caste •Sub-Castes •Caste from Chandragupta Maurya to Harsha •Curse of Inequality

2. **Condition in Medieval Period** 51
Impact of Islam

PART TWO: ERA OF AWAKENING

3. **The Pioneers** 69

4. **Mahatma's Patronage** 83
The Conditions

5. **Babasaheb's Crusade** 153

PART THREE: PROBLEMS AND ISSUES

6. Role of Society 197

7. Role of Economy 211

8. Role of Religion 223

9. Role of Various Castes 237
Present Position •Public Activities •Servants Outside

PART FOUR: PROSPECTS

10. The Modern Era 259
Individuals as Reformers •Social Awakening and Democracy •Non-Brahmin Movement in Maharashtra •Jyotiba Phule Movement •Shahu Chhatrapati •The Revolt of Untouchables •Kala Ram Temple and Burning of Manusmriti •Simon Commission •Non-Brahmin Movement in South •Narayan Guru: Izhavas and Vaikam Satyagraha •Other Non-Brahmin Movements in South •Role of Naicker •Non-Brahmin and Dalit Movement in North India

11. The Emancipation 307
Education •Economy

12. Identity in the New Millennium 339
Delhi Seminar •World Conference against Racism •Beating of Drums •Hidden Apartheid •Discrimination •Fight in Delhi •Dalits made themselves to be Heard •India's Official Stand •Bhopal Document •Affirmative Action Programme

Bibliography 367

Index 371

Preface

Humanity has witnessed a sea-change over past several thousand years. A new social and political culture has replaced the old one. People have developed politically, socially, culturally and economically, but, an unfortunate section of our society is still forced to live under the same hostile circumstances, they are known as Dalits. These 'have nots' are supposed to be the most deprived lot in our society, at the lowest strata. Some people may hold the view that they have no soul, spirit or life in them. But in fact, Dalits are full of enthusiasm and dynamism. They have played, and are still playing a vital role in our social life.

Dalits have a whole world of their own, but this world is sill to have been discovered and explored. The community deserves a fair conduct from the nation, polity and society. We owe a great responsibility to our brothers – the Dalits to do justice to them.

Looking into the causes and searching for the roots of the problems and seeking their remedies is a great task in itself – a remarkable service, which intellectuals and scholars can offer to a fellow community. This work is an humble effort in this context.

Not that, there is dearth of literature on Dalits, as there are hundreds of books available. Still, very honestly, I feel, there is a room for a comprehensive and authentic work on Dalits. Hence, I have made an attempt to fill that vacuum. I have no faint idea that this small book would prove to be the last word on the subject. But, I hope, this modest attempt would at least create a stir among those, who think and want to act.

Here is a brief but exhaustive, research-based work, the result of a painstaking search and toilsome job, spanned over years.

Hopefully, this single book would provide the reader with a new, reassuring experience. I have tried to cover not only the larger issues and major problems but, have also made all efforts to study the whole thing in an earnest manner, virtually bringing all important topics in a few hundred pages.

It must be taken as an accomplishment, if this petty contribution of an humble fellow, proves to be able to create a sort of awareness, among academics, social activists and those, who are at the helm. If this book achieves this much, I would feel honoured and privileged, to have made a small but vital contribution.

Dalit world is a world in itself and Dalit Studies, as a branch of knowledge, is vast like an ocean. I feel great pride in making my humble offering to this treasure.

Author

Introduction

It's an irony that the structural basis of the Hindu society is caste, which is a rigid social division of the society governed by the concept of pollution, purity and professional restrictions. Caste system restricts feeding, drinking, social intercourse, imposes civil religious disabilities, privileges of marriage and choice of occupations to different sections. In a feudal agrarian system and static village economy of an organised Aryans, the non-Aryans – the Dravidians or the natives were kept and forced to live like slaves and a servile class, with minimal, occupational and spatial mobility. They formed the lowest strata of society.

For centuries the so-called village republics dominated by the caste Hindus have been the dens of superstition, ignorance, stronghold of caste hierarchy and fortified posts of slavery and subordination. There are enough references in the Hindu scriptures, Buddhist literature and Jaina canons and other religious works that prior to Aryan invasion in India, the natives or the Dravidians were the earlier settlers who lived peacefully and inherited a rich indigenous culture and civilization. In due course of time the new settlers defeated and enslaved the non-Aryans who became marginalised social groups, ignored and isolated.

No one can deny that the institution of caste, from the ancient days to the recent times, has done great harm to the society as well as low caste people. In the remotest past the original inhabitants of India were conquered by the invading Aryans. The dominating priestly class of invaders divided the society according to the occupations they followed. While the

Brahmins, the Kshatriyas and the Vaishyas enjoyed all the power, prestige and privilege, the fourth Varna or the Shudra class were either craftsmen or slave labour.

The Chandalas, the Nishadas and the Pukkasas were the most degraded and despised of the Aryan social order. They were a defeated race and not allowed to live within the walls of villages and towns. Some of them were hunters and criminals and lived in thick forests. They were more or less casteless classes.

The social segregation has made them totally crushed and cursed, discriminated and deprived class. The divine theory to govern and suppress the masses was actually invented by the Brahmins and the ruling feudal class. The feudal landlordism in league with the priestly class oppressed and dehumanised the Shudras and the Chandalas for nearly five millenniums. The Hindu doctrine of racial supremacy has remained powerful and triumphant because of division in the society. In a caste ridden society, the dominance of religion was manifest in every sphere of life and because of its influence the upper castes enjoyed special rights and privileges over the lower castes.

In the evolution of society, the Shudras or the artisans class formed their own occupational groups or organisations. We can easily trace the germs of the modern functional classes or castes related to a specific occupation since ancient times. By their social status they were always inferior to the dominating classes. Since long, the Shudras, the untouchables, which form the bulk of the total population were landless labour, servile class or engaged in their ancestral but primitive handicrafts, cottage industries, hunting, fishing and performing arts.

Buddhism was a revolt against caste system and the practice of untouchability, which certainly has been a living norm of the Bahujanas (the masses) and a social force in India from the sixth century B.C. to the twelfth century A.D. Buddhism was, in fact, one of the several heterodox movements in India, who in one way or the other were all against Brahmin supremacy, ritualized orthodoxy, animal sacrifices in Yajnas and institution of caste gradation. Vedic religion which had denied human rights to the Shudras and the Chandalas, lost its former glory and many abuses and superstitions crept into it. Buddha himself not only opposed Vedic ritualism and prevailing caste system but embraced the fallen men and women and untouchables and initiated them to his Sangha, the pious society of Buddhist monks.

Though Buddhism denounced caste system and practice of untouchability in theory, but in social life castes existed as an important factor. The Chandalas, Pukkasas and Nishadas were not fairly treated and the Brahmins, Kshatriyas and Vaishyas dominated the social life. The Chandalas were the most despised class, the Pukkasas probably plucked flowers and the Nishadas lived by hunting and fishing. Slavery existed in Buddha's time.

If we go through the pages of history carefully, we can easily find that Varna or Jati system remained intact from Vedic period to Buddha's emergence and from Maurya dynasty to the reign of Harshavardhan.

The life of a Hindu was always guided by the Dharma Shastras. A Brahmin was always supreme in the society. At every stage of social life farm labour, artisans, slaves and servants were required to attend to various duties or perform certain jobs. For an upper caste Hindu, religious laws and mundane duties were more important than deities. They took every care in eating, drinking, marrying and all sorts of social intercourse in keeping with the law of one's Varna, Jati and Ashrama. Only the masses belonging to the low castes were attracted to the principles of Buddhism, which opposed caste system. However, Buddhism flourished in a big way under the patronage of ruling chiefs. Many Brahmin scholars also joined Buddha's religion.

The Muslim invaders during 7th to 14th century A.D. destroyed the Buddhist institutions and Buddha temples throughout the country. Hindu temples were also destroyed by them. The untouchables and Shudras were the worst sufferers. They were the slaves and the captives of the new rulers and oppressed in several ways.

The Muslim rulers created sardars, rajas and noblemen from the caste Hindus and empowered them. Even the Brahmins were offered high places in the military and other establishments. There is enough historical material to prove that during the medieval Islamic period, the untouchables and the Shudras were denied human rights, equal treatment in society, liberty of occupations and right to education and worship. The Brahmins and other dominating and ruling classes enjoyed all privileges and respect in the eyes of the Muslim invaders.

In the army of Shivaji, the Kolis and Mahars fought against the Mughals, therefore the Mughal rulers harassed and suppressed them after his death. Shivaji, the founder of the Maratha empire was ill treated by the priests of Maharashtra who refused to participate in his coronation and in recognising him as a king because he belonged to a low caste. He was helpless in abolishing the caste system and untouchability, and so much so that Brahmin Peshwas played tricks and hatched conspiracies after his death to eliminate his successors.

The entire period of Muslim rule in the history is a period of suppression and isolation of the Shudras and the untouchables. Even when palaces and forts, mosques and gardens were built, the Shudra artisans and menial labour were made captives and hardly paid for their work. They were behaved as prisoners of war.

In the history of literature we see religious, social, literary and reformative movement known as Bhakti Movement during 13th to 16th century, which in conceptual and dogmatic nature opposed the Hindu orthodoxy, Vedic ritualism, caste system and practice of untouchability. Bhakti cult also preached communal harmony, brotherhood, equality and universalism. Bhakti Movement was purely a liberal and humanistic religious movement. For them rich and poor, caste Hindu or untouchable, Brahmin or Shudra were all human beings before God. The Bhakti Movement from South to North and East to West was actually led by the saint-poets, who belonged to the lower classes; either were Shudras or untouchables, i.e. weaver, cobbler, potter, gardener, tailor, carpenter, barber, agriculturist or meat seller. They were not highly educated. They were all innocent and pure religious people. But they all believed in humanity. They raised their voice against Chaturvarna, Brahmanic supremacy, social odds and superstitions. The Bhakti cult created awakening and consciousness amongst the masses. The message of the saint-poets was of love, peace, equality and above all oneness in the eyes of God. They raised the banner of revolt against caste system and ritualism which has hampered the growth of the society since ancient days. They were against superstition and ignorance. They strengthened the feelings of national and emotional integration. The colour and warmth of liberalism, equality, universalism and humanistic touch in the devotional songs of the Bhakti cult poets and saints enriched the intellectual vitality and put a powerful break on religious conversion. On popular and philosophical level their voice became the voice of the masses, a voice against caste prejudices. Chokhamela, a 13th-14th century untouchable Maharashtrian saint-poet in the Bhakti tradition opposed untouchability and caste system. Another saint poet of Maharashtra, Eknath though a Brahmin, raised his voice against social rigidities, untouchability and caste system. In Northern India, Kabir, Ravidas, Dhanna, Pipa and several other saint-poets raised the banner of revolt against caste system, priestcraft and untouchability.

Mughal emperors hardly cared for the uplift and welfare of the untouchables and the Shudras. The great Mughals are seen either fighting wars or making compromises with the Rajputs and caste Hindus.

During colonial rule of the Company the problem of the untouchables was not taken seriously. The British Government hardly cared for them till the formation of the Indian National Congress. Both Gandhi and Dr. Ambedkar did excellent work during pre-independence days in bringing awakening amongst the Dalits, in elimination of untouchability and caste system.

While Gandhi maintained that removal of social injustice and the stigma of untouchability as a religious duty of the Hindus, Dr. Ambedkar's views were more radical and reformative and he always insisted on constitutional safeguards, representation in services and political reservations. Gandhi alone was not the first to cryout against untouchability, there were several other leaders and reformers who raised their voice both against caste system and untouchability. Gandhi's passionate oratory and his practical vision was not always appreciated by the orthodox Hindus. He raised Harijan Fund and started the Harijan Sevak Sangh in Delhi-an organisation for service to the untouchables.

Gandhi virtually inherited the Congress ideology on untouchability. In 1917 it recorded a resolution urging upon the people of India the necessity, justice and righteousness of removing all disabilities imposed upon the depressed classes. Since then removal of untouchability became a much debated concern and a constructive action programme of the Congress under the leadership of Gandhi. Interestingly, he possessed unchanging belief in Varnasharama Dharma the divinely ordained division of society into four Varnas: Brahmin, Kshatriya, Vaishya and Shudra. His views were somewhat of a saintly Hindu and on certain occasions he rather tried to correct himself.

Dr. Ambedkar intended to integrate the untouchables into Indian society in the light of India's democratizing political developments and constitutional reforms. While Gandhi will be remembered for his saintly greatness who tried to change the minds of the caste Hindus to be liberal and helpful to the untouchables, Dr. Ambedkar will be known for his radical and reformative ideas on socio-economic and political rights and privileges, removal of earlier social disabilities, awakening, self-respect, creating interest in socio-political life and sharing in governance. Very truly the 20th century has been the harbinger of great humanistic ideals, social transformation and far reaching economic-cultural changes. The advent of India's independence followed by adoption of the Constitution of India is unique in the history for achievement and fulfilment of progressive social ideals and democratic norms of freedom, liberty, equality and fraternity.

The democratic system and the legal revolution, no doubt, has empowered the marginalised social groups and there is widespread social awakening in them. Though the organised and affluent political elite is using them as a potential vote bank in capturing the levers of power, a current of strong leadership seems to be emerging in these sections. While India is at the threshold of a Dalit Revolution, promising options are being suggested before the depressed sections of society in power sharing. In an emerging coalition-culture, and philosophy of governance through alliances, the governability is sure to change hands. New developments are taking shape. Efforts are being made to correct the socio-economic ills, educational and cultural deprivations and to break the barriers of social injustice and isolation. Non-Dalit reformers including Gandhi, had a very liberal but limited vision of removal of untouchability and equal status of Varnas. But, for Dalit reformers restoration of human rights and constitutional safeguards are more important as a vehicle of transformation of society. For them equality means equal but preferential social, economic, educational and political opportunity. No doubt, for over a century or so in the modern age, the Dalits, the untouchables and the unprivileged and marginalised sections of society have struggled effectively to overcome the oppressed state of dehumanisation and slavery into one of socio-economic equality, political safeguards and sharing in governance. But still they have to go a long way. Education, social unity, revolutionary spirit and right type of leadership is the need of the hour.

In American society the dark-skinned Negro population have been racially harassed and discriminated by the whites for more than 300 years. According to George E. Simpson and M. Yinger "even in America because of racial segregation and discrimination the Negros are treated somewhat of different social world. There have been race riots and a Negro is a victim instead of beneficiary of economic and social progress." In a most prosperous and highly civilized American society the members of disadvantaged groups however, take advantage and gain through American federal laws and the relative status of these groups seem to be improving.

In Indian context there seems to be no racial discrimination, but the continuance of caste discrimination still is a great handicap and main hindrance in their social uplift and economic prosperity compared to the upper castes. Superstition, ignorance, poverty and many social abuses can only be removed through education, social and economic planning. No doubt caste discrimination is worst than racial discrimination. And in the Durban conference an unsuccessful voice was raised to internationalise the caste discrimination and bring this problem in UN Agenda. Dalit NGOs presented papers and propagated against social ills and the monster of caste.

On the other hand, Kanshi Ram's role in the revival of Ambedkarism is unique in the history of Dalit movement. He built a leadership among the common masses or the Bahujan Samaj in Northern India, which has become a committed mass movement. No doubt there had been a remarkable new development in social, religious and political field when Kanshi Ram formed the Bahujan Samaj Party, to achieve and fulfil the ideals of Phule, Shahu Maharaj and Dr. Ambedkar. Alongwith Mayawati, as his right hand, Kanshi Ram attempted to bring Dalit, Muslim, and Other Backward Classes voters together in order to capture the levers of power in the Hindu heartland. Kanshi Ram has a widespread following in Uttar Pradesh, Maharashtra, Madhya Pradesh, Punjab, Uttaranchal and Delhi etc. The political base and influence of Bahujan Samaj Party under the leadership of Kanshi Ram and Mayawati no doubt has increased amongst the downtrodden people and common masses. Today, Mayawati is a dominant national figure in India's social and political life. She is not only a leader and spokesperson of the Dalits, Backward Classes and the minorities but also a prominent figure and decision maker for her own suppressed class. She has won the battle to gain power for her people, to raise the socio-economic status of Dalits and Other Backward Classes equal to the higher castes. It is a big achievement for her as leader of the masses, in an atmosphere of emerging coalition culture.

In India several other Dalit leaders are trying to reshape and strengthen the Dalit movement, and several national parties are also trying to attract them, as well as promising better deals to uplift their socio-economic and educational conditions. Our Constitution contains many provisions designed to uplift the Dalits and attempts to abolish their disabilities and provides special opportunities for advancement of education and employment. But Dalits are still grossly under-represented in judiciary and other high positions.

In the present age of science and technology, computer discipline and globalisation it is still doubtful if India will try an 'affirmative action' in its new market economy and concepts of social transformation. While Dalits are mistreated in social life, some high caste circles feel that 'merit or 'suitability' is ignored. But it is not true at all.

PART ONE

Backdrop

ONE

Origin and Roots

India is a laboratory of races, religions and various cultures. From ancient times, India has been a much attracted land for the people of foreign origin, the outsiders, more correctly the invaders. The historians, anthropologists and sociologists think that the Dravidians came to settle down on this land from some other parts of the world, even before Aryan-invasion. It is believed that the pre-Dravidian settlers were the natives, the aborigines of India. It was a savage and primitive society. According to the continental drift theory, the geographers and climatologists believe that the northern part of Australia was linked with the southern part of India, another eastern part of Africa was enjoined with the western part of India's sea coastal Maharashtra, Kutch, Gujarat and Sindh, now in Pakistan.

Pre-historic Period

The pre-historic stage of social development marks the starting point in the evolution of India's life and thought. The remotest past, as is generally held, represents the age when man lived in a state of nudity and barbarity. There was, however, a simple, democratic and dynamic state of primitive society, which marched towards a civilized living only by slow stages. The natural simplicity, the hunger-satisfying activity and indiscriminate sexuality were the modes of human relationship in primitive societies.

The story of Indian history started when Saraswati flourished or Indus Valley civilization itself emerged. The barbarism of civilization came to an end with the emergence of this civilization. But it took thousands of years and social transformation was not so easy. From barbarism to primitive age of civilization there have been struggles between man and man and between men and animals etc.

Stages of Development

The early inhabitants of India were supposed to be the Palaeolithic men, who belonged to a very primitive stage of civilization. They lived on trees and natural caverns. River side dwellings mostly under trees were preferred by them in due course of time. They ate roasted flesh of wild animals. Their life was not organised.

After Palaeolithic culture Mesolithic culture developed. The people of Mesolithic culture like their predecessors were mainly hunters. They knew hunting, fishing, ate wild fruits, nuts and forest products. According to Dr. R.C. Majumdar they knew pottery. This was great achievement. The life was still very hard and full of struggles.

The link between Mesolithic cultures and Chalcolithic is Neolithic men who covered their bodies with leaves, made rough stone implements, knew construction of huts of dry grass and leaves, produced fire and prepared food. They worshipped spirits, trees and even performed animal sacrifices. Neolithic culture of the primitive native Indians was widespread. It is not possible to form a clear picture of that primitive stage for want of proper evidence.

Chalcolithic people used arms and utensils of stone, and gradually shifted to copper and bronze. They knew agriculture, besides hunting and fishing. They became familiar with domesticated animals. They worshipped 'Mother Goddess' and developed a system of burial of dead.

Dravidians

Social scientists believe that Dravidians formed another stage of social development in the remotest past. In ancient India they developed their own civilization and culture which was more advanced than Palaeolithic, Mesolithic and Neolithic people.

They knew farming and domesticated animals. They were the earliest people to build dams across rivers for irrigation. They constructed houses and fortifications. There is a possibility of village republic system, mainly governed by primitive petty chiefs as still found in tribal people. It was probably a matriarchial society. Under the Dravidian tradition mother with their children formed the nucleus of a settled and developed society. The caste system had not developed till then. The male members often went away from their huts either for hunting or fishing and mother kept children and thus occupied an important social status. A sort of tribalism was present in the Dravidian people and people grouped under small groups each possessing its own totemism. Animals, trees and birds etc., occupied an important place in totemism which grew as a religion of the ancient Dravidian and Chalcolithic people.

Even before Aryan settlers Dravidians came to this land. The Indo-Greeks, Sakas, Scythians, Parthians, Pallavas, Kushanas, Huns, Christians, Jews, Zoroastrians, Muslims, Mughals and many small groups of tribes and races from time to time came in waves and settled down in this vast Indian subcontinent from the dawn of human civilization.

A continuous synthesis is a part of our nation. At the very beginning the assimilation of the Aryan and Dravidian culture laid the very basis of Hindu civilization.

The Dravidians were an organised race and first attacked the aboriginals of India. They were basically nomads and wanted a settled life. The defeated race of natives or aboriginals joined the social life of Dravidians and got mixed up in due course of time. But those who fled away in the thick-inaccessible forests and mountain areas remained aloof for centuries from the Dravidians, leading uncivilized and barbarous life. The pre-Aryan Dravidians were materially prosperous which is proved by Indus civilization.

According to historian Stanley Wolpert the Dravidians reached a higher stage of development. They had a developed civilization as compared to the other races.

The Aryans have given various names to the natives. But the monumental excavations of Harappa and Mohen jo-daro have emphatically reversed the relative cultural status of India's Aryan conquerors and her pre-Aryan peoples. The pre-Aryan 'Dasas' or 'slaves' whose darker skin differentiated them from 'Aryan colour' were suddenly revealed as more advanced sophisticated and technologically pre-conscious than the semibarbaric hoard of Aryan invaders from the West, whose only civilized advantage seem to have been some superior weaponry and the use of harnessed horses.

Thus India's aborigines, the natives or the mixed race of the Dravidians have reached a high stage of development. In the words of Dr. Ambedkar, "the necessary blood-relationship, which occurred among the people of one race with another helped much in obliterating the distinctions between the natives and the Dravidians.

It seems all aborigines and natives were mixed up with the Dravidians in due course of time. The Indus Valley civilization emerged and flourished much before Aryans settled in India. It was totally non-Aryan civilization.

The Aryan Race

The Aryan race entered in India in groups. Gradually the Aryans had won over the natives, the Dravidians. In the process of diffusion, centuries old confrontation and contact with the indigenous people, the Aryan society underwent important changes, in their way of life, social thinking and culture. They were interested in permanent dwellings and establishment of tribalist socio-political system. With the passage of time the Varna system, which was initially social gradation, was on its way towards crystalisation. In support of the above view we may quote Romila Thapar's conclusion that "for some points of view the coming of the Aryans was a backward step, since the Harappan culture had been far more advanced than that of the Aryans who were as yet pre-urban."

It is a fact as Jagjivan Ram says that "when the Aryans

entered in India, they had outgrown the stage of tribal endogamy. Among them were only three divisions conforming to the primitive functional divisions of priest, warrior and artisan. Varna in this Trivarnic society indicated a particular social function and a distinct level of culture and way of life."

The clashes and conflicts between the Aryans and the Dravidians and aboriginals accentuated not only the social and cultural but even the occupational and functional division. In order to avoid large scale intermixing of the natives amongst the invading race of Aryans, a fourth caste, the Shudras came into being when they were conquered and enslaved and later employed by the organised society of the Aryans, as a forced labour.

The conquered aborigines, or the Broken-men, were deprived of all claim for a place in the divinely ordained social order and on the community land. They were forced to live outside the village, and occupations regarded low and contemptible were assigned to them. They were the ancestors of the untouchables (now a distinct number of castes) and were known as the Asprashyas or the Panchamas. They were attached to the Hindu society and yet did not belong to it, having been assigned no place in the social hierarchy of caste in the Chaturvarna.

In the process of conquest and compromise settlement and customs changed. Some native tribes who easily submitted to the Aryans and accepted their faith and belief, rituals and cultural pattern were graded higher and those who did not submit and accept their faith were tortured and kept as untouchables. Thus, the Trivarnic society became Chaturvarnic. It was, however, "a deliberate attempt to introduce gradations in rank according to the place of origin. These lower ranked people, or the Shudras "were apparently a conquered race.

The idea of caste struck its roots deeply into Hindu social life. For Hindus the caste became a social and political package and for the Shudras and untouchables it became a curse, a licence of slavery and serfdom.

In the words of Iyer: "Few topics within the sphere of Indian sociology present more difficulties than those connected with the origin and evolution of caste. Scholars have devoted considerable time to the research and study of the subject, and have come to no conclusions. Various theories have been propounded by scholars. They can be roughly divided into two schools. The older school based its arguments on the sacred literature of the Hindus, and arrived at different conclusions; but all agree in ascribing to caste extreme antiquity, and regard the system as the artificial product of the Brahminic hierarchy. Of late, fresh light has been thrown on the subject by the study on inscriptions, and by the patient investigations of Buddhist and Jain literature, the authors of which were directly opposed to the Brahmins, and gave quite a different account of early society. And there is the new school of theorists `who postdate of the origin of caste to comparatively modern late times by looking for its origin in the nature of the elements composing the early Indian society and for its development in the working of social forces on these lines.' Thus, none of the theories commands universal approval. Further, information on the early Hindu society is still meagre, and the discovery of any new fact will lead to the revision of the best of the theories." It was the Brahminic or priestly class which created the Indian caste system (Varna System).

In the present social set up the eradication of caste system is very much desirable in the best interest of democratic traditions and national unity. But it is not so an easy task.

Rig Veda

The earliest work which the Aryans left to posterity is the Rig Veda. Aryan people believed in theistic and deterministic social system. In Aryan society family formed the basic unit. Monogamy was the fashion. The Rishies (the teachers) were all family men. Gradually the Aryans got domination over the aboriginals and the indigenous people, and Aryan culture underwent major changes. The pre-natives (Shudras) seems to be a conquered race. The defeated Dasyus became slaves (Dasas) who in the beginning did not accept Vedic authority. The word 'Shudra' was actually used for an inferior or lower race, Kshudra. Whosoever transgressed the rules of Varna system was a rebel and an outcaste; and finally crushed.

"Most of the tribal people, believed in the institution of social collectivity. The Mina could not withstand the onslaught of domination by the aggressive Aryans." Dravidians compromised with them. Dasyus. However, fought with Aryans, and carried on an uneasing warfare against them."

According to Iyer: "The earliest reference to caste is found in the Rig Veda, in which mention is made of four castes which originate from Brahma, the Supreme Being. The Brahmin came from his mouth, the Kshatriya from his arm, the Vaishya from his thighs and the Shudras from his feet." This statement is somewhat allegorical. It means that the Brahmins are the instructors of mankind, the Kshatriyas are the warriors, and the Vaishyas and Shudras are the agriculturists and servants respectively. Similar references to the origin of caste are found in Satapatha Brahmana (II-4-11), the Taittiriya Brahmana (III-12-9), Vajasaneya Samhita, and the Atharva Veda. But from an examination of the legends contained in the Brahmanas, it is seen that the accounts vary.

From the beginning of the Vedic period to the middle of the Sutras or Buddhist period, the fourfold division represented only classes, and this can be proved by the statements in the Srauta-Sutra of Drahyana and the Puranas regarding the functions of priests and warriors.

The Puṛusha Sukta of the Rig Veda divides the entire society of Aryans and non-Aryans into four classes, known as Varnas: The Brahmin, the Kshatriya, the Vaishya and the Shudra created from Prajapati's mouth, arms, thighs and feet respectively. Rig Veda says: "Brahmin was his mouth, Rajanya was made from his arm. Vaishya his thighs and Shudra sprang from his feet." (X. 9,12).

Brahmins or priests were just like Bureaucrats of today.

They were virtually powerful. The Kshatriyas as/or warriors were the military personnel, the rulers. Vaishyas were merchants and cultivators, while the Shudras were menials and labours. Below Shudras were certain primitives and criminal tribes defeated as well as degraded Brokenmen.

"The Brahminic literature is a proof that the priestly class or the Brahmins were the intellectual and spiritual leaders. It was believed that learning and spiritual knowledge were esoteric virtues and their cultivation needed exclusive attention. Manual labour, therefore, became taboo for the Brahmins. It also became taboo for the Kshatriyas, with whom the Brahmins shared power and who were their rivals and equals. The aristocratic order of the Kshatriyas could not be sustained by mere force. So, the Brahmins framed elaborate rules laying down not only the status and grade of the various social and cultural groups but also prescribing distinct rituals and ceremonies for each." This exercise was only to control and rule over the Shudras.

Max Muller states: "The three occupations of the Aryans in India were fighting, cultivating the soil and worshipping the gods. Those who fought the battles of the people would naturally acquire influence and rank and their leaders appear in the Veda as Rajas or kings. Those who did not share in the fighting would occupy a more humble position and they were called Vish, Vaishya or householders and would no doubt have to contribute towards the maintenance of the armies." Brahmins were given supremacy in caste hierarchy.

In the ninth book of the Rig Veda, there is famous passage referring to the various crafts. It is said that the organisation of castes was fully developed at the period of Brahmanas, and is codified in the laws of Manu. The four castes were fully established. The rites and duties of the Brahmins were in complete accord with modern descriptions, and necessary purity of the race was fully inculcated. The caste was ignored by the persistent neglect of initiation.

Undoubtedly, the germs of abhorrent practice of

untouchability and slavery oriented caste system are alive since Rig Vedic period. "The orthodox Hindu, on the other hand, considers the caste system to be a divine institution, and that there have existed since the beginning four distinct orders of men, Brahmin or priest, Rajanya, Kshatriya or noble, Vaishya or tiller of the soil, and Shudra or the servile class. There is a great difference between the first three and the last. The former are said to possess light colour, and the Dasyus dark colour. It is also said that before the end of the Rig Vedic period, a belief in the divine origin of the four orders of men was firmly established, but there are no references to the sub-division of these orders." "In the next period, the period of the Yajur Veda and the Brahmanas, are found the division of the Aryan society into four classes with distinct functions. The term denotes a social order, independently of any actual difference of colour, and we hear of the mixed Varnas, the offspring of parents belonging to distant orders." Descent is the chief factor, though not the sole one. Tribal connection, religion, and occupation combine with descent to consolidate the social groups and keep them apart. "Throughout the Vedas," says Blunt, "there is not a single reference to connubial or commensal restrictions to any of the characteristics of the modern Hindu social system."

Buddha attacked practice of untouchability and caste system. This will be discussed in the next chapter in detail. He said individual's merit may be taken into consideration and not the caste. For him a learned Brahmin and Sramana are of the equal status.

In the Jatakas, a collection of folktales, there is an account of Hindu society in early Buddhist times. The colour distinction so prominent in the Vedas has faded into the background, though its memory survives in the word Varna, used for the social classes, namely, Kshatriya, Brahmin, Vaishya and Shudra. Here the Kshatriya leads the list. The lords spiritual have not assumed the pride of place at the expense of the lords temporal. The Brahmin is held in status inferior to the Kshatriya nobility. The Varnas have not yet developed to make them close corporations. Vaishyas and Shudras rise to the rank of Kshatriya. Anybody can become a Brahmin by becoming a priest. There is no endogamous restriction; a Brahmin marries a Kshatriya widow, and according to one Jataka, Buddha himself, a Shakya Kshatriya, married a Koli girl. Marriage within the clan is considered preferable to marriage outside it. But social prejudice and social convention stand in the way of the latter. Below the Varnas there are Hina Jatyo, low tribes, of barbers, potters or weavers-for example, a remnant of the Dasyu tribes on the outskirts of civilization. The lowest of all are the Chandalas and other outcaste tribes."

In the Vedic period and according to Manu, Vaishyas were basically herdsmen and after settling took to agriculture: During the Vedic period, Visha (a house or district) signified people in general, and its adjective Vaishya was afterwards applied to a householder. The Vishas or clans afterwards became the 'Vaishyas', the third classical caste. Before they entered India, the Aryans were pastoral people, their domestic animals being the horse, the cow and, perhaps, the sheep and the goat. The horse and the cow were specially venerated, and they were the chief means of transport. The Vaishyas must, therefore, have been herdsmen and shepherds who entered India, took to agriculture and settled down to the practice of cultivation. The word Vaishya signifies a man who occupies the soil, a cultivator or a merchant. According to Manu, God ordained them to tend cattle, give alms, offer sacrifice, to study, to cultivate, to trade, and learn the Vedas."

The institution of caste created by Rig Veda is exclusively Indian phenomenon. It was just to maintain the gradation in Hindu society, to broaden the scope of enslavement and serfdom. It was purely an Aryan concept, nowhere found in the world. Brahmanas have argued that the primary object of the caste system was to protect and maintain purity of blood.

In the Varna system a calculated conspiracy was made to divide the society. "The persons who possessed knowledge of the sacred lore, officiated in religious ceremonies and received gifts, were called Brahmins; those who fought, owned land and wielded political power were classed as Kshatriya, the general mass of the people-the traders, the agriculturists, the craftsmen were grouped under the term Vaishya, and the persons, reserved for menial services were called Shudras, who generally belonged to the vanquished people."

In the beginning this was mainly an occupational division, like trade guilds. But this division of class or labour guilds turned into rigid caste in due course of time.

Right from the pre-RigVedic age to the epic period the development of India's social thought and social condition, the Brahminism continued to be a dominating force. The Brahmanas, the Sutras, the Puranas, all played the role of degrading and suppressing the self-employed class of artisans and agriculturists. The religious revivalism helped the Brahminism to regain its power and position for nearly five thousand years.

The Rajnyas or the ruling class fully supported the Varna system and the percepts of Hindu Dharma had encouraged priestcraft to divide the society with the sword of scriptures.

The unity and awakening in the Shudras was crushed. Since Vedic age the central purpose of all Brahmanical literature have been to keep supremacy of Brahmins over the sub-merged sections of society, the defeated non-Aryans, the artisans and the untouchables. This viewpoint can be examined by going through the available sources.

The Brahmins

The Brahmanas deal with the ritualistic aspect of Vedic social life. They have, combined Vedic philosophy with rituals and sacrifices. Brahmanas accepted the divine authority of the Vedas for the guidance of social behaviour. The sacrifice was performed for gaining earthly profits and a prosperous life. The increasing dominance of the idea of sacrifices gave rise to the office of priesthood. The flexible class system gave way to rigidity of the caste system. Varnas came to be distinguished from each other.

In the age of Brahmanas there was emphasis on sacrifice, supremacy of the priest, the eternity of the Veda and observance of Varnashrama Dharma. The Varna system became more and more rigid. Shudras could not revolt against this Vedic-Brahminic theory of social injustice, and were crushed for raising any voice. The Rig Vedic division into the Aryan and non-Aryan (Dasa) was replaced by that of Daivya (godly) and Asurya (of Demons). The Brahmin was supreme and represented divine Varna, while the Shudra was the lowest in the social order and thus Asur. The Brahmins were 'veritable gods on earth.' The Shudras were inauspicious, condemned persons and 'were not to be seen' what to talk of 'touch.'

The Brahmin was always higher than Kshatriya and Vaishya, while a Shudra was the servant and meant to serve all others, to be removed, beaten, tortured and even killed. In order to maintain the continuity of religious tradition and the supremacy of Brahmins, the caste system or the Varna Vyavastha was engineered as divine authority." We see the roots of forced labour and slavery in this age, which had continued till today.

The Upanishads

The Aranyakas and the Upanishads are the concluding parts of the Brahmanas.

The hymns are the creations of poets, the Brahmanas are the works of the priests and Upanishads are the results of meditations of the philosophers. These are the strong philosophical protests against the rigid social thinking and religious performances of Brahmanas.

The Upanishads belong to the revealed literature (Sruti) and provide means for spiritual freedom. The Upanishads uphold the Varnashrama as an essential part of Karma doctrine. Man is required to perform his duties and serve the society. The duties depend on man's individual capacities, divided into four Varnas.

The Upanishads, however, could not entirely break the bonds of the caste system, but opened the gates of spirituality without any distinction of caste and sex. The Upanishads could not revolt against oppressive features of the priestly class which encouraged sacrifices and ritualism and maintained serious distinctions between man and man and Varna system.

The sages of Upanishads emphasized that the ascetic aspect of human life was important than society.

The age of Upanishads failed to register any protest against growing sacrifices, the Vedic rituals and orthodoxy. The priesthood ruined the moral values in society. The Varna system created inequality and the practice of untouchability. Though the Upanishadic concepts of Atman and Brahma (Soul and God) abolished distinctions between man and man spiritually and morally, but practically they could not eradicate inequalities and oppressive features in life.

In fact, Upanishadic age witnessed more and more sacrifices, priesthood, inequality, caste system, exploitation of Shudras and torture of lower castes.

Kalpa Sutras

The Kalpa Sutras basically deal with Vedic sacrifice, household ceremonies and social laws. Literally, Kalpa means ritual. Therefore there was much ritualism. They provide a good account of early social life in India. The complete Kalpa Sutras comprise of the Srauta Sutras which deal with sacrifices known as Srautayajanas. The Grihya Sutras conduct household ceremonies like marriages and Upanayana and Dharma Sutras deal with rights and duties of different classes in society.

In the age of Sutras the social life was the same as in the Vedic period. The first three castes were allowed to perform Upanayana, whereas the Shudras were denied the right to sacred thread ceremony. (Surprisingly, this practice has continued till today). This created two divisions the Dvijas or the 'Aryans' and Advijas or the non-Aryans. In the age of Kalpa Sutras the caste system became even more rigid. There was great emphasis on the purity of the Varnas. It was the revival of Brahminical traditions. The Shudras became a distinct group of oppressed and suppressed class without any voice of revolt. In the social process, the Brahmin, Kshatriya and the Vaishya, known as Dvijas became powerful and dominating class, who were allowed to have Upanavana, the tudy of Vedas, status in the society and above all social-political power in hand.

The Smritis recognised monarchy. A divine origin was attributed to the king. The clever class of Brahmins took powers from the king to define Dharma in order to supress and enslave the Shudras.

Some Shudras were however allowed to perform small domestic Yajnas and Shraddha, but recitation of Vedic Mantras by them was strictly denied. A Shudra girl was also allowed to marry a Dvij without chanting Mantras. The Shudras mere neglected in social and cultural function, organised by the Brahmins, which were more religious and ritualistic. Shudras were only allowed to watch.

In social prestige and power sharing Kshatriyas were very close to the Brahmins. The Shudras suffered many disabilities, which continued for centuries. The population of Shudras was scattered over in various castes and sub-castes with gradations and they could never unite and revolt against the Brahminical order. They were also socially-culturally deprived and exploited economically.

In the age of Sutras the legal institutions were all based on Dharma Shastras, which were definitely against Shudras. The power of legislation and codification was in the hands of the Brahmins. The dominating priestly class, who fully supported the Vedas. They enjoyed almost divinely status in society. Without Upanayana, which was no more than an oppressive signal an individual of low caste was doomed to social degradation, ignorance and poverty. This was the actual state of the Shudras. The egalitarian social system became a myth.

In the Karma theory, the doctrine of transmigration is an essential part which has close relation with Varna social system.

The soul transmigrates according to the acts of an individual. Therefore it gets the birth, for which it deserves. This was totally a misconception to prove that Shudras in their previous birth have not done good acts and have deviated from Dharma. Because of their past sins they have a wretched life in the present times. The Dharma Sutras state explicitly that good acts lead to higher birth and evil deeds to a lower one.

There was in fact no social awakening in this age among the Shudras, the oppressed, Dalit people.

The Epic Age

The Ramayana and Mahabharata are the two great epics of the Hindu society. They preach supremacy of Brahminism and divinely order. The epics seem to have imposed the Varna system as originated by the gods themselves. The Kshatriyas are also placed in high position. The theory of Karma with transmigration of soul is combined with Varna Vyavastha as the central doctrine of the epics. The author of the epics declare that various functions and duties of the Varnas are allotted to men in accordance with their nature which they inherit from their past. By doing service and Bhakti to the gods they can attain Moksha.

The Ramayana is a complete work which believes in divine government and the entire universe is governed by God's dispensation. All castes are supposed to perform their duties, which have been assigned to their Karmas of the past birth. The Ramayana has clearly accepted the authority of the Varnashram Marina. The Mahabharata also accepts the authority of the divine social order, Karma and transmigration. It believes that a man is born in high or low caste because of his Karma in the previous birth. The central theme, which is identical with Gita is that one should perform his duties without caring for the reward (Nishkam Karma). Mahabharata has the complete faith in the divine origin of Varna Vyavastha. It resembles almost with the doctrine of Purusha Sukta of Rig Veda.

Surprisingly, the epics deny the right of Upanavana of Shudras, and re-establish the Brahmin supremacy which was challenged by the Upanishads. Epics thus revive the hold of priests on Shudras, who were treated as Asuras, Demons, Raskhasas, Chandalas etc.

Social Deterioration of Vaishyas

In the Buddhist period, as Dr. Dutt says, "Vaishyas and Shudras were not to be found as pure castes, nor did they represent groups anywhere. There is no mention anywhere of a member of any particular professional caste belonging to either Dasya Varna or Shudra Varna. The real distinction existed only during the Vedic period. Even during the early period of the Brahmanas, the distinction had almost vanished, and in later periods still more so. It was so in practice as well. In the early Buddhist period mention is made of Gahapat or Grahpati, as a landowning and mercantile class which ranked below Kshatriyas and Brahmins. The word is synonymous with Kudumbika (householder) living in towns and villages. Gradually the Vaishyas underwent a kind of social degradation. The reasons were:

1. Rapid increase in the number of Kshatriyas, coupled with the expansion of the Aryan domination, and the advance from tribalism towards feudalism and oligarchy;
2. The advancement and separation of the sacerdotal class from the common people, and their domination over them. The Vaishyas, according to Taittiriya Samhita, lived only to be exploited by the Brahmins and Kshatriyas. Numerous passages attest to their inferiority to the first two twice-born classes;
3. The abundant availability of slave labour in farming, pasturing and industrial arts, and the close association with certain branches of industry, together with a growing contempt for manual labour which brought the industries themselves low in the estimation of the

higher classes. The separation of Rathakaras (chariot makers), Takshan (carpenters) and Kamaras (workers in brass) from the Vaishya community is an instance in point. Thus the artisan classes were separated from the Vaishyas, among whom there were merchants and farmers. At the outset there was no distinction, and gradually a Vaishya farmer was looked upon as inferior in status to a Vaishya merchant. In the Jataka literature, it is said that merchants alone formed what might be called the Vaishya community, while others sank to the status of Shudras;

4. During the Vedic period all professions and industries were in the hands of the Aryans. But after the intermingling of the Aryan with non-Aryan races the industrial and economic life of the people became very much changed. A large number of occupations fell to the lot of lower classes;
5. When the colour bar and purity of blood came to be considered, the cultural and the ruling classes adopted a policy of segregation and refrained from intermarriage and interdining with the non-Aryan peoples. The rank and file of the Vaishyas, owing to their number and association with the Shudras in various fields of activity, received a large admixture of non-Aryan blood. This also resulted in a lowering of the status of the Vaishyas.27

The Shudras

According to Senart and Wilson the Shudras were the aboriginals, conquered by the Aryans; and forced to live as a servile class. They were also not allowed to mix up with the Aryan society. They picked up arts, crafts and various type of cottage industries.

Senart points out that the division of the four castes appearing in the post-Vedic literature does not continue on the same lines. There were two groups, one composed of the three higher castes, the other of the Shudras, or the lowest. The higher caste constituted the fraternity to which admission was obtained only by the religious ceremony of initiation and investment of the sacred thread. The Shudras were excluded, and could take no part in sacrifice. The punishment for the commission of grave offence by a Brahmin was degradation to a Shudra or outcaste. Dr. Wilson remarks: "They were the original inhabitants of the land, who confirmed to the Brahminic rules, and received certain privileges. They constituted the fourth caste, with the designation of Shudra. Manu has ordained that if Shudra are unable to maintain their families they might subsist by handicrafts. The Shudras were ordained not to wear the sacred thread. They were regarded as a servile class whose duty it was to minister to the twice-born."

It seems right from the Brahmanas to the Epic age, the Shudra's voice was suppressed. They were not allowed access to scriptures and knowledge. Even Shudra ascetics and truth seekers were brutally liquidated. There were long wars between the Aryan race and the Shudra Kings.

Chandalas

The Chandalas were the most despised of the Hindu society. They were not allowed to live within the walls of the town. The Pukkasas like Chandalas were also despised people. They were excluded from the category of castes. In the Dharma Shastras the occupation of a Chandala is to carry the dead bodies of men who have no relations or friends, and to execute criminals. In the fivefold division of society in the Madhyadesa (Middle country), Brahmin, Kshatriya, Vaishya, Shudra and Nishada are found. In the Buddhist Jataka literature also, the social divisions are on similar lines. The authors of Dharma Shastras, relying on the Vedic texts as authority, excluded them from the fourfold division. The fifth caste was of rejected souls, and the Nishadas, Chandalas and Pukkasas were under casteless classes (Manu 4 et. seq).

But in the later Sanskrit works like Raj Tarangiiai by Kalhan, Chandalas have been placed as a martial or warrior race. Here the word Chand or Prarhand is used to depict one who is brave.

Trade Guilds

During the Vedic period the number of professional classes went on steadily increasing, and their organization bore a close analogy to the medieval guilds of Europe. The former were influential corporations in Buddhist times. Even Manu, Yagnavalkya, Narada and other law-givers opined that they became dangerously powerful. They were the financers of the age, and even kings were their debtors. The many privileges, which they enjoyed were granted in return for their assistance in money. "They had their own family inheritance and apprentice laws with which the king could not interfere. They tried their own law suits, and could be taxed only with their approval. It is even laid down that the kings must approve of whatever the guilds do for other people, whether it be kind or cruel. Each guild was ruled by a president (Sreshti) and a council of four members, who used to decide both domestic and business disputes. There was also a merchant who exercised his authority over all the guilds in a particular city and in its neighbourhood." He was called Mahasreshti. Disobedience to the guild's orders was punished with fine or even expulsion. Wrong done by one member of a guild to another was treated as a wrong done to the whole community, and awarded with severe punishment. A common fund was also raised for religious offerings, and also for promoting the common interests of the guild.

A guild is not a caste. There is no community of one blood. Membership ceases on abandoning the trade or industry common to the guild. The caste is a homogeneous community, and membership is retained even when the occupation is given up. The functional castes have many things in common with the guilds. It is primary rule among them that a member cannot deprive another of his privileges. So strong is the proprietory sense that the recognized rights of certain families are sometimes sold like a goodwill, mortgaged and even given in dowry. An encroachment on another man's rights is severely dealt with, even to outcasting in some places. In fact, encroachment of any kind was vehemently resisted.

It is in these guilds that Dahlman and other modern writers find the germs of modern functional castes. These powerful and well organized corporation must have exercised a considerable influence on the development of the Hindu social system. A survival of it is found at present in Bombay and Baroda. Guilds of weavers (Tantushalas) during Mahavira and Buddha's period consisted of richest persons. Now weavers are paupers and exploited Dalits.

Caste Definition

The word 'caste', Dr. Wilson states, is not of Indian origin, but is derived from the Portuguese 'casta' signifying race, mould or quality. The Indian word for caste is Jat or Jati which has the original meaning of birth or production of a child, and hence denotes good birth or lineage, respectability and rank. Jatha means well born. Thus Jat or Jati now signifies a caste as every Hindu is born into a caste, and his caste determines his social position throughout life.

The two main ideas denoted by a caste are a community or persons following a common occupation and a community whose members marry only among themselves. A third distinctive feature is that the members of a caste do not as a rule eat with outsiders with the exception of other Hindu castes of a much higher social position than their own.

The coming of foreign races in India created many racial, political and social problems in the earliest period of history. The problem of Varna system, formerly a mere division of labour became a tool of oppression and suppression in the hands of the dominating races, very similar to Plato's idea of justice, with each man doing his proper duty in the state.

Varnashrama Dharma is a conceptual division of society into four categories according to the Hindu classics chiefly the Vedas and Dhanna Shastras. Notwithstanding the later innovations in face of existential realities Varnashrama Dharma represented the harmonious inter-relationship of the four Varnas or social order. The Brahmin was invested with spiritual and instructional duties; the Kshatriya was the guardian of temporal powers; the Vaishya was occupied with commercial pursuits; and the Shudra was meant to provide menial services to the first three Varnas. In theory, the Hindu classics ensured a harmonious working of the society by prescribing the right and obligations of each of the Varnas.

It seems Dr. Wilson's opinion is somewhat soft to the early Aryans.

In the opinion of Nehru caste was probably neither Aryan nor Dravidian. "It was an attempt at the social organisation of different races, a rationalisation of the facts as they existed at the time. It brought degradation in its train afterwards, and it is still a burden and a curse, caste began with a hard and fast division between Aryans and non-Aryans, the latter again being divided into the Dravidian races and the aboriginal tribes."

The word caste had been variously defined, and none of the definitions is satisfactory. These are given below:-

1. Caste is defined "as endogamous group or a collection of such groups bearing a common name, and having the same traditional occupation, claiming a common descent from the same source, and commonly regarded as forming a single homogeneous community." (Sir E.A. Gait)
2. Sir Herbert Risley defines caste, "as a collection of families bearing a common name, claiming a common descent from a mythical ancestor, human or divine, professing to follow the same hereditary calling, and (are) regarded by those who are competent to give an opinion and forming a single homogeneous

community. The name is always associated with a specific occupation;

3. Emile Senart has a more comprehensive definition. Caste, according to him, "is a close corporation, exclusive and in theory at any rate, rigorously hereditary; equipped with certain traditional and independent organizations including a chief and council; meeting on occasion in assemblies; bound together by a common occupation; observing certain usages which relate more particularly to marriage, to food and to questions of occasional pollution; and ruling its members by the exercise of jurisdictions, the extent of which varies, but which succeeds, by the sanction of certain penalties and above all, by the power of final or revocable exclusion from the group, in making the authority of the community effectively felt."

The test of caste is not intermarriage and interdining, but defilement by eating and touching what is unclean. On this consideration, Sutras show only the beginning of that formal theory of defilement which results in a pure man of the upper class being defiled by the shadow of an impure man and in the taboo of all contact with the impure. "According to Gautama (Dharrna Sutra XVII, 1), a Brahmin may not eat food given by any of the reborn who are the worthy members of his caste, and in need of food to support his life. He may take food and other things even from a Shudra. Food forbidden is that defiled by hair or insects falling into it, and that touched by a woman in her menses, by a black bird (crow) or by its foot or given by an outcaste, a woman of bad character, a person accused, an hermaphrodite, a police officer (Dandika), a carpenter, a miser, a jailor, a physician, a man who hunts without using a bow, i.e., a non-snarer of animals, a man who eats refuse or the food of a multitude, of an enemy," The list contains the taboo of food offered disrespectfully and of certain animals. "Apastamba (Dharma Sutra, 1,6.28. II) allows the acceptance of gifts, including a house from the low caste (Ultra), though like the later law books this code stages that a priest may not eat in the house of any one of the three orders (Varnas) below him, but he may eat the food of any caste except that of the Shudras, and eat even their food in times of distress. Forbidden by him is the food of an artisan, of people who let houses or lands, a spy, an unauthorised priest (a Buddhist), besides that of a surgeon, usurer and others. Caste is Varna or Jati, colour and kin, the former embracing the latter as a social including clans and families."

Amongst the various theories on caste which have been formulated by scholars, the most important are given below:-

1. According to Sir Denzil Ibbetson, occupation is the chief basis of the division of caste. Every separate occupation has produced a distinct caste, the status of which depends now either partially or entirely on its occupation. The fact that there may be several castes pursuing the same occupation, as agriculture or weaving, does not invalidate this any way. If a caste changes its occupation, it may gradually change its status in a corresponding degree. Caste sometimes tends to rise or fall in social position with the acquisition of land or other forms of wealth or dignity. Strictly speaking, a man inherits the social position of the caste in which he is born and retains it through life without the power of altering it. It is now the caste as a whole, or at least one of its important sections or sub-castes, which rises or falls in social position, and the process may extent over generations or centuries. This theory, though applicable to a large number of castes, does not cover the whole ground.

2. Caste, according to Nesfield, is used to designate common occupation. It is the centre round which caste has grown up, and its social gradation corresponds precisely to the different periods of civilization during which their traditional occupation originated. The primitive tribes inhabiting the hills pursue the occupation of hunting, and the pursuit of wild animals was the earliest stage in the

development of human industry, next in order comes fishing castes fishing being considered superior to hunting because the water is a more sacred element than land among the Hindus. There is less apparent cruelty in capturing fish than in the slaughtering of animals. Above these come the pastoral castes. Above the pastoral castes are the agricultural castes and the various tribes included in them. Following the order in which these occupations are adopted during the progress of civilization, the others are mentioned. Above them are various occupational castes. The higher group includes those castes whose occupations were coeval with the age of metallurgy, those who work in stone, wood, metal, and make ornaments. At the top of the system stands the Kshatriyas, or the warrior class, whose duty it is to protect all the lower castes, and the Brahmin who is their priest, spiritual guide.

lyer writes further: The gradation of society given above is in the scientific order of precedence, and it is likely that these divisions arose from the divisions of the principal social organisations of India in the village community.

According to this theory, the caste system springs from the regular evolution of social life, starting, from the lowest level and following in its slow progression. This theory cannot be reconciled with the relatively late date to which Nesfield refers to the constitution of society. He also affirms that the Brahmin was the first born of castes, the model upon which all the other castes were subsequently formed, extending gradually from king or warrior to the tribes practising hunting and fishing whose rank is no higher than that of a savage. The Brahmins who formed themselves into the Levite guild set an example which was followed by others. It was he who invented for himself, the rule prohibiting marriage with a woman of another caste. There is a curious contradiction of later passages where he derives the regulation of marriage from the traditional usages of the tribe. The Vaishyas, according to him and the Shudras in particular, have never been anything except a kind of rubric intended to embrace a multitude of heterogeneous elements.

Ibbetson's thesis is less complete and less forced than that of Nesfield, but is based on the same data. He summarise the various stages which are to be discerned in the history of caste:

(i) "The organization of the tribe common to all primitive societies; (ii) the guilds founded on heredity of occupation; (iii) the exaltation peculiar to Indian of sacerdotal function; (iv) the exaltation of Levitical blood by the importance attributed to heredity; (v) the consolidation of the principle, by the elaboration of a series of entirely artificial laws derived from Hindu beliefs, regulating marriage and fixing the limits within which it may be concentrated, declaring certain occupations and foods to be impure, and determining the conditions and extent to the community of occupation and the constitution of the tribe: The status of the Brahmin is reversed. They are represented as contributing to the spontaneous organization of the country. The real weakness of the system consists in the inordinate importance attributed to community of occupation. If this really constituted the primitive bond of castes, the latter would have shown less tendency to split up and disintegrate.

3. It is in race that Risley unlike Nesfield, seeks the SOUI of caste. He lays stress on the difference of colour between the dark Dravidian or non-Aryan races and their conquerors, the fair skinned Aryans. The conquerors take the daughters of the land as concubines, but give their own daughters in marriage only among themselves. Race is substituted as the generating principle. The nasal index is the formula for the proportions of the nose, and is the most unerring criterion of race. There seems reason to suppose that the contact of the Aryans with the indigenous people of India is mainly responsible for the growth of the caste system, and the main racial divisions may perhaps even be recognized, though their basis has to a great extent vanished. But when we come to individual castes and sub-castes, the scrutiny of their origin is based more on certain Puranic stories than on the supposed racial traits. Risley bases

his argument upon the use of the word Varna and the conquered races, the white and the black, as the germ of distinction. The endogamous laws are the foundation of the system. He arrives indirectly at the general acceptance of the orthodox Brahminic system, and believes in the dominance gradually acquired by the priesthood. The theory of mixed castes is, according to him, an invaluable proof of crossbreeding. For Nesfield, caste is a matter of profession; for Risley, it is a matter of marriage.

The Vedic Varna system is so deep-rooted that it has given rise to social injustice and colossal vice like untouchability, slavery, degradation of womenfolk, uprooting from land, ancestral poverty, exploitation and under employment to a vast majority of non-Aryan races. The scriptures and the Hindu social order legally handed over and concentrated all resources of power and privileges in the hands of the Aryans, the dominating communities and propagated absurd and baseless theories of divine origin.

In Vedic literature, according to N. K. Dutt the Dasas (Dasyus) are "black skinned noseless, of unintelligible speech, not sacrificing, worshipping no gods, following strange customs." Risely on the basis of ethnographic study describes them "of low stature, black skin, long head, broad nose, ... related to aborigines of Australia and linguistic affinity with Australian dialect."

French Scholar Emile Senart observes "..... they are definitely of inferior race, isolated by geographical conditions and by history ...... but culturally they were by no means inferior."

Rig Veda (in its 104th hymn of the first book) describes them having "castles and great wealth of natives whose womenfolk bathed in milk."

Dahlman defines caste as a "class of the community which disowns any connection with any other class and neither intermarry, nor eat or drink with any but the person of their own community."

Bonnerjee says that Aryan invaders were primarily responsible for the institution of caste.

Ibbetson emphasises on the exploitation of the position by the Brahmins which he supposes to have degraded all occupations except their own. He explains caste as arising from a combination of tribal origin, functional guilds and a Levitical religion.

Sarat Chander Roy accepts that caste is an outcome of interaction between the Indo-Aryan Varna system on one hand and the tribal system of pre-Dravidian and the occupational class system of Dravidian on the other. These have been cemented by Indo-Aryan concept of Karma and a certain taboo-holiness.

According to G.S. Ghurye caste has arisen largely as a result of racial differences. Probably Aryans wanted to be the unquestioned supreme power for all time to come and strengthened their ideology through their viced literature. The caste institution found a religious status, beyond scientific scrutiny, logical questioning, critical evaluation and social challenge."

Mixed Union of the Four Castes

"From early times by an ordinance of Manu, men of the higher castes or classes were permitted, after marrying a woman of their own caste, to have subsidiary wives from any of the classes below them. This custom seems to have been prevalent, and no definite rule was prescribed that the children of such unions should necessarily be illegitimate, and in many cases there is no doubt that their descendants ultimately became full members of the caste of the first ancestor. According to Manu, the children of a Brahmin by a Kshatriya woman could attain Brahminhood in the third generation, and those by a Vaishya woman in the fifth".' Such children could also inherit the family property. According to the Mahabharata, (Chap. XIVII) if a Brahmin had four wives of different castes, the son by a

Brahmin wife took four shares, that by a Kshatriya wife three, that by a Vaishya wife two, and that by a Shudra wife one share. Manu gives a slightly different distribution, but also permits the son by a Shudra wife to have a share of the inheritance." Thus the fact is clear that the son of a Brahmin even by a Shudra woman had a certain status of legitimacy in his father's caste, as he could marry in it, and must therefore have been permitted to partake of the sacrificial food at marriage, and could also inherit a small share of the property. The detailed rules prescribed for the state legitimacy and inheritance show the recognized unions of this kind of subsequent prohibitions. This must have led to mixture of blood in the different castes. There is still a survival of it in the practice of hypergamy.

The Tribe

Both tribe and caste are loosely applied to a social group. The tribe is defined as 'the largest body of people, speaking about what they themselves regard as one language, and having a common language for themselves as well as sense of solidarity which expresses itself in regarding other people as strangers.' A tribe is not a close corporation. In its original form, it is an aggregate of persons who have or believe themselves to have a common origin. This together with common political interests, and mutual defence, holds them together. Sometimes, it admits of aliens who wish to throw in their lot with it especially women obtained by purchase or capture. It is not endogamous though circumstances tend to favour endogamy. It differs from caste in as much as the common name does not usually imply occupation. Its members occupy or profess to occupy a definite tract, but they do not necessarily marry among themselves. The modern tendency for such tribes is to be transformed into a caste. In fact, a tribe is a prospective caste. Thus a tribe took thousands of years to become a caste.

Class and Caste

The two names caste and class are often confounded with each other. They correspond neither in extent, in character, nor in natural tendencies. Each one among the castes which would belong to one and the same class is plainly distinguishable from its fellows. The class subserves political ambitions. The caste obeys narrow scruples, traditional customs and local influence, which have generally no relation to class interests. More than that the class clings to the safeguarding of an integrity which is the subject of deep concern and sensitiveness even with the humblest. It is the distant echo of the class struggles handed down by legend with which tradition resounds. By the reaction of principles on facts, two institutions have become fused together. They are none-the-less essentially independent. The hierarchic division of the population into classes is universal. But the caste system is a unique institution. The Brahminic ambition has taken advantage of it in order to make more securely its domination possible, but not obvious. A caste system is not necessarily the basis of theocracy. It's theory has confused the two sets of ideas. This is a fact of secondary importance. For the sake of historic development they have to be carefully distinguished.

In the Vedic literature the Brahmins are said to be the trustees and repositories to the civilization. Both Buddha and Mahavira and some other contemporary philosophers revolted against Brahmin supremacy and Vedic wisdom. Buddhism guided and shaped the human history and human thought discarding inhuman sacrifices, too much ritualism, caste system and practice of untouchability.

With the entry of the British in India, the Trade Guilds changed to modern factory system, now owned by the capitalist class. There is a definite change in ancestral or traditional occupation of a particular caste, which is a signal of eradication of caste system. R.V. Russell observes:

"The abandonment of the traditional occupation has become a most marked feature of Hindu society as a result of equal opportunity and freedom in the choice of occupations afforded by the British Government, coupled with the rapid progress of industry and the spread of education. So far it has no very markedly disintegrating effect on the caste system, and the status of a caste is still mainly fixed by its traditional occupation but signs are not wanting of a coming change."

"As several castes have the same traditional occupation in other parts of the country, the distinctions of occupation therefore, are not a sufficient basis for a classification of caste. Nor can caste be simply defined as a body of persons who marry only among themselves or, as it is termed, an endogamous group; for almost every important caste is divided into a number of sub-castes which do not marry and frequently do not eat with each other. But, it is distinctive and peculiar feature of a caste as social institution that it splits up the people into a multitude of these divisions and bars their intermarriage and the real unity of the system and the basis of the fabric of Indian society is this endogamous group or sub-castes.

Sub-Castes

The sub-castes, however, connote no real difference of status or occupation. They are little known except within the caste itself and they consist of groups within the caste which marry among themselves, and attend the communal feasts held on the occasions of marriages, funerals and meetings of the caste panchayats or committees for the judgment of offences against the caste and there expiation by a penalty feast.

Caste from Chandragupta Maurya to Harsha

Megasthenes, who was an ambassador in the court of Chandragupta (Sandrokotus of the Greeks) in 300 B.C. wrote an account of the social system of his day in a work compiled by him, and this was preserved by Strabo, Arrian and other writers. His classification of the people of his day into seven groups is somewhat confusing. He speaks of the philosophers, the herdsmen and hunters, the traders and labours, the fighting men, the overseers, the councillors, and the judges and administrators. From the above list, Brahmins and Kshatriyas are easily identified. The third and fourth groups include Vaishyas and Shudras. The fourth would include all the guilds of armourers and ship-builders of which Megasthenes speaks as possessing special privileges. The sixth and the seventh of Megasthenes groups refer to professional classes. According to Strabo's version, "no one is allowed to marry out of one's own caste or to follow more than one business. An exception is made in the case of the philosopher, who for his virtue is allowed this privilege." Arrian endorses this view. From the above mentioned facts three important things may be inferred, namely, prohibition of intercaste marriages, the importance of heredity, and the exemption of Brahmins from the above rules. Nevertheless there were violations. Chandragupta was of mixed descent. There were mixed marriages at a much later date, and perhaps there were exceptional instances in the fourth century B.C.

Regarding the six centuries between 300 B.C. and 300 A.D., informations on the development of caste is rather scanty. Some attempts were made to prevent the intermixture of caste. During this period, there occurred the invasions of the Sakas, the Yavanas, the Pahlavas and the Kushans. These must have left their mark on the Hindu society, though very little is known except in the case of the Huns, about their intermixture with the population of the country.

Quoting earlier researches and writings of Blunt and Dutt as well as Institution of Manu, Iyer traces the growth of Varna system, which is complex from the very beginning. He observes:

"The Institutes of Manu and the chief Puranas in their present form are ascribed to the Golden Age of Sanskrit Literature under the early Gupta kings (330-450 A.D.) The Brahmins and Kshatriyas the 'sacerdotal' and ruling and military castes respectively are shown as occupational. The

Vaishyas and Shudras are not clearly defined. They are identical probably with trading, industrial and menial classes. The Vratya and Vrishala castes are the degenerate descendants of the twice born classes who have neglected to perform the prescribed rites. Among them are included Khasa, Dravira, Yavana, Saka, Pahalva and China, and these names clearly show, what Manu's Vratyas and Vrishalas were. These must have been the names of aboriginal tribes and races, that have partly or wholly merged in the then Hindu tribes and caste. Manu's Institutes contain a fairly good account of the social system as it existed in his time. Many tribal castes must have sprung from foreign invaders, after their adoption of Hinduism. In this connection, it must be remembered that many of the invaders were barbarous, and their manners and customs would have become repugnant to the Hindus. It is very likely that these groups would have gradually become endogamous communities. Further, the real position of the Kshatriya cannot be ascertained. It is said that Chandragupta Maurya was of mixed birth; the Andhra dynasty is usually regarded as of Shudra extraction. Harsha of Thanesvar, the last great Hindu king, was a Vaishya, but ranked as a Kshatriya. It seems, therefore, that the ancient Kshatriyas, like the modern Rajputs, were a social class to which all rulers by virtue of sovereignty were recognized as belonging to ruling race. Thus Kshatriyas, may be regarded as an occupational caste following the Hindu ritual land becoming rulers."

Iyer further writes: "In the early Buddhist period the Kshatriya was socially supreme. In Manu's account, the supremacy passed to the Brahmin. That the Kshatriya power decayed and reverted to the Brahmin, cannot be denied. In fact, as Blunt says, the causes may be found in the history of the time. During the three centuries from 200 B.C. to 500 B.C. India was subject to foreign invasions by powerful barbarian hords, which led to the extirpation of the ancient Kshatriyas, who were also liable to be attacked from within. Buddhism, which was a new religion, founded by a Kshatriya prince, was opposed to Brahminism. The two religions went on side by side for ten centuries till at last Brahminism gained the ascendency after the death of Harsha of Thanesvar in the middle of the seventh century AD. It is also said that Parasurama extirpated the Kshatriyas. Thus the Kshatriya became extinct, and his power as ruler passed by right of sword to the foreign Sakas, Pahlavas and Kushans, each of whom in turn usurped the throne with the title of Kshatriya. Thus the kings and kinglets of India were often Hinduized foreigners who never attained to the rank and pre-eminence of the ancient Kshatriyas. This low position of the later Kshatriyas afforded an opportunity to the Brahmin, who in the meantime, increased his authority and consolidated his position. In the Vedic period he was an acolyte at sacrifices, and assistant to the head of the family who officiated as priest. During the period which ended with the advent of Buddha, in the midst of a people that was intensely religious, and still more intensely ritualist, he had become the hereditary priest, the sole master of religious ceremonies and doctrine, and as such had won himself an almost unassailable supremacy.

Further, as philosopher and statesman, by sheer force of learning he had acquired considerable temporal power. The king's minister was a Brahmin and was no more a figure head. Chanakya overthrew Nanda kings, put Chandragupta Maurya on the throne, and acted as his minister. The first Brahmin dynasty after the Kanvas was the Shahya dynasty of Sindh in the tenth century. During the Buddhist period Brahmin power suffered a little; Buddhism was a revolt against Brahminism and its metaphysics. But Brahminism was never entirely destroyed. Under the Gupta dynasty the Brahminic culture was widely diffused. The Brahmin ascendancy both temporal and spiritual revived. It increased during the troubled period which came with destruction of the old Arya nobility. The Brahmin, 'the chief remaining link with the past, obtained the social hegemony, never again to lose it.'

In fact, from ancient days, as Dr. Ambedkar rightly

observes: "The caste problem is a vast one, both theoretically and practically. Practically, it is an institution that portends tremendous consequences. It is a local problem, but one capable of much wider mischief, for as long as caste in India does exist, Hindus will hardly intermarry or have any social intercourse with outsiders; and if Hindus migrate to other regions on earth, Indian caste would become a world problem." Theoretically, it has defied a great many scholars who have taken upon themselves, as a labour of love, to dig into its origin.

According to well-known ethnologists, the population of India is a mixture of Aryans, Dravidians, Mongolians and Scythians. All these stocks of people came to India from various directions and with various cultures, centuries ago, when they were in a tribal state. They all in turn elbowed their entry into the country by fighting with their predecessors, and after a stomachful of it settled down as peaceful neighbours. Through constant contact and mutual intercourse they evolved a common culture that superseded their distinctive cultures. It may be granted that there has been a thorough amalgamation of the various stocks that make up the people of India, and to a traveller from within the boundaries of India the East presents a marked contrast in physique and even in colour to the West, as does the South to the North. But amalgamation can never be the sole criterion of homogeneity as predicated of any people. Ethnically all people are heterogeneous. It is the unity of culture that is the basis of homogeneity. Taking this for granted, it can be said that there is no country that can rival the Indian Peninsula with respect to the unity of its culture. It has not only a geographic unity, but it has above all a deeper and a much more fundamental unity-the indubitable cultural unity that covers that land from end to end. But it is because of this homogeneity that caste becomes a problem so difficult to be explained. If the Hindu society were a mere federation of mutually exclusive units, the matter would be simple enough. But caste is a parcelling of an already homogeneous unit, and the explanation of the genesis of caste is the explanation of this process of parcelling.

According to common belief among scholars caste system has either been imposed upon the docile population of India by a law-giver or grown according to some law of social growth. Dr. Ambedkar believed Manu as dirty and tyrant law-giver who had given the law of caste. Caste existed much before Manu. He as an upholder philosophised it, codified existing caste rules and preached caste Dharma.

In his opinion the theories of scholars are typical and mostly based on occupation, survival of tribal organisation, rise of new belief; cross-breeding and migration. They have dealt with the problem that why occupational group turned into an occupational caste.

The earliest Hindu society in common with other societies was composed of following classes (i) The Brahmins, or the priestly class; (ii) the Kshatriyas, or the military class; (iii) The Vaishyas, or the merchant class; (iv) The Shudras (Sudra) or the artisan and menial class.

In the opinion of Dr. Ambedkar: "This was essentially a class system. Individuals when qualified, could change their class, and therefore classes did change their personnel. In the history of Hindus, at some time, the priestly class socially detached itself from the rest of the body of the people and through a closed-door policy became a caste by itself. The other classes being subject to the law of social division of labour underwent differentiation, some into large other into very minute groups."

The Vaishya and Shudra classes were the original inchloate plasm, which formed the sources of the numerous castes of today. The Kshatriya were warriors and administrators and there was very little minute sub-division.

The Europeans have unnecessarily emphasised the colour in the caste system. Dr. Ketkar is correct that all princes whether Aryan or Dravidian were basically Aryas. Whether a family or a tribe was Aryan or Dravidian was question which never troubled the Indian mind, until foreign scholars came and began to draw a line.

Curse of Inequality

The institution of caste created inequality. Hinduism did not attach importance to individual merit but to caste of an individual.

According to Dr. Ambedkar, inequality is the soul of Hinduism. The morality of Hinduism is only social. It is immoral and inhuman to say the least.

The state of civilization of the Primitive Tribes in the Hindu social order "includes the entire period of human progress from savagery to barbarism and from barbarism to civilization. The transition from one to other has been marked by some discovery or intention in some department of knowledge of art resulting in advancing the onward march of man."

These Aborigines of the Primitive Tribes, who were the forefathers of the present day workforce, the artisans, the agriculturists, the lower classes, invented fire and its use, discovered bow and arrow and other earlier tools (of wood, stone or metals), domesticated wild animals, kept domestic animals. Hunting, fishing and collection of food from forest were their main occupations. They were basically meat-eaters. They lived on trees and in caves, and have no hesitation in eating worms and insects, as well as dead animals and birds.

The next group was of Criminal Tribes. They lived in forests as Primitive Tribes. They were barbarous and engaged in criminal activities. A few were engaged in agriculture and domestic industries but most of them took to nefarious practices. Besides these two classes there were untouchables. They were the lowest among the Hindu social order. A vast majority of people were made slaves. The Broken-man was almost a captive.

It is a naked truth that the Hindu social order for centuries denied human rights to these people. Right to education and knowledge was denied. The status was denied in the society. Physical, social and economic growth was hampered. According to Dr. Ambedkar, "The Hindu social order 60 does not recognise the individual as centre of social purpose. For the Hindu social order is based primarily on class or Varna, and not on individual the unit of the Hindu society is not the individual Brahmin or the individual Kshatriya or the individual Vaishya or the individual Shudra or the individual Panchama. Even the family is not regarded by the Hindu social order as the unit of society except for the purpose of marriage and inheritance. The unit of Hindu society is the class or Varna to use the Hindu technical name for caste."

In the Hindu social order, there is no room for individual merit and no consideration of individual justice. If the individual has a privilege it is not because it is due to him personally. The privilege goes with the class, and if he is found to enjoy it, it is because he belongs to that class.

The Vedic Aryans excluded the Shudras from the mainstream of social, cultural and religious life. Their economic powers and activities were restricted. They were discouraged to adopt Vedic faith and denied education. There is no doubt the practice of untouchability was promoted by the Aryan society to oppress and exploit the menial class in a planned and calculated manner. Aryan race accepted many invaders who were later on Hinduised and even the Arabs, Turks, Mughals etc., were tolerated who ruled over the Hindus for over 1000 years, but treated the untouchables as slaves.

Thus the principle of 'graded inequality' became the order of Brahminic or Hindu social system.

The institution of Manu codified such laws which socially and economically condemned millions of untouchables for centuries. In India, the institution of slavery in the form of graded caste system, alongwith abhorrent practice of untouchability, has no parallel in the history of the human race in the whole world.

Every attack on caste and untouchability, social and

cultural deprivation of untouchable was treated as an attack on Aryan supremacy by the Hindu orthodoxy. Surprisingly, every field of knowledge and power was monopolised by a single ethnic group. Kshatriyas and Vaishyas supported the ideological base of the Brahminical order to keep alive the feudal landlordism, exploitation and the institution of caste discrimination, the worst form of social degradation and slavery for centuries.

TWO

Condition in Medieval Period

Impact of Islam

The removal of untouchability and the caste system were never the concern of the Muslim invaders, who ruled over this vast land because of India's social weaknesses for about one thousand years. On the contrary there are historical evidences when Islam prompted mass conversions and compelled the Shudras, the untouchables and even so-called caste Hindus, and the ruling chiefs to embrace Islam and follow their religious and social traditions.

On the eve of the Islamic invasion there was no paramount power in India and the society was divided into castes or Varnas. Only so-called martial races of the ruling chiefs or Kshatriyas were eligible to participate in wars but they always faced defeat. The Dalits, a class of exploited people suffered heavily when Turk, Afghan, Mongol and Mughal invaders one after another attacked India. Some historians, social scientists and ideologies rather derive conclusions on the basis of some 'Persian' texts and other historical evidences that there was all peace and prosperity, communal harmony and goodwill in Delhi and around (perhaps Northern India) after Muslims have conquered this vast land and have settled here permanently.

Our historians have traced little of the medieval period untouchables. When Bhakti cult influenced the sub-merged sections and artisan classes to follow the teachings of the Saints and Bhakti poets to live unitedly and rise in revolt against the tyranny of the foreign rulers. The Shudras and untouchables were all landless farmers and artisans. They were kept and treated as a servile class, slaves and bonded labour both by the caste Hindus, dominating communities as well as the new masters.

Before Hiuen-Tsang, Chinese pilgrim Fa-Hien visited India during the reign of Chandragupta-Vikramaditya, and stayed here for six years (405A.D-411 A.D.). His deep authentic writings provide insight into the social life and status of Shudras of that period who were being harassed by the Brahmins and upper castes.

Only half a century of earlier invasion of the Arabs, the Chinese pilgrim Hiuen-Tsang visited India between 630 and 644 A.D.

Hiuen-Tsang's account reveals that 'the towns and villages have inner gates. The walls are wide and high, the streets and lanes are tortuous and the roads winding. The thoroughfares are dirty and the stalls arranged on both sides of the road with appropriate signs. Butchers, fishermen, dancers, executioners, scavengers, and so on, have their abodes outside the city. Incoming and going of these persons are bound to keep on the left side of the road till they arrive at their homes. Their houses are surrounded by low walls and from the suburbs.'

'...Brahmins did not participate in industrial activity of the country. Agriculture was in the hands of the Shudras.' The lower class were a crushed lot, and worked as slave labour.

Hiuen-Tsang tells us further that 'caste system dominated the Hindu society. The Brahmins performed religious duties. Kshatriyas were the governing class, and very often were the kings. The Vaishyas were traders and merchants. The Shudras did the agriculture and menial work. Mostly they were artisans. But inferior in status.

'....There were no inter-caste marriages. There were restrictions among various castes with regard to food. There was no widow re-marriage. The system of Sati was known.

The untouchables lived in the outskirts of the village or town in thatched huts. They were not allowed to mix up' with the people. Even the artisans and agriculturists of some Shudra class practiced untouchability with them. They were known as Chandalas. There was no forced labour.

It is clear the Shudras were a working class of agriculturists and artisans, they all were hand to mouth, whereas the socially discarded untouchables were known as Chandalas. They were 'Broken-men'.

Another Chinese pilgrim Itsing visited India between 672 and 688A.D. He tells us Buddha preached to the lay followers in a very simple language and treated all human beings equal. He was against caste system. For Buddha even a low caste Chandala after embracing Buddhism and becoming Sramana was equal to a Brahmin. Buddha believed most of the sins of the people could be removed by the regulations of Sheela or morality.

Thus from the time of the Chinese pilgrims to the Muslim invasion and their long stay the Shudras remained as low caste people, a socially and economically exploited poorer section. The Chandalas were kept away from the society. Their life was very miserable.

According to Edwards, V.A. Smith, D.R. Bhandarkar and other historians, after Harsha the political and social unity of India was broken. A large number of states came into existence in northern India and there was struggle for supremacy among them. So was also the condition of the Deccan.

The most outstanding feature of this period was rise of the Hindu ruling chiefs. They claimed to be the lineal descendents of the Kshatriyas of the Vedic times, while Shudras and untouchables were an ignored lot who mainly lived in villages in muddy thatched huts.

According to Col. Tod, the Hindu ruling chiefs were the descendants of the Sakas, Huns, Kushans, etc., who came to India either as invaders with imperial designs or seekers of fertile land and settled here. They married Indian wives and formed separate war like class, while the lower classes began to be known as Gujars, Jats, Ahir etc. Even the tribal Kshatriyas of Buddhist period, Shakyas, Koliyas, Mallas, Lichchavis,

Maurya," etc., were recognised as leading castes in Hindu society and were treated above Brahmins during Buddha period. It was Buddha himself who broke the caste system and attacked untouchability. Historians like C.V Vaidya and G. S. Ojha do not accept the theory of foreign origin of Rajputs.

The caste system was acceptable to the Hindu ruling chiefs. The Shudras were placed very low in social ladder, while Brahmins were placed very high. Shudras were very poor and exploited class. So were the untouchables, the wandering-gypsy castes who lived outside the villages and towns.

The rigid caste system kept 'the people in ignorance fed with unwholesome superstition and beguilded with gorgeous and never-ending festivals.'

The upper caste Hindus as a society had lost their assimilative power and vitality. The caste rigidities and orthodoxy made them self-centred, materialistic, proud but unprogressive. People of the higher classes became rich and prosperous. The fame of their riches and wealth and the jewellery which their ladies used to wear virtually invited the cupidity of the Muslim invaders.

The ornaments of kings and queens and the wealthy mercantile people as well as deities placed in temples were made of precious stones. This attracted the attention of Arab attackers. The society was already divided into various castes and ancient martial races made untouchables the 'Broken-men'.

It is most unfortunate that our historians, thinkers and literatures have not written much on the social conditions of the untouchables and the Shudras, of the medieval period of History-what they did, how they lived and the reasons of their poverty and social neglect in the hands of the powerful class. Earlier when Buddha established his order, they embraced Buddhism which denied caste system and untouchability. Arabs knew well that India was divided in various castes. Shudras were a suffering lot because of upper caste domination. Therefore, they had planned to plunder and crush this land which the Greeks did earlier.

This fact cannot be ignored that continued hatred and growing social separatism and discrimination towards low castes, the Buddhist monks and the lay votaries of Buddha and the wealth of Hindus encouraged the Arab invaders, in the beginning of the 8th century.

'India's major centres of Buddhism, including the great university at Nalanda, where more than ten thousand monks lived and studied, were sacked by Muhammad Ghori in the end of the 12th century, driving thousands of Buddhists to flee towards Nepal and Tibet and killing uncounted lower caste people, who weren't swift enough to escape. The severity of Turko-Afghan persecution directed against centres of Buddhist monasticism was so unrelenting that the religion of the Buddha was now sent into exile from the land of its birth.

This also resulted in massacre of the people of the lower classes who were Buddhists. The Shudras were further enslaved by the Arab invaders.

As stated earlier, under the influence of unwise Brahmin priests and the scripture's authority the Hindu failed to unite themselves as Indians. The untouchables and the Shudras were the worst sufferers during this prolonged Muslim invasion. Many of them were either killed or enslaved.

Ignoring all these facts the Brahmins in their priestly wisdom blamed that it was due to their sins committed during the previous life and carelessness in observance of religious rites. And this carelessness must have offended some deity who has thus fulfilled his desire to destroy them. Where these fanatic notions prevail and the authority of the Brahmin is unquestioned, it follows as a necessary consequence that the disadvantaged people under the fear created by priestly class, are bound to suffer because of ignorance and superstitions. Brahmins imposed doctrine of transmigration and Karma explaining the defeat. These ideas indeed have exercised a dumb, depressing, fatalistic influence upon the whole society, making people lazy, selfish and projecting the failures on some unknown agencies overtly the angry Hindu gods. The worst harm that Brahmins did to non-Brahmin Hindus and to the country was perpetual subordination, suppression of intellectual and moral growth, imposition of inferiority, submergence of religion in a flood of ritualism and above all creating an impression that their religion was tolerant to others and believed in non-violence belying all historical facts. Infact, it was not tolerance but jealousy, dynastic intrigues, internal dissension combined to create political vacuum which the first comer who knew his own mind was irresistibly impelled to fill.

Based on written documents, Jiloha observes: "Indian history is a record of invasions. Wave after wave of conquest or armed occupation has swept over the face of the country, but at no time were the invaders confronted with resistance organised on a national basis or inspired by a patriotic enthusiasm. Military service was the group concern of professional castes and failure of Hindus to organise a national resistance to the advancement of Muslim invaders, an organisation of plunder to inspire Hinduism with the spirit of active patriotism, was the core of Brahminism which adheres, not to the defence of the country but to the defence of caste system and this attitude has been given the name of non-violence. Man's loyalty was to the caste rather than to the community as a whole; and not at all to the state. The local chieftains fought for independence as Porus opposed Alexander and Prithvi Raj Chauhan resisted Muhammad Ghori, their nearest rival hastened to offer his sword to the foreign enemy. India has never attained the idea of the state or of the fatherland, the sphere of interests at such occasions has contracted rather than expanded. In the ancient republics the class concept tended to develop into the wider idea of the city; in India it grew more sharply defined inclining to confine itself within the narrow limits of the caste. Real interest was not in who governed, but in how they governed without interference in caste affairs. It is for this reason that inspite of the instability of the state the social conditions remained unaffected by change of the ruler because the social conditions i.e. caste structure had supposedly divine origin which placed them out of political control."

These facts are beyond dispute and a pointer to the inevitable conclusion that the national sentiment in India can derive no encouragement or pride from the study of India history.

All pervasive in Hindu-life was caste, which attracted the notice of early Muslim immigrants, who had not seen its like anywhere in the Muslim world, a segment of the same society diffusing and atmosphere of impurity was forbidden to enter high caste quarter of the village and was compelled to announce their own approach by a special cry. They were puzzled at such a logic of tolerance of Hindu. They also observed that Hinduism transfused by mysticism and ecstatic devotion and resting ultimately on the esoteric teaching of transcendental philosophy, knows nothing of open proselytism and attained its ends in a different and more subtle fashion. On the other hand their own religion was a force of volcanic sort, a burning and integrating force, which under favourable conditions could make even a nation, melting and fusing together and reducing their internal structure to one uniform pattern in which no survival of preexisting usages could be detected.

According to Srivastava there is another viewpoint also: "Islam condemned caste restrictions, discouraged infanticide, diminished the importance of birth and heredity, encouraged widow marriage and preached equality".

In cities the Brahmins and upper caste people were afraid of Muslim rule. They altogether surrendered and many of them started praising the invaders. However in villages, the Brahmin or upper caste supremacy remained intact. Shudras and Dalits were still subject to torture and inhuman treatment. They were mainly artisans, farm labour, herdsmen and forest dwellers.

The process of conversion has already begun in oppressed

classes. For them slavery was slavery, whether the masters were Hindus or Arabs. Islamic equality and feeling of universal brotherhood, and absence of caste hatred, suppression and untouchability attracted them.

Al-beruni (973-1048 A.D.) a scholar, who came with Mahmud Ghazni, gives a vivid account of social, religious and political life of this country during that period. Hindu records of that time only sing songs in the praise of Brahmins and the polluted Hindu mind as he mentions,"... Indian scribes are careless and do not take pains to produce correct and well collated copies...", it was not possible with a Hindu mind to be neutral observer in the matter of caste. Al-beruni concludes, "...they spent most of their care on the division of their subjects into different classes and orders, which they tried to preserve from inter-mixture and disorder. Therefore, they forbade people of different classes to have intercourse with each other and laid upon each class a particular kind to work... they did not allow anybody to transgress the limits of their class..."

During this period, caste-system in India was in its full bloom and had its impact on every aspect of human-interaction in Hindu life. No matter what one's aptitude was, he had to confine his interests to the jurisdiction of his caste. Other than the four castes Al-beruni describes fifth caste of Antyaja after Shudras, not reckoned among any caste i.e. Chandalas, living away from the main village or town, not coming near caste Hindus, addressed from far off, remaining naked except for their private parts, eating carrion and even flesh and caretakers of cremation grounds.

Al-beruni himself a prolific writer, linguistic and a Sanskrit scholar writes about the linguistic competence of Hindus " ....boast of enormous range of their language, whilst in reality it is defect." Writing about their attitude towards others and their religious prejudice he says, "...their fanaticism is direct against those who do not belong to them..." against all foreigners. They call them Mlechcha i.e. impure and forbid having any connection with them ...in all manners and usages they differ ...frighten their children with us, with our dress and ways of customs declaring us to be devil's breed. Hindus believe that there is no country but theirs ,...no religion like theirs..." fact was the Hindus lost their motherland because of caste distinctions and disunity.

In fact, Sanskrit, a language of priestly class, was beyond the reach of common people and probably it was a deliberate attempt to keep the working class (the untouchables and Shudras) ignorant of what the cunning designs of the priestly class were.

Al-beruni's account reveals that the Hindus of that period were like frogs of a well whose world is within the well and cannot perceive anything beyond that. Hindus of that time operated at a primitive level of thinking like an infant whose entire world is within himself and by virtue of his magical thinking he could destroy the whole world at will. Hindu psyche is a collection of wishful thinking and merely at will any Hindu god could reach anywhere to the rescue of his devotee in distress.

For untouchables it did not matter whether the ruler was a Hindu or a Muslim because they had to lead the same life of serfdom and obligation, strongly under the grip of superstitions and ignorance, more than an ordinary Hindu, except for those untouchables who were unhappy with their status in the Hindu fold, got an opportunity and platform to switch over to Islam as it treated all alike. Some of them whole-heartedly co-operated with the newcomers and got an opportunity to raise their material position (Yusuf Hussain 1962 pp. 120-121). Perhaps this was the beginning of social mobility among untouchables. A large-scale conversion to Islam took place from the underprivileged sector of Hindu social order; they hoped by accepting the religion of the conquerors, to participate in some way in the advantages of religious identification. During the same period Muslims explored different ways and means to acclimatise themselves to the Indian environment, and they found it not only favourable but also encouraging of the proliferation of Islam.

When Hindus emerged from the twilight of these invasions they found that Islam had comfortably encroached upon Indian territory almost the same way as they themselves had grabbed India a couple of millennia earlier.

Lower Hindu castes took Sufism as a liberal-reformative Islamic saintly movement which has no place for caste. However, "Sufism, Islam's mystic thread, which evolved primarily as a legacy of Persian influence upon orthodoxy, struck a responsive chord in the mass of Bengal's population, especially among the lowest class of Hindu outcastes and former Buddhists, who were left without a priesthood to turn to for spiritual guidance after 1202; it appealed as well to many poor Muslims, for whom it revitalized the message of Islam.

Three orders of Sufi saints had appeared in India by the thirteenth century; the Chisti, Suharawardi, and Firdausi, all of which appealed to the same mystical yearning for union with God, experienced by so many Hindus as well as Muslims and other 'God-intoxicated' seekers the world over. The fervent love of God, which played so important a role in the passionate yearning for 'the mother goddess' that had characterized Bengali religious consciousness from time immemorial, may well have its roots in the same lush alluvium, fed by torrential monsoons which gave birth to 'golden' jute, the premier crop of Bangladesh. The ineffable blend of love and sorrow, of human frailty and poverty amid the awesome forces of nature's lush wealth, helped fashion the uniquely sensitive, passionate and mercurial temperament characteristic of Bengal; it seems also to have predisposed millions of Bengalis to the ardent appeal of Islamic mysticism. The wandering Pirs (sufi preachers), who went into Bengal's remote villages to bring their message of divine love to impoverished peasants, sounded much the same as Hindu Bhakti (devotional) saints offering salvation through worship of the mother goddess, or Mahayanist Buddhists bearing the promise of divine salvation by grace of a Bodhisattva's blessing. Bengali translations of epic Sanskrit literature were encouraged by court patronage during this era of independent Muslim rule, serving at once both to weaken the grip of Brahmin Pundits over the people and to provide the national mortar of a literary vernacular language to this culturally fecund region. Under a succession of independent Muslim dynasties, Bengal was to retain its sovereign status, free of interference from Delhi, till the peak of great Mughal power and Akbar's conquest in 1576. The Sufis, no doubt influenced the social life class the lower class Bengal peasants. It was a cool-fresh air in polluted Hindu social order, which considered the peasants and artisans as slaves.

When the Muslim rule in India got fully secure it became a geographical compulsion for both Hindus and Muslims to stay together as neighbours. Though they never tolerated each other's presence, they started assimilating each other's ideas, customs, beliefs etc. Seldom in the history of mankind has the spectacle been witnessed of two civilizations so vast and so strongly developed, yet so radically dissimilar, as the Muslims and the Hindus, meeting and mingling together, the wide divergence in their culture and their religion make the impact peculiarly instructive. As minorities cannot resist absorbing the characteristics of majority, Muslims were influenced by Hindus and as a consequence Muslims too started looking down upon untouchables the way the caste Hindus were doing. To avoid it there was a large-scale conversion of untouchables to Islam which provided a very fertile ground for the spread of Islam as well as an alternative to untouchables, to lead a better life, to participate in some way to the advantage of religious identification. Forcible conversion of caste-Hindus to Islam also took place which helped Hinduism to become more orthodox, more strict in caste rules such as Pardah system and its mobility toward Islam created many a non-caste professions which were adopted by neo-Muslims with a fair degree of acceptance in Islam. The fear of defilement closed those occupations to the Hindus; this fear spread and became general among the inferior population owing to the religious influence of the immigrants and of their priests. The sections were graded according to the degree of impurity.

It is said Kabir was put to harassment and torture by the Delhi Sultanate as he raised the banner of revolt against Hindu and Muslim orthodoxy and established rituals. Kabir's biggest social contribution is that he saved Hinduism from Islamic influence and Hindu society from embracing Islam.

Gorakhanath, a low caste Yogi started Nath Panth and majority of its followers were from suppressed castes who denounced caste system and privileges of Brahmins. They adopted Tantric and Yogic methods. This movement subsequently got reduced to a particular caste group and became a community in itself.

The Hindus as a defeated race took shelter in idol-worship, pilgrimage and observance of fasts and never cared for the Shudras. Hindu kings had already surrendered, so also the priestly class. The Hindu society practically remained static throughout the medieval age. It is strange, caste system and untouchability continued.

Lower castes searched their identity with the saints, and Muslim Pirs (Sufi Saints). But despite the wave of Bhakti Movement, caste-system existed in full vigour and as a class untouchables remained oppressed and lived in continuous fear of one and all belonging to higher castes. They were constantly harassed by the unsatiable demands of all kinds. A word from Zamindar was enough for 'his man' to go to locality of untouchables impressing upon them the number of persons required for work. They were supposed to receive wages for their services but they remained more or less at the call of others, no matter what their own commitments might have been. There were certain duties which they had to perform for the landlord for which they were awarded certain privileges like collection of left-over grains from the harvested fields, graze their cattle in the fields of the land-lord and receipt of caste-off clothes from the family members of their master.

There were however, many instances where they could be summoned to work without pay under the direction of any caste Hindu or officer of the Nawab. They had to live in a hopeless state of degradation and serfdom, their womenfolk could be raped in broad day-light if they willingly refused to satisfy the sexual lust of henchmen of the land-lord. If an untouchable offered immoral services of his wife or daughter, he was fortunate enough to get the cultivating right and safety of his house.

It was hoped that with the change in political conditions by virtue of Muslim rule, there would be decline in the influence of Hindu religion and thus improvement in the situation of the untouchables but the speculations proved contrary to the fact. With the establishment of Muslim rule and change of dynasties over dynasties, caste system emerged stronger and stronger leading to ever-increasing enslavement of untouchables. Bhakti Movement came, challenged and undermined caste system, and in due course of time it perished but caste system stood immortal.' Even the Muslims treated the untouchables as inferiors and degraded, as Hindus have done. Many backward and untouchable castes embraced Islam but their status was unchanged.

Islam brought terror that oppressed the masses. Hindu feudal lords also suppressed the poor people in villages. However, there is no denying the fact that the Brahmins lost much in prestige and power with the fall of Rajput kingdoms to Muslims and with the challenge of Bhakti Movement to their unquestioned superiority. Brahmins realised that their grip on the caste had become slippery and people were not so enthusiastic to feed them with sumptuous meals and had also started ignoring their elaborate rituals.

There is no doubt Ramayana written by Tulsi Das openly advocates the supremacy of the Brahmins and Kshatriya and the prince of Ayodhya as an incarnation of God. It condemns and dehumanizes the untouchables, the Shudras and the tribals; and compels them to follow Brahminic rule. Since medieval times when it was written Ramayana has done much harm to the Dalits and tribals of India as it preaches inequality, casteism and principle of divine theory of kings to rule over the land which is a feudal thought. It is all against an egalitarian concept of democratic society. Ramayana stands as a document of Hindu revivalism.

According to Ramayana, Shudras had no respect in Hindu society. They are only meant to serve the kings and feudal landlords. The position of women in the society is also not quite encouraging, when Tulsi Das writes: 'drum, illiterate Shudra, animal and women in society, all deserve to be punished. In some parts of South India the Brahmin priests encouraged sex exploitation of Shudra women in the name of god. Devadasi system of South is a glaring example in this regard which has been in practice in the temples of South, till now. The Priests in the temples has misused these poor Dalit women by creating Devadasi system to satisfy their lust. During 16th and 17th century in big way slavery existed in South. Logan says: "In 1792 when British rule commenced in South, a proclamation was issued against dealing with slaves. In 1819, the Collector banned selling slaves. Women slaves fetched good price. According to S. A. Iyar social position of these miserable beings was. "very low indeed. A Dalit should stand at a distance of thirty feet, was the law of the day. He was not allowed entry in a Brahmin village, temple or tank. They could build only muddy huts. In the native states of Cochin and Travancore where Brahmin influence was in the ascendant their position was miserable."

In whole of northern India, during Mughal rule the Brahmins and Kshatriya landlords promoted the practice of forced labour, and slavery in several forms. It was worst type of oppression and serfdom and an ugly form of physical economic exploitation.

Dynasties came and dynasties went, but they hardly influenced the village social set up founded by the Aryans and other invading races. During this period Vedic Varna system prevailed, authority of scriptures and Manu's codification remained intact.

According to Edwards and Garret though India was politically divided but religiously and culturally one and the Bhakti cult brought general masses of artisans class nearer and nearer. The teachings of great apostles of the Bhakti Movement set aside the caste distinctions. There have been some social and spiritual awakening in the oppressed people because of Bhakti Movement. Muslim Sufi saints had also influenced the people of low origin.

Frequent battles and invasions generally disturbed the peace but the village remained largely unaffected. Babar's autobiography in the form of memoirs Tcezuk-I-Babri mentions that its people have no good looks, lack social intercourse, genius and capacity none, manners none, ... peasants and the people of low standing go about naked. This shows the real picture of the Shudras and the untouchables.

Babar's memoirs have been described as a great literary work of historical importance by Elliot and Dowson, E. Demison Ross and Rushbrook Williams etc. Since Babar's time, the Mughal policy was not to interfere in social matters of the Hindus. Mughal emperor's hardly cared for the well being of the lower class and the untouchables who lived mostly in villages. There have been no change in the lives of the untouchables who suffered stigma of untouchability and caste discrimination for centuries. The Mughals tried to associate Hindu rulers, learned and scholarly persons with their administration and many of the Hindus occupied high offices in civil and military services. It seems people of low birth who were to be easily identified kept away from good service, whereas according to Abul Fazl the caste Hindus both Brahmins and Hindu ruling chiefs marked out their career in several administrative fields in Mughal courts.

It is evident from Akbarnama that there was social mobility among upper castes and Vaishyas could perform the role of a Kshatriya, but all doors were closed for Shudras for such mobility. Shudras were suppressed and circumstances forced them to serve the masters whether Hindus or Muslims. Akbar framed separate rules for the Shudras under the influence of upper castes. Akbar was always busy in pleasing Brahmins and Hindu ruling chiefs and liked to promote their interests. He never took interest to set right the caste ridden social life of the country. As usual, bulk of Shudras worked as farm labour, artisans, labourers and menial servants. Mughal administrators engaged them as building workers to construct their forts, palaces and mosques. Thousands of such people were kept as slaves, courtiers and informers on low wages and compelled to embrace Islam. The famines, sometimes heavy rains and floods, day to day battles and revolts, epidemic diseases adversely effected the lives of the artisans and working class. While artisans were crushed by the moneylenders, the peasantry by the Zainindars and Nawabs.

According to A. L. Srivastava: During Muslim rule the Shudras have chosen their ancestral occupations and also worked as field labour and the caste system and the practice of untouchability was so strong that no Shudra was allowed to choose the occupation of the higher caste. In case of Brahmins who could not earn their livelihood by scholastic pursuits were allowed by the new Smritis to pursue agriculture through hired Shudra labour. In times of distress they could themselves cultivate the field. It is however very strange, the Shudras were kept out of forces because of fear of pollution or touch, otherwise country may not have been enslaved by the foreign invaders. Brahmins suffered in prestige due to loss of wholesale patronization by the new rulers. Islamic tradition finally have broken their religious supremacy. Even though their influence in villages where ignorance and superstitions ruled and influenced the society much, was intact. Undoubtedly the social life of the Dalit Shudra classes and untouchables was of utter neglect and complete isolation, extreme sufferings and suppression in the medieval period of history. They were all an ignored class.

PART TWO

Era of Awakening

THREE

The Pioneers

Since, ancient period, the curse of untouchability received the attention of the great Acharyas. Sankaracharya, the prince amongst them for all practical purposes, acknowledged an untouchable as his Guru. His famous work 'Mane-eshapanchakam' bears eloquent testimony to this. But his over-zealous disciples, drawn mostly from the twice-born dwija castes, converted this unknown untouchable into none else than Lord Siva. Untouchables may, therefore, pat on their backs for one of them becoming Maheswara for the moment to initiate the boy Sankara — a rare privilege. But why should have Sankara preferred the garb of a truncated Chandala, despised and dehumanised? So far, none has given a cogent explanation to this question. However, this great Acharya does not seem to have said or done much for the emancipation of the untouchables. There may be two reasons for this—one, all records pertaining to Sankara's benevolence for the well-being of the untouchables might have been destroyed wilfully or, secondly, Sankara might have been very busy in rehabilitating decadent Hinduism so as to scuttle Buddhism which was, by then, though still powerful and popular, in the process of disintegration. Whatever be the reason, Sankara had not gone on record as a bold benefactor of this beguiled and bedevilled lot of human beings. But his non-dualism (*Advaita*) had opened the eyes of the orthodoxy to the immeasurable damage done to the society through its rigidity which often approximated to absurdity. He attacked Vedic ritualism and advocated purposive renunciation. He regarded Ultimate Reality to be te pure consciousness without subjective or objective relation. According to him, the subjective or objective relation is illusory and is due to Avidya or Nescience. His philosophy has been summed up as "Brahman alone is real, the world is illusory and there is identity between the soul and the Brahman (*Brahmah satyam Jagatmithya Jivo Brahmaiva naparah*)". The word *mithya* has, later on, developed into *maya*. Nothing would matter to a person who refuses to recognise the world as a reality. *Na varna Na varnasrama-charadharma...* as his emphatic refutation of mephitic caste system of Manu. Sankara summed up beautifully his philosophy of non-dualism, abstruse yet absorbing, in his 'Dasa Sloki'. He was a born teacher and fulfilled his mission before he discarded his mortal coil at the age of thirty-one years.

Ramanujacharya was a benign personality. He gave the description of a true brahmin—with a heart softer than fresh butter—as indicated in Mahabharat. He authored the Visithadwaita, qualified monism. He rejected Sankara's theory of super-imposition and nescience. Avidya, he averred, was not testified by any means of knowledge (Pramanas) such as perception, inference, and revelation. He opined that the relationship between the individual self and the Absolute is not imaginary as Sankara believed, but very much physical. In other words according to him, the relationship of man and god in religious experience was a matter of mutual inclusion.

Unlike other seers of his age he was positive in his attitude towards untouchables. He attempted to restore them to their legitimate place of honour in the society. He is said to have an un-touchable amongst his disciples. Accompanied by the saint used to go to river Kaveri for his morning ablutions. Coming back from the river to the temple of Lord Sriranganatha on the banks of Kaveri, he would lean on the shoulders of the untouchable disciple. This was resented by others and one day they asked Ramanuja why he was humiliating them by being partial to the untouchable. Ramanuja gently smiled and said softly "He is purer than myself". This may very well be a legend, but it gives an insight into his mind.

Ramanuja resented the word 'Pariahs' applied to untouchables and named them 'Tirukulattar', i.e., people of noble descent. It is chronicled that an untouchable devotee was living far away from the 'sacred' Srirangam as the entry into the town for him was forbidden. Like Orpheus, famous for swaying the beasts and moving the trees and rocks to follow the sounds of ethereal notes on his lyre, this disciple, by his ecstatic singing, used to cast a spell on every passer-by. Of course, he sang the psalms composed by the Alwars, devotees of Lord Vishnu, including Tiruppan Alwar, despite being an untouchable, was considered a saint amongst saints. One day, while returning from the river, Ramanuja entered the untouchable's hovel and listened rapturously to the melodious hymns he sang. When the guru carve out, his face radiated spiritual glow transcending all barriers of caste and creed.

In the Vaishnava temple in Melkote, Mysore, Ramanuja ordained that for three days during the annual festival period, priests from among the untouchables only should attend to the ceremonies and the pilgrims should treat them with equal reverence. This, some say, he did in deep appreciation of their devotion to him and the risks they ran in order to save his life from Jain fanatics.

Madhvacharya stands as the most powerful propounder of Dwaita philosophy. Born of humble Brahman parents and known then as Vasudeva, he joined the Ekadandi order of the Ekanti-Vaishnavas when he was just sixteen. Even as a student he was never at home with the Advaita. Fired with zeal, his young heart longed to resucitate the ancient theism of the Veda Sastras. According to him, there are two orders of reality—one the Independent and the other Dependent. He identified the Independent Reality with Hari or Vishnu who formed the link between Vedic, Upanishadic, Epic and Puranic phases of thought which struck deep roots in the spirituality of Hinduism. He said that the soul of man was potentially divine and the spirit of inquiry in man had to be awakened. He proclaimed that the world was real and Hari was the supreme reality whereas the individual soul is different from *Paramatma*. Tall and handsome, he was such a strong athlete that he easily swam across the Ganges in floods on his way to Vyasasram. Proficient in music and endowed with a deep sonorous voice, specially fit for Vedic recitation, he soon gained popularity as a savant of rare ability and incisive intellectual clarity. Prodigious memory and faith in his mission brought to him innumerable disciples, most of them being the stalwarts of other faiths.

Unlike other Acharyas, Madhva had a deep mystic strain in him. Though he stood for the revival of the best in the Prasthanathraya (Vedas, Upanishads and Gita), he was never inclined to toe the line of orthodoxy. He was opposed to ceremonies that were irrational. He preferred merit to birth. He stood for social reconstruction based on correct understanding of the purpose of life, which he called philosophy of Brahman. He openly declared that the Sudras and Antyajas (untouchables) should be allowed to worship the God. Society according to him, was the creation of a political organisation and, as such, it was the duty of Government to establish an environment in which all were considered to be the children of God. Indeed, it is due to this enlightened outlook inculcated by him that the Madhvas are somewhat liberal towards the untouchables though they did not protest with any vigour the system of inhuman treatment meted out to them. Nor did they invoke the intervention of Vishnu, their God, for a better deal for those exploited.

Basavacharya, looked as the fire-brand amongst the social reformers, had blazed on the horizon of Hindu theology as a meteor of resplendence. He was a veritable Prometheus. Like the Greek demi-god, he suffered heavily for making man self-confident and self-reliant. The social revolution brought about by him had put an end, though temporarily to the dismal ritualism and degrading casteism. He felt that the Hindu society was in a deplorable state because of moral weaknesses originating from superfluous ceremonials, irrational canonical laws and false religious ideas.

Basava felt that there was a general lack of love of knowledge amongst the people and that study of arts and sciences was neglected. He could not tolerate the higher castes oppressing the lower and the strong ill-treating the weak. His receptive mind located the disease and was anxious for its cure corroding the mind of man. Caste tended to weaken the rank and file of the society. Basava planned to create a single community, integrated and well-knit, the brotherhood of Veerashaiva, fully dedicated to the worship of Lord Siva. He introduced far-reaching reforms to promote social cohesion and promote fraternity amongst all. He was against Varna and Varnashramadharma. Basaveswara showed the hollowness of the much vaunted varna, caste system of the Hindus.

This great seer never minced matters. He was straightforward in his preachings. "There is no high-born for me, nor low-born... I am the least of men", he said. He was stung to the quick when he saw anyone deride the lowly and the meek. In righteous indignation.

So universal is his teaching ! The gist of the Eight-fold Path of the Buddha, the quintessence of the Sermon on the Mount and the essence of the Vedic wisdom as embodied in Upanishads are epitomised in these few lines for creating a new society beaming with the spirit of social justice for the happiness of mankind.

Basava's teachings spread a fresh buoyance in the minds of the people. He gave them a new sense of belonging. He offered them something which was new and something grand, which they never knew how to achieve. He breathed a new spirit into the contemporary decaying religion. Women were given equal status and were encouraged to have an independent outlook. Trades and occupations were supported and manual labour was given a new dignity. The spirit of modernism in him challenged the primacy of birth. He threw open the sacred literature to everyone. As against this, he insisted on primacy of character. He was the harbinger of a new social order, helping the fusion of all forces including political, economic and moral. He emphasised the need for establishing unfettered social justice. He was not fascinated by gods and angels. He was pained to see the misery all around. His teachings carried an uncanny fire in them and he imbibed a sense of militancy to his followers. His movement spread like wild fire burning all impediments to ashes. His genius pervaded all fields of activity and, within a decade, he revolutionised the society by instilling confidence and courage in the masses. Under his inspiration, Jangamas toured extensively, singing bellicose ballads exhorting people to eschew caste, establish equality and foster brotherhood. But this glory was short-lived. Basava had a spark in him of the great Vishwamitra who, in his time, had tried to create a new social order based on social justice. Though his movement did not prove effective enough to sustain the society for long, it did refine the religion, perhaps for a short duration, of its age-old impurities.

If the Himalayas have separated India from the rest of Asia, the Vindhyas have divided the country into — the North and the South — two regions. If the sea has served as a natural moat, the Eastern and Western Ghats form the formidable ramparts to our foot. Our great rivers like Indus, Narmada and Tapti, flow towards the West whereas all others wend their way towards the East. Had Indus and Ganges coursed across from the North to the South as the Nile in Egypt, one wonders, what would have been the history of India. But Rishi Bhagiratha had pre-determined the course of Ganga according to the great epic Valmiki Ramayana.

For times unknown, the Deccan plateau along with the divaricated Dandakaranya was an area unknown, unpredictable and to some extent disliked by the people living in the North. It was Agastha, the great Aryan Missionary, who ventured to go to the South, to spread the Aryan culture there. He and his beloved, the dynamic Lopamudra, played an important role in bringing the North and the South closer.

Despite various differences, such as climate, terrain, language and occupation, India always stood united and unified. Yet, there seems to be an un-written law providing the North and the South different functions, especially in the fields of religion, theology and philosophy. The North has been fortunate to be the birth place of Hindu gods. All the ten incarnations of Vishnu, have all taken place in the North. Vamana, Parasurama, Rama and Krishna, to name a few, were from the sacred Aryavatra. No one knows why Vishnu was so partial to the North. This is not a place for describing the incarnations, but in passing, it may be said that Rama and Krishna stand out in bold relief, the former a symbol of Duty and the latter of Beauty. Had there been a harmonious combination of these two imperishable attributes of mankind, Hinduism would, undoubtedly, have been the largest single religion of the world today. If North leads in the matter of God-incarnations, South seems to have enjoyed the bliss of producing great Acharyas like Sankara, Ramanuja, Madhva and Vallabha hailing respectively from Kerala, Tamil Nadu, Karnataka and Andhra states. The Acharyas enunciated boldly principles of monism. Although the source material was the same yet the commentators differed widely and sometimes violently perhaps due to the fact that each one was the product of his times. Sankara had to combat against the degenerated but still popular Buddhism. Ramanuja was fortunate to see the Christianity and Islam in action. So it can be surmised that he borrowed certain healthy practices from these faiths. Madhva had an inveterate antipathy to Advaita, and, as such, his commentary was composed to suit his thesis. Vallabha interpreted Prasthana-Trayi so as to support his Ideal monism. It is, therefore, amusing to find that while all the four Acharyas differed from each other in their individual approaches, their goal was the same. What would happen if the four were to meet now?

The evolution of religions throught in India cannot be taken to be an accident. The edifice was built by brick and it took ages to assume a definite shape and style. The pre-Vedic theological systems are yet to be unravelled. The deciphering of the Harappa and Mohanjedaro inscription might provided enough information on the subject. It is generally accepted that the proto-Dravidian culture and civilisation were of a high order. The archaeologists have given exhilarating accounts of these people and their times. When we come to the Vedas we see animism in full blast slowly devetailing into polytheism leding to final unification in monetheism. But Max Muller thought that Hindu worship approximated to henotheism which gave everyone liberty to invoke different gods each one of them being the paramount for the time being. What in reality is one, is called by the wise by different names is the dictum of Rig Veda and this lends support to the above view. But ritualism dominated the whole field and at times in practice it became oppressive. Uninhibited in thought and unattached to the fruit of their labour, the great Rishis probed into the mysteries of creation and the immanence of the Creator. They pondered a great deal over the permanence and the transitoriness of the world we see and the force behind it. They probed deep into the misty regions of metaphysics in search of solutions of various problems that confronted them. If Vedas are considered to be a gift from God, Upanishads were undoubtedly a boon from men of renunciation and learning, most of them being Kshatriyas. It may be the reason why they were unanimous in their anti-ritualistic attitude. Each one of the Upanishads is a mine of pure gold going deep into thinking, clear analysis and bold enunciation. They tried very hard to capture the essence of the holy Vedic hymns, hence the name Vedanta, end of Veda. Vyasa was a beginner in evolving a harmonious and unified system of philosophy out of the apparently inconsistent and self-contradictory teachings of the Upanishads. The subsequent mostly trusted upon Badarayana's Brahmasutras for people who write note of their own commentaries. The splendid mansion of Vedanta is held aloft by the three pillars, namely the Upanishads, the

Brahmasutras and the Bhagwatgita, collectively known as Prasthana Trayi. Though occasional indirect references were made here and there by the commentators, Vedas always happened to stay in the background.

Ever since the days of Upanishads the general idea of Indian philosophic thought happened to be rather supra-cosmic and supra-terrestrial. This is too much for a non-professionally qualified man. The common man adheres pure intellectualism. He would wish to have something which can have control on his mind and sway his inner feelings. This is brought into practice by spiritualism. The aim of every religion is to forbear a spiritual base to its adherents. Spirit is man's essence. Unimpeded, it opens him out into a saint. The real examination of a religion has its power to produce saints. It is saints who would animate the life of man with divine grace. It is the basis of this that the Bhakti cult of the middle ages is welcome as it provides relief to the otherwise provoking picture of internecine inter-religious quarrels and feuds. Here also South India was the initial point. In a way the celebrated Acharyas, especially Ramanuja and Madhva, began the sacerdotal saga and Basava reached the zenith. Bhakti is high devotion and when it is pointed towards God, it is doubly sanctified.

Narada, the mythological court singer of Vishnu, feels that a devotee is one who always thinks of God with his throat choked and tears running down his cheeks. The devotee talks with immensed love and pleasure with others. He purifies not only his family but the whole world. Amongst the devotees of God there is no difference of birth, learning, external appearance, family, wealth, religious difference in observance and the like since they all belong to Him. Sandilya holds that devotion is the way to liberation. Sankara feels that Bhakti is meditation on the Supreme Self. Ramanuja prescribes meditation coupled with yoga to acquire perfect Bhakti. To Madhva, service to all living beings and constant meditation on Hari is Bhakti. In brief Bhakti means to train the mind to have a vision of God everywhere and love. His display of objects with renunciation as Prahlada did. Bergson considers that divine love is not some thing related to God, it is God itself. This Bhakti cult spread all over Indian thought for many generations and helped to restrain the minds of the people, it rid the society of its evils and ill elements and provided various means for nobler aspirations.

This point is to be noted is that Bhakti is not self-taught. It has to be first brought about by a Guru, Teacher. Hence the doctrine of personal Guru is there. In other words, rules of Bhakti show us that there should be a personal god, and a teacher should constantly guide and guide the devotee into the realms of God's vision. This cult of devotional supplication is not something new to India. It can be compared as old as India's civilisation. The Vedas comprises of a few indirect references to this and Epics have quite elaborate account of saintly personages. But it is only in the Gita we come across a detailed discussion of the theme by Lord Krishna himself. Having dealt with the various systems finding to attainment of salvation, Krishna assured Arjun—"Abandoning all righteous deeds, seek me as thy sole Refuge; I will liberate thee from all sins; do thou not grieve." He confided: "Knowing for certain that my devotee never perishes—so invaluable in his devotion to me." This seems to be the refined of Gita to the laity.

But there is a strong wave of public opinion amongst the scholars that Islam and Christianity had a helping hand in enlivening of Bhakti cult in the middle ages. It is quite right that these religions of Semitic origin arrived South India through the sea routes years before they made their show up by land in the Gangetic plain. There was a well coordinated and managed Church in South India from the Sixth Century. Islam reached Malabar Coast during the first century of Hijra, 7th Century A.D. The intellectual Dr. Tara Chand is of the view that most of the elements in the Southern schools of devotion and philosophy taken singly were brought about from ancient systems but the elements in their totality and their uncommon emphasis betray a singular approximation to Muslim faith and, therefore, make the arguments for Islamic influence probable. He strengthens his argument by giving stress that Islam has made an indirect contribution to the increasing emphasis on monotheism, emotional worship, self-surrender (prapatti), adoration of the teacher (Guru Bhakti) and, in addition to them, carelessness in the rigours of the caste system and indifference towards mere ritual. He firmly believes that Ramanuja copied the Teacher-Disciple system from Islam as absorption in God through devotion to a teacher which is a significant Muslim conception. It started with the Shias and blossomed very well amongst the Sufis. It cannot be gainsaid that Ramanuja, Madhva and later Basava were highly influenced by these new religions, whose impact on India was widely to affect the text of history of this sub-continent.

Amongst the various saints of India, Kabir is peerless. He was not as ascetic. He was a family man. Ever immersed in perfect happiness having no fear in his mind, Kabir spoke immortal words which became beacon lights to many subsequent seekers after truth. Temples and mosques were insignificant for him. He was neither influenced by Kaaba nor Kailas. He brushed aside dogmas and doctrines. He attracted many disciples from all communities who formed the Panth to spread his message of equality and fraternity amongst all the people, Hindus as well as Muslims in India.

Tulsidas, who entirely created the soul stirring epic, *Ramcharit Manas*, was another source of inspiration for people to follow the path of piety. A Brahmin himself and highly learned, he adjusted his mind to the fervid felicity of divine love. He set himself so deeply that he lost himself in ecstasy in delineating the divine qualities of Rama. He scoffed at caste barriers and kept the self-esteemed quiet by declaring that sinners too could become saints and untouchables were not excluded from this privilege.

Kanaka Dasa, whose profession but a prince among saints, went the whole hog against casteism. Here is what he said:

"The world is crying hoarse, saying caste, caste, caste. But really what is the caste to the Sadhu and to the good man? Is not the lotus, that grows in a muddy pond, used to adorn God? Is not the milk which is produced from the cow used as the drink of the highest castes? Is not the musk that is used as the head-mark of the Gods obtained from a deer? What is the caste of God Narayana? What is the caste of Siva? What is the caste of the Atma? What is the caste of Jiva?" It was not in anger that he attacked the caste. He was right in making a revolt against the oppressive orthodoxy.

Chaitanya, who entirely devoted his life to Lord Krishna, recommended dance and music to produce a certain state of ecstasy so as to enjoy and celebrate God-vision by Bhaktas. His disciples belonged to all castes. The school of Chaitanya, through Karta Bhajans, propagated an entirely new way of life based on purposive. It created a brotherhood which had nothing to do with caste and creed.

Namdeva is worshipped throughout Maharashtra as brave advocate in possession of divine love and emotional integration of mankind. He along with others made an effort to rub off the sharp edges of various sects and faiths. He had Mahar disciples for whom his heart shivered with tenderness.

Tukaram belonged to the same time of Sivaji and more than anyone he helped the Marathas to weld themselves into a 'people united in common aims and aspirations'. He completely denied Vedic sacrifices and attempted a fusion of the ideals of Islam and Hinduism. According to him, Rama and Rahim were different names for one and the same consistence. Of course, he was against caste system.

Eknath is another great soul who was delighted to enter an untouchable's hut and eat the food served by an untouchable woman who adored him for his saintliness. A great dinner was arranged at Pandharpur in which the contemporary saints like Guroba, Sanvata, Chokhoba, Parisa Bhagwat, with different backgrounds and others took part along with Namdeva and Gnaneswar. A day after this feast, Gnanadeva was declared to have entered Sanjivan samadhi at the age of 21. We come to know about many miracle stories of these devotees in the South who visited the land preaching divine love. The Alwars of Vaishnavism and Nainars of Saivism created a warmth amongst the masses for a better, fuller and richer life for everyone to live happily.

Even amongst untouchables there have been renowned and greatly revered Bhaktas like Ravidas in the North, Nandanar in the South and Chokamela in the West. How could this community produce such saints in spite of the consuming flames of unequality and distinction? But devotion and dedication to God are not the close preserve of any set of people. Striving to realise divinity is not the monopoly of any single caste or community, according to Bhardwaja. The gods in temples may be claimed as belonging to either this or that caste. But the all-pervading God who is the unseen seer, unheard hearer, unthought thinker and unknown knower is love and respected by everyone, the sentient and the insentient.

FOUR

Mahatma's Patronage

In our society, the untouchability akin to the race and colour problems in the West, rested upon the idea of the superiority of one section of people over another on account of their birth. A Brahman might be as poor as the untouchable, but he was not ill-treated by our society on account of his poverty. Gandhi called these so-called religious sanctions as a serious stigma on the fair name of a society which have deep-rooted cultural and historical traditions to support its identity.

The disease of untouchability is quite old in our society. It led to social hatred and discriminatory feeling of high and low, and as a result the later category suffered for centuries in the hands of the former. Time and again, ceaseless attempts were made by social reformers to alleviate the status of downtrodden and bring them to a level by which they could breathe and subsist with some confidence in the society. This was, however, a most complex problem, the complete or satisfactory solution of which could not be evolved in spite of attempts by prominent personalities including social reformers, educationists and political leaders of our society. For example, Buddha, Mahavira, Kabir, Nanak, Dayanand and others played their social and religious role at one time or the other. Besides numerous socio-religious reform movements had deep association with the cause of the untouchables who were labelled as a serious stigma on the fair name of Hinduism.

The idea of social discrimination was first experienced by Gandhiji in South Africa where he engaged himself against the discriminatory attitude of the South African Government against Indians. The problem was similar to that of untouchability as the migrants were treated as inferior to the local population which enjoyed numerous basic rights legally not available to Indians. As a youngman Gandhi started realizing how much hellish was their life which had weakened their social and moral fabric essential for the growth of physical and economic features of human beings. In India, too, he was faced with this problem when he returned to his motherland in 1915, during the second year of the First World War.

For him the reconstruction of the life of the nation was of utmost importance. This could be achieved by alleviating the social status of the untouchables. He always considered untouchability as a cruel and inhuman institution. It violated human dignity. He did not believe that the imperial ambitions of Britain were alone responsible for our slavery but it was the negligence of our national duty which was primarily responsible for it. A reformed India, he stated, would be a free India. Untouchability in its extreme form always troubled him so much because he regarded himself as a Hindu of Hindus saturated with the spirit of Hinduism. As he always considered it as an excrescence in Hinduism, he had even no hesitation in renouncing Hinduism itself. To remove untouchability was a penance that caste Hindus owed to Hinduism and to themselves. Thus the purification needed was not of untouchables, but of the so-called superior castes.

The apathy of the high-caste Hindus worried him much. He, however, dealt with them as best as he could. During his discussion with Harijans, at Ahmedabad, he observed, "This is a movement for the purification of Hinduism. Think what contribution you can make to it. If you bestir yourselves, if you shed your unclean habits, if you reform your way of living, irrespective of what the high-caste Hindus do, I assure you their superiority of birth will automatically disappear. Superiority consists in clean and pure living and I assure you that in spite of your unclean occupations you can live cleaner and purer lives than the rest of us. Yours is a service without which the community cannot do. I want you to be conscious of the dignity of your profession, to learn to practise it in a clean manner and I am sure you will be able to dictate your terms. Depend on yourself, stand on your own legs and work your own salvation."

Gandhi felt that the so-called caste Hindus had a personal obligation to fulfil towards the Harijans which they must do attaching any conditions and it was to be their atonement. "Whether in this world or the next, it is for each one to free oneself from bondage by one's own effort. Harijans should not look upon themselves as lowly, weak or crippled."

Time and again, Gandhi exhorted the Harijans to magnify their own faults so that they appeared to be as big as mountains and then make regular attempts to overcome them. In it lay the key to obtaining the rights which they wanted. "Never believe that since others have the same faults we need not mind our own. No matter what others do, it is your dharma to overcome the feelings which you find in yourselves.

......You will not be able, at the behest of others to overcome what you yourselves do not look upon, as failings. Hence, it should suffice to say that you should shake off whatever faults you can find in yourselves.

In the process of regeneration of the nation, Gandhi waged an unrelenting and systematic war. "If we are children of the same God how can there be any rank among us." For him, there was only one *varna* in India—the *Sudras*. Indeed the *Sudras* are those who serve. He desired that all the Hindus voluntarily call themselves *Sudras*.

He was critical of any person who would claim superiority over fellow-men. In his view there was no such thing as inherited or acquired superiority. He was happy and felt satisfied to call himself a scavenger, a spinner, a weaver and a labourer. He wrote in the *Harijan*, I have intentionally described myself as a *Bhangi*. In man-made social ladder I want to be at the bottom.

He indeed was much troubled to see the appalling plight of untouchables in different regions of the country. Its eradication greatly agitated his mind and he devised ways and means, from time to time, through his speeches and writings. He wrote in *Navajivan,* "By passing resolutions and talking about their problem we have raised hopes in them. It was absolutely necessary to do this. It was necessary also that hopes should be raised in them and to tell those *antyaja* friend that what has happened should be sufficient answer to them. Another answer can be that they lay the entire burden on me. I can understand the sting in their words. They accuse me of being satisfied with the more or less that I do myself and of being gullible enough to be taken in by others who only befool me. However, if I do something, there are others who may be doing less but still they do it."

Gandhi called Harijans as men of God and felt that all the religions of the world consider God pre-eminently as the Friend of the friendless. Help of the helpless and Protector of the weak. He stated that leaving the rest of the world aside, in India who could be more friendless, helpless or weaker than the forty millions or more Hindus of India who were classified as 'untouchables'. If, therefore, anybody of people could be fitly described as men of God, they were surely these helpless, friendless and despised people. He observed, "when Caste Hindus have of their own inner conviction and, therefore, voluntarily, got rid of the present day untouchability, we shall all be called Harijans; for according to my humble opinion, Caste Hindus will then have found favour with God and may, therefore, be fitly described as His men" Gandhi had the opinion that "If we came into power with the stain of untouchability unaffected, I am positive that the 'untouchables' would become worse under that *Swaraj* than they are now, for the simple reason that our weakness and our failings would then be buttressed up by the accession of power."

Through his speeches in public and writings in *Young India* and *Harijan,* he stressed the problem of untouchability and its removal from its roots. He hated untouchability with his entire soul. The Mahatma had the feeling that in Hinduism there was no sanction for treating any single human being as untouchable. The Bhagavadgita has never taught that a *Chandala* was in any way inferior to a Brahmana. A Brahmana is no more a Brahmana, once he becomes insolvent and considers himself a superior being.

Gandhi considered himself a Sanatani Hindu, because he obeyed the eternal precepts of the faith as embodied in the Shastras as he understood them. He had no doubt that there are many interpolations in the *Smritis* and the other scriptural books. He rejected as interpolations everything in the *Smritis* or other writings that were not consistent with Truth and Non-violence or other fundamental and universal principles of ethics. He opined, "The idea of superiority and inferiority is repugnant to the most elementary principles of morality. A Brahmana who regards himself superior to any single creature of God ceases to be a Brahmana. If we are children of the same God, how can there be any rank among us? ... What will happen to the body, if these members begin to quarrel about rank ? ... The verses in the Smritis about Sudras deserve to be summarily rejected as being contrary to the spirit of humanity."

Gandhi believed that untouchability would not be removed by the force even of law. It could only be removed, he opined, when the majority of Hindus felt that it was a crime against God and man and were ashamed of it. In other words, it was a process of conversion, i.e. purification, of the Hindu heart. The aid of law had to be invoked when it hindered or interfered with the growth of the reform as when, in spite of the willingness of the trustees and the temple going public, the law came in the way of the opening of a particular temple.

There are innumerable castes in India. They are a social institution. This institution has superadded to it restrictions which in my opinion, are undesirable and are bound to go in course of time. The difference, therefore, between the caste system and untouchability is not one of degree, but of kind. An "untouchable is outside the pale of respectable society. He is hardly treated as a human being. He is an outcaste hurled into an abyss by his fellow-beings occupying the same platform.

The difference, therefore, is somewhat analogous to the difference between heaven and hell."

He summarised the social position of untouchables as follows: "Socially they are lepers. Economically they are worse than slaves. Religiously they are denied entrance to places we miscall 'houses of God'. They are denied the use, on the same terms as the Caste Hindus, of public roads, public schools, public hospitals, public wells, public taps, public parks and the like ... The wonder is that they are at all able to eke out an existence or that they still remain within the Hindu fold. They are too downtrodden to rise in revolt against their suppressors. It is only ceaseless effort that can raise these downtrodden fellow beings from degradation, purify Hinduism and raise the whole Hindu society and with it the whole of India."

Regarding inter-dining and inter-marriage, the Mahatma held the view that marrying and dining were matters of individual preference and no one had a right to ask to choose a girl for wife or to dine with anybody against his will. He, however, elaborated his point thus: "But my answer is at the same time 'yes' because if a person refused to take food touched by another person on the ground of untouchability or inferiority, he is observing untouchability. In other words, untouchability cannot constitute any ground for restraint on interdining or marriage."

An important organization, known as the *Harijan Sevak Sangh* which was not a part of the Congress came into being as a result of the fast which the Mahatma undertook in 1932 when he was in jail. G.D. Birla was its President and Thakkar Bapa its Secretary. "it is the duty of Harijan workers and Caste Hindus to do sweepers' work themselves. These reforms do not cost much. They require intelligence, hard work and love of an ideal. We may not relegate sweepers work to one particular class. Therefore all should learn it in the same way as cooking. Each person should be his own sweeper. If this ideal were to be put into practice in society, the miserable condition of sweepers would at once be rectified."

The system of forced labour exacted by petty landowners from Harijans and other classes called backward is almost universal in India. The petty landlords are generally Hindus. "It is the privilege of Harijan Sevaks, no matter to what organization they belong to befriend Harijans, to study their condition in detail, to approach Savarna Hindus and show them as gently as possible what their duty is towards those whom they have treated as outcastes of society and deprived even of legal rights."

He always preached among the Harijans, the importance of cleanliness, abstention from carrion-eating and intoxicating drinks and drugs, requirement of taking education themselves and giving it to their children, also abstention from eating the leavings from Caste Hindus' plates. He stated, "On the contrary, I suggest to Caste Hindus that the shortcomings are not inherent to Harijans but that they are due to our criminal neglect of—even deliberate suppression of—these brethren of ours.... We must approach Harijans as penitents or debtors, not as their patrons or creditors extending generosity to the undeserving."

Besides Gandhi suggested that common schools and wells should be opened where the existing ones were not available for Harijans either due to the violent and successful opposition of the neighbours or some other unavoidable cause. Harijans, he observed, could not be left uncared for in matters of necessary services till public opinion had matured. National schools, to be worth the name in terms of *Swaraj* for the attainment of which they have been brought into existence must be conducted in order to advancing the national programme in so far as it is applicable to educational institutions. Thus, for example, national schools must be the most potent means of educating the untouchables and abolishing the curse of untouchability from the schools. Whilst in theory the (present national) schools are open to the 'untouchables' very few, as a matter of fact, have untouchable children in them. I have no hesitation in advising that teachers should run the risk of closing down their schools if the condition of running them requires the exclusion of untouchables.

Thus the Mahatma stressed the fact that preliminary training should consist in teaching Harijan children manners, good speech and good conduct. "A Harijan child sits anyhow; dresses anyhow; his eyes, ears, teeth, hair, nails, nose are often full of dirt; many never know what it is to have a wash. Their lesson should begin for the first three months with teaching them cleanliness. They should be taught also how to eat properly. If this preliminary training is to be given in all Harijan schools, pamphlets giving detailed instructions for teachers in their languages should be prepared and distributed, and inspectors of schools be required during their inspection to examine teachers and pupils on this head and to send full reports of the progress made in this direction."

In fact, Gandhi never reconciled himself to untouchability. He always considered it as an excrescence in Hinduism. He stated forcefully that a religion that established the worship of the cow could not in all probability have countenance or warrant a cruel and in human boycott of human beings. I should be content to be torn to pieces rather than disown the suppressed classes. Hindus will certainly never deserves freedom, nor get it if they allow their noble religion to be disgraced by the retention of the taint of untouchability.

He warned the Hindu brethren against the tendency which he saw of exploiting the suppressed classes achieving their political ends. He stated that to remove untouchability was a menance that Caste Hindus owed to Hinduism and to themselves. The purification needed was not of 'untouchables' but of the so-called superior castes. There was no vice that was special to the "untouchables", not even dirt and insanitation. It is our arrogance which blinds us, superior Hindus, to our own faults and which magnifies those of our downtrodden brethren whom we have suppressed and whom we keep under suppression. That religion and that nation will be blotted out of the face of the earth which pins its faith to injustice, untruth or violence. God is Light, not darkness. God is Love, not hate, God is truth, not untruth. God alone is great. We His creatures are but dust. Let us be humble and recognise the place of the lowliest of His creatures. Krishna honoured Sudama in his rags as he honoured no one else. Love is the root of religion.

For the opening of the roads was not the last but the first step in the ladder of reform. Temples in general, public wells, public schools must be thrown open to the untouchables equally with the Caste Hindus.

"I want my Harijan brother, if he wishes, to share this temple, worship with the millions of his co-religionists the so-called Caste men. It is the latter's duty to throw open their temples to their Harijan brethren. Temple worship supplies the felt spiritual want of the human race. It admits of reform. But it will live as long as man lives."

The Mahatma considered untouchability as the greatest blot on Hinduism. He developed this feeling when he was a child. He mentioned how he did not like numerous Hindu customs which promoted the feelings of high and low in Indian society. He felt sorry that Hinduism had sinned in giving sanction to untouchability, and Indian society had suppressed 'our brethren'. I regret untouchability as the greatest blot on Hinduism. This idea was not brought home to me by my bitter experience during the South African struggle is not because of the fact that I was once an agnostic. It is equally wrong to think—as some people do—that I have taken my views from my study of Christian religious literature. These opinions date as far back as the time when I was neither enamoured of, nor was acquainted with the Bible or the followers of the Bible.

Gandhiji stated, "while at school I would often happen to touch the untouchables, and as I never would conceal the fact from my parents, my mother would tell me that the shortest cut to purification after the unholy touch was to cancel the touch by touching any Mussalman passing by. And simply out of reverence and regard for my mother I often did so, but never did so believing it to be a religious obligation. After some time we shifted to Porbandar, where I made my first acquaintance with Sanskrit. I was not yet put into an English school, and my brother and I were placed in charge of a Brahmin, who taught us *Ramaraksha* and *Vishnu Puja*. The text *Jale Vishnuh Sthale Vishnuh* (there is the Lord present in water, there is the Lord present in earth) has never gone out of my memory. A motherly old dame used to live close by. Now it happened that I was very timid then, and would conjure up ghosts and goblins whenever the lights went out and it was dark. The old order, to disabuse me of fears, suggested that I should mutter the Ramaraksha texts whenever I was afraid, and all evil spirits would fly away. This I did and, as I thought, with good effect. I could never believe then that there was any text in the *Ramaraksha* pointing to the contact of the untouchables as a sin. I did not understand its meaning then, or understood it very imperfectly. But I was confident that *Ramaraksha*, which could destroy all fear of ghosts, could not be countenancing any such thing as fear of contact with the untouchables."

More Extracts:

"The *Ramayana* used to be regularly read in our family. A Brahmin called Ladha Maharaj used to read it. He was sticken with leprosy, and was confident that a regular reading of the *Ramayana* would cure him of leprosy, and indeed, he was cured of it. 'How can the *Ramayana*', I thought to myself, in which one who is regarded now-a-days as an untouchable took Rama across the Ganges in his boat, countenance the idea of any human being untouchable on the ground that they were polluted souls?" The fact that we address God as the 'purifier of the polluted' and by similar appellations, shows that it is a sin to regard anyone born in Hinduism as polluted or untouchable—that it is Satanic to do so. I have hence been never tired of repeating that is a great sin. I do not pretend that this thing had crystallized as a conviction in me at the age of twelve, but I do say that I did then regard untouchability as a sin. I narrate this story for the information of the Vaishnavas and orthodox Hindus."

"I have always claimed to be a Sanatani Hindu. It is not that I am quite innocent of the scriptures. I am not a profound scholar of Sanskrit. I have read the Vedas and the *Upanishads* only in translation. Naturally therefore, mine is not a scholarly study of them. My knowledge of them is in no way profound, but I have studied them as I should do as a Hindu and I claim to have grasped their true spirit. By the time I had reached the age of 21, I had studied other religions also."

"There was a time when I was wavering between Hinduism and Christianity. When I recovered my balance of mind, I felt that to me salvation was possible only through the Hindu religion and my faith in Hinduism grew deeper and more enlightened. But even then I believed that untouchability was no part of Hinduism; and that if it was, such Hinduism was not for me. True Hinduism does not regard untouchability as a sin." I do not want to enter into any controversy regarding the interpretation of the Shastras. It might be difficult for me to establish my point by quoting authorities from the *Bhagavat* or *Manusmriti*. But I claim to have understood the spirit of Hinduism. Hinduism has sinned in giving sanction to untouchability. It has degraded us, made us the pariahs of the Empire. Even the Mussalmans caught the sinful contagion from us, and in South Africa, in East Africa and in Canada, the Mussalmans no less than Hindus came to be regarded as pariahs. All this evil has resulted from the sin of untouchability."

"I may here recall my proposition, which is this: So long as the Hindus wilfully regard untouchability as part of their religion, as long as the mass of Hindus consider it a sin to touch a section of their brethren, Swaraj is impossible of attainment. Yudhishthira would not enter heaven without his dog. How can, then, the descendants of that Yudhishthira expect to obtain Swaraj without the untouchables? What crimes for which we condemn the Government as Satanaic have not we been guilty of towards our untouchable brethren?"

"We are guilty of having suppressed our brethren; we

make them crawl on their bellies; we have made them rub their noses on the ground; with eyes red with rage, we push them out of railway compartments—what more than this has British rule done? What charge that we bring against Dyer and O'Dwyer may not others, and even our own people, lay at our door ? We ought to purge ourselves of this pollution. It is idle to talk of Swaraj so long as we do not protect the weak and the helpless, or so long as it is possible for a single Swarajist to injure the feelings of any individual. Swaraj means that not a single Hindu or Muslim shall for a moment arrogantly think that he can crush with impunity meek Hindus or Muslims. Unless this condition is fulfilled we will gain Swaraj only to lose it the next moment. We are no better than the brutes until we have purged ourselves of the sins we have committed against our weaker brethren."

"But I have faith in me still. In the course of my peregrinations in India I have realized that the spirit of kindness of which the poet Tulsidas sings so eloquently, which forms the cornerstone of the Jain and Vaishnava religions, which is the quintessence of the *Bhagavat*, and which every verse of the *Gita* is saturated with—this kindness, this love, this charity is slowly but steadily gaining ground in the hearts of the masses of this country."

"Many a fracas between Hindus and Muslims are still heard of. There are still many of those who do not scruple to wrong one another. But as to the net result, I feel that kindness and charity have increased. The Hindus and Mahommedans have become godfearing. We have shaken ourselves free from the hypnotism of law courts and Government schools and no longer labour under any other hallucination. I have also realized that those whom we regard as illiterate and ignorant are the very people who deserve to be called educated. They are more cultured than we, their lives are more righteous than ours. A little study of the present day mentality of the people will show that according to the popular conception, Swaraj is synonymous with Ramarajya—the establishment of the

Kingdom of Righteousness on earth. If it can bring any comfort to you, my untouchable brethren, I would say that your question does not cause so much stir, as it used to do formerly. That does not mean that I expect you to cease to have misgivings about the Hindus. How can they deserve to be not mistrusted having wronged you so much ? Swami Vivekanand used to say that the untouchables were not depressed, they were suppressed by the Hindus who, in turn, had suppressed themselves by suppressing them."

"I suppose I was at Nellore on the 6th of April. I met the untouchables there and I prayed that day as I have done today. I do not want to attain *moksha*. I do not want to be reborn. But if I have to be reborn, I should be born an untouchable, so that I may share their sorrows, sufferings and the affronts levelled at them, in order that I may endeavour to free myself and them from that miserable condition. I, therefore, prayed that if I should be born again, I should do so not as a Brahmin, Kshatriya, Vaishya or Sudra, but as an Atisudra."

"Today is much more solemn that the sixth. It is hallowed by the memory of the massacre of thousands of innocents. And I prayed, therefore, also today that if I should die with any of my desires unfructified, with my service of the untouchables unfinished, with my Hinduism unfulfilled, I may be born again amongst the untouchables to bring my Hinduism to its fulfilment."

"I love scavenging. In my Ashram, an eighteen-year-old Brahman lad is doing the scavenger's work in order to teach the Ashram scavenger cleanliness. The lad is no reformer. He was born and bred in orthodoxy. He is a regular reader of the *Gita* and faithfully performs *sandhyavandana*. His pronunciation of Sanskrit verses is more faultless than mine. When he conducts the prayer, his soft, sweet melodies melt one into love. But he felt that his accomplishments were incomplete until he had become also a perfect sweeper and that if he wanted the Ashram sweeper to do his work well, he must do it himself and set an example."

"You should realize that you are cleaning Hindu society. You have therefore to purify your lives. You should cultivate the habit of cleanliness, so that no one may point his finger at you. Use alkali ash or earth if you cannot afford to use soap to keep yourselves clean. Some of you are given to drinking and gambling which you must get rid of. You will point your finger at the Brahmins and say that even they are given to these vices. But they are not looked upon as polluted as you are. You must not ask the Hindus to emancipate you as a matter of favour. Hindus must do so, if they want, in their own interests. You should, therefore, make them feel ashamed by your own purity and cleanliness. I believed that we shall have purified ourselves within the next five months. If my expectations are not fulfilled, I will think that although my proposition was fundamentally correct, yet I was wrong in my calculation; and I will again say that I had erred in my calculation."

"You claim to be Hindus; you read the *Bhagavat*. If, therefore, the Hindus oppress you then you should understand that the fault does not lie in the Hindu religion but in those who profess it. In order to emancipate yourselves you shall have to purify yourselves. You shall have to get rid of evil habits like drinking."

"If you want to ameliorate your conditions, if you want to obtain Swaraj, you should be self-reliant. I was told in Bombay that some of you are opposed to N.C.O. and believes that salvation is only possible through the British Government. Let me tell you that you will never be able to obtain redress by discarding Hindu religion and courting the favour of a third party. Your emancipation lies in your own hands."

"I have come in contact with the untouchables all over the country; and I have observed that immense possibilities lie latent in them of which neither they nor the rest of the Hindus seem to be aware. Their intellect is of original purity. I ask you to learn spinning and weaving, and if you take them up as a profession, you will keep poverty from your doors. As regards your attitude towards the Bhangis I will repeal what I said at Godhra. I cannot understand why you should yourselves countenance the distinction between Dheds and Bhangis. There is no difference between them. Even in normal times their occupation is as honourable as that of lawyers or Government servants."

"You should now cease to accept leavings from plates, however clean they may be represented to be. Receive grain only—good, sound grain, not rotten grain—and that too only if it is courteously offered. If you are able to do all I have asked you to do, you will secure your emancipation, not in four or five months, but in so many days", he added.

Gandhiji further described, "The Hindus are not sinful by nature—they are sunk in ignorance. Untouchability must be extinct in this very year. Two of the strongest desires that keep me in flesh and bone are the emancipation of the untouchables are the protection of the cow. When these two desires are fulfilled, there is Swaraj, and therein lies my own *moksha*. May God give you strength to work out your salvation."

In a huge assembly of students at Nagpur on 9th November 1933, the Mahatma opined that he was not confined to Hinduism, and if untouchability was removed from the Hindu heart, he hoped far-reaching consequences and a great change in Indian society. The barrier of untouchability, he said, was a great hindrance towards achieving of any kind of unity. He was, however, not sure if his dream about the removal of untouchability would be achieved during his life time.

He said, "I know this tussle between English and Hindi is almost an eternal tussle. Whenever I have addressed student audiences, I have been surprised by the demand for English. You know, or ought to know, that I am a lover of the English language. But I do believe that the students of India, who are expected to throw in their lot with the teeming millions and to serve them, will be better qualified if they pay more attention to Hindi than to English. I do not say that you should not learn English; learn it by all means. But, so far as I can see, it cannot be the language of the millions of Indian homes. It will be confined to thousands or tens of thousands, but it will not reach the millions. Therefore, I am delighted when the students ask me to speak in Hindi."

"You, both the speakers, have spoken of me in terms, which if I believed to be true of myself, I do not know where I would be. But I know my place. I am a humble servant of India and is trying to serve India. I serve humanity at large, I discovered in my early days that the service of India is not inconsistent with the services of humanity. As I grew older in years, and I hope also in wisdom, I saw that the discovery was well made and after nearly 50 years of public life, I am able to say today that my faith in the doctrine, that the service of one's nation is not inconsistent with the service of the world, has grown. It is a good doctrine. Its acceptance alone will ease the situation in the world and stop the mutual jealousies between nations inhabiting this globe of ours. You have said truly that, in taking up this war against untouchability. I have not confined myself to Hinduism. I have said more than once that if untouchability is removed in its fulness from the Hindu heart, it will have far-reaching consequences, in asmuch as it touches millions of human beings. As I said last night to the great meeting in Nagpur, if untouchability is really removed from the Hindu heart, that is, if the high caste Hindus purge themselves of this terrible taint, we shall soon discover that we are all one and not different peoples, Hindus, Muslims, Christians, Parsis, whatever we may call ourselves. We shall feel the unity, once the barrier of untouchability is removed. As I have often said, untouchability is a hydra-headed monster, appearing in many shapes. Some of them are very subtle. If I have jealousy for any human being, that also is a species of untouchability. I do not know if my dream about the removal of untouchability will be fully realized while I am living. All those who are religiously inclined, those who believe not in formal religion but in the essence of religion, cannot but believe in the removal of a subtle type of untouchability that affects the lives of a vast mass of humanity.

If Hindu hearts can be purged of this evil, our eyes of understanding will be more and more opened. It is not possible to estimate the gain to humanity when untouchability is really removed. You can now have no difficulty in understanding why I have staked my life for this one thing."

"If you, the students who have assembled here, have followed me so far and understood the implications of this mission of mine, you will soon extend the help I want from you. Many students have written to me asking what part they can take in helping this movement. It is a surprise to me that students are obliged to ask this question. The field is so vast and near you that you need not ask the question as to what you may do and what you may not. It is not a political question. It may become one, but for you and me, for the time being, it is not connected with politics. My life is governed by religion. I never lost sight of the principle that governs my life when I began dabbling in politics. As this is a humanitarian campaign, students must devote a part of their spare time, if not the whole, to the service of thousands of Harijans. By giving me this magnificent purse you have certainly equalled the brightest records of students meetings which I have addressed in my many pereginations throughout the length and breadth of India. But I want much more from you. I have found that, if I get many helpers who can give their spare time, much work can be done. This work cannot be done by hired labour. With hired labour we cannot go to Harijan quarters and sweep their roads, enter their houses and wash their children. I have described in the columns of the Harijan what students can do. A Harijan teacher has shown what a Herculean task it is for him to tackle. Even wild children are better than Harijan children. Wild children are not sunk utter degradation, as the Harijan children are, nor do they live in such filthy surroundings. This problem cannot be tackled by hired labour. No amount of money can enable me to do this. It must be your prerogative. It is an acid test of the education received by you in schools and colleges. Your world will not be measured by your ability to make faultless English speeches. Your worth will be measured by the services you render to the poor and not by Government posts worth Rs. 60 or Rs. 600 that you may have got. I wish you would do this work in the spirit I suggest. I have not met a single student who has said that he cannot spare one hour per day. If you write your diary from day to day, you will find that you waste many a precious hour in the 365 days of the year. If you want to turn your education to good account, you will turn your attention to this work while this hurricane campaign lasts. Erstwhile students are serving Harijans within a radius of 5 miles round about Wardha. They are doing good silent work; therefore, you do not know them. I invite you to see their work. It is hard but pleasurable. It will give you joy, greater than your cricket or tennis. I have repeatedly said that money come if I have real, intelligent, honest workers. As a boy of 18 I began my education in begging. I have seen that money can be found easily if we have the right kind of workers. Money alone will never satisfy me. I would ask you to pledge yourselves to devote a definite number of spare hours to Harijan service. As you, Mr. President, have said, I am a dreamer. I am indeed a practical dreamer. My dreams are not airy nothings. I want to convert my dreams into realities as far as possible. Therefore, I must hasten to auction the gifts I have received from you."

There was much difficulty in running schools for Harijan boys. In spite of allurements of fee-concessions and scholarships to them, their attendance in the schools was not upto the mark. The Mahatma suggested ways and means for the improvement of their lot by devising novel schemes by the teachers attached to these schools. "One who is responsible for the management of over twenty-five Harijan schools writes a long letter stating the difficulties experienced in the management of the schools and ask how I would conduct them if I had the direct management thereof. I need not recount his difficulties which he has described carefully. What I am about to say is an attempt to answer them."

"While we are bound to give scholarships and other help to those Harijan boys and girls who attend the established schools, there is no reason whatever slavishly to reproduce the mode and methods of those schools in the ones under our own management."

"We have to recognize that we get Harijan children with great difficulty to attend any school at all. We cannot expect any degree of regularity in them and, thanks to our past criminal neglect, they are so unkept that we have, in the beginning stages, to handle them in a manner wholly different from the ordinary."

"On first admission their bodies have to be minutely examined and thoroughly cleaned. Their clothes might have to be cleaned and patched. The first daily lesson, therefore, will for some time consist of applied hygiene and sanitation and simple needle-work. I should use no books probably for the whole of the first year. I should talk to them about things with which they are familiar and, doing so, correct their pronunciation and grammar and teach them new words. I should note all the new words they may learn from day to day so as to enable me to use them frequently till they have them fixed in their minds regularly. The teacher will not give discourses but adopt the conversational method. Through conversations he will give his pupils progressive instruction in history, geography and arithmetic. History will begin with that of our own times, and then, too, of events and of persons nearest us, and geography will begin with that of the neighbourhood of the school. Arithmetic will begin with the sums applicable to the pupil's houses. Having tried the method myself, I know that infinitely more knowledge can be given to the pupils through it, and without strain on them, than can be given through the orthodox methods, within a given time. Knowledge of the alphabets should be treated as a separate subject altogether. The letters should be treated as pictures which the children will first be taught to recognize and name. Writing will follow as part of the drawing lesson. Instead of making daubs of their letters, pupils should be able to make perfect copies of the models placed before them. They would not, therefore, be called upon to draw the letters till they had acquired control over their fingers and the pen. It is criminal to stunt the mental growth of a child by letting him know as much only as he can get through a book he can incoherently read in a year. We do not realize that, if a child was cut off from the home life and was merely doomed to the school, he would be a perfect dumee for several years. He picks up information and language unconsciously through his home, not in the schoolroom. Hence do we experience the immense difference between pupils belonging to cultured homes and those belonging to uncouth homes, which are no homes in reality.

"In the scheme I have adumbrated, the schoolmaster is expected to treat his occupation seriously and feel one with his pupils. I know that, in putting the scheme into operation, the want of schoolmasters of the right type is the greatest difficulty. But we shall not get the right type till we have made the right beginning.

"I must postpone the consideration of the stage when we have to arm the pupils with books", he added.

Gandhi's constructive programme was devoted to social reform and development of the backward communities His objective was to regenerate a new spirit, a new thinking and self-reliance amongst the Harijans. This kind of feeling, he believed, would greatly enhance their prestige and self-respect. They could hold their heads high by becoming economically stronger by hard work and incessant labour.

It was made evident at numerous meetings and through his writings that untouchability was a cruel and inhuman institution. It always violated human dignity by compelling untouchables to do work which was unclean and degrading. It was viewed that untouchability was against the spirit of democracy which made no distinction among citizens of a free country. It has also led to economic problems. The untouchables were the poorest section of Indian society. Their avenues of employment were very limited. They lived apart, in unhygienic surroundings, on the outskirts of villages and cities. Though they were Hindus and believed in and worshipped Hindu gods and goddesses, they were not allowed to enter Hindu temples. Public institutions like schools, hostels, etc., were not open to them.

To boost up the work for the upliftment of Harijans, Gandhi laid the foundation of the *Harijan Sevak Sangh.* Its main function was the removal of all such disabilities which hindered the progress and development of Harijans. As it had in its fold some dedicated workers it did remarkable work. So far so, Gandhi brought a Harijan family in the *Ashram* and he adopted their daughter as his own. He also offered his blessings on the eve of marriages which were conducted between Harijans and Caste Hindus. A few such marriages were celebrated in his own Ashram.

In an article on 'Task before Harijan Sevaks', Gandhi stated that the growing number of reformers should be active in the execution of several programmes and should not sit still. Rather they should be shown by their acts that change can be brought about with hard work. He was sure that the change to full self-reliance would never come unless all the workers realized that this was essentially a religious movement. He opined that propaganda among Caste Hindus could only be successfully carried out by influential persons with a remarkable capacity in them.

He wrote, "Though I have concurred with the policy of centralization I have always desired, as I have no doubt the Board too has desired, decentralization at the first opportunity. But that could only be done when the Provincial Boards were ready and able to raise their own funds, I would love nothing so much as that every village had its Harijan Board and was able to find its own funds. When that day comes, it will also be one of complete abolition of untouchability in every shape and form. For the present it has to be unfortunately admitted that the cause is still led by a handful of earnest reformers scattered all over the country. Not all of them are able to raise funds locally nor are they all sure of the policy to be followed. I use the word policy deliberately. For while everyone knows the goal, everyone does not know the grave limitations under which the reformer labours. The slightest error of judgment, a hasty action or a hasty word may put back the hands of the clock of progress. Policies have, therefore, to be cautiously evolved in the light of experiences daily gained by the few who have no other thought but that of serving. Harijans and riding Hinduism of its greatest blot."

Further, he stated "Ever since the inauguration of the *Harijan Sevak Sangh* the central organization has been feeling, every properly, the provincial branches. But the time has certainly arrived for the branches to stand on their own and be self-sustained even though it may be at the sacrifice of a part of their programme. The work in each province, and for that matter in each district or taluka, should be an unequivocal demonstration of active Savarna support. For the chief mission of the Sangh is to touch the Savarna heart and change it. Supposing the central organization had collected from two or three reformers a crore of rupees, and with it established branches all over India to cover it with schools and hostels for Harijan boys and girls, it would not have hastened the day of the doom of untouchability. For the Savarna heart would remain as stony as ever. Supposing conversely that without cost of a single pice, by some stroke, of good fortune, the Savarna heart was changed and untouchability became a thing of the past, the whole object the Sangh would be fulfilled. For in that case every public school, place of worship and other institutions would be open to Harijans precisely on the same terms as to Caste Hindus. That day may be far off or much nearer than many people expect. Anyway that is the goal of the Harijan Sevak Sangh, and never the opening of separate schools, wells, temples and the like for Harijans and consequent perpetuation of untouchability. At present these things are undoubtedly done, but they are done only as a means to the end. They have become necessary because the Savarna heart is slow to change.

"The growing number of reformers must not sit still and make protestations of removal of untouchability from themselves. They must demonstrate that change by their visible conduct. The spending of their purse for the Harijan cause is a tangible proof of the change and, therefore, an essential part of the programme. But immediately it becomes a corner confined to a few individuals who salve their conscience by liberal donations, it ceases to be a token in the manner indicated by me. Hence it becomes a matter of duty for the Central Board to invite the attention of the branches to this fundamental part of the programme and for the branches to appreciate it and prepare the way to becoming wholly self-reliant. Indeed the burden has been progressively thrown on provincial boards of financing their own institutions. But the time has come for definite and decisive action in the direction.

"This change to full self-reliance will never come unless all the workers realize that this is essentially a religious movement. We are a nation spending lavishly for causes which the masses believe to be religious. One has only to go the places of pilgrimage to have an ocular demonstration of the fact. A study of the history of religious endowments will reveal the tragic story of fortunes being entrusted to them by credulous millions without ever caring to know-how they were spent. It is enough for people to believe that they pay their mite to a cause which in their opinion is religious. Harijan workers have a cause that is wholly religious in the best sense of the term. If they have a living faith in it, if they do not move mountains, they will at least get from their surroundings enough for the institutions in their charge."

To certain questions, Gandhiji had answered in the following manner:

Q. The Harijan Sevak Sangh is looked upon as a part of the Congress. But very few Congressmen are Harijan workers. Why?

A. The Sangh is not a part of the Congress. It was the outcome of the fast I undertook in 1932 when I was in jail. The meeting of Hindus drawn from every class, which was held under the Presidentship of Pandit Malaviyaji and which gave birth to the Sangh, deliberately decided to keep the organization separate from the Congress and non-political. It was this quality of the Sangh that enabled Seth G.D. Birla to become its President and Shri Thakkar Bapa its Secretary. Nevertheless there are ought to be many Congressmen in the Sangh, because practically all reformers are drawn into the Congress fold. But it is true that there are plenty of non-Congress persons in the Sangh. It is also true that those Congressmen who are only interested in politics do not come into it. It is, therefore, sometimes wrongly thought that Congressmen do not take an interest in the Sangh. It is the duty of every Congressman to remove untouchability, root and branch, from his life.

Q. Harijan service has really developed into mere Harijan uplift. Practically no work is done among Caste. Hindus for the removal of untouchability. What is the remedy for this?

A. Experience shows that propaganda among Caste Hindus can only be successfully carried out by influential persons whose words carries weight with the general public. Such persons are hard to find. But it is within the capacity of every Harijan worker to carry on mute propaganda. Our Caste Hindu workers are often satisfied with mere uplift work among the Harijans, which is not sufficient. Many workers, while they do not observe untouchability themselves; are unable even to convert their own families. How then can they influence the outside world? Moreover it is my confirmed opinion that every Harijan worker has to make a point to beg for even one pice for Harijans from those Caste Hindus with whom he comes in contact. If all devoted themselves, heart and soul, to this task very good results would ensue.

Q. Should not the Sangh take upon itself the service of those Harijans who have been converted to Christianity or Islam and are yet treated as untouchables? Are we not out to remove untouchability root and branch and, therefore, help all who come under its sway?

A. This question has already been answered in the columns of *Harijan* but must bear repetition so long as it is raised. The moment untouchability is utterly banished from Hindu society it will, *ipso facto*, disappear from elsewhere too. Whatever the merits or demerits of the case, it is clear that our interference with converts will be the cause of strife with Muslims and Christians. Such converts have either broken off all contacts with, or they have been in their turn boycotted by Hindus. They have thrown in their lot with other sects whose leaders will not allow them to maintain their old contacts. Hence the *Harijan Sevak Sangh* quite rightly decided from its inception to confine its area of work to Harijans who had not left the Hindu fold. A convert, having left his original fold, is no longer guided or controlled by it.

Q. What should be the attitude of the Sangh, if Harijan boys wish to enlist in the army?

A. They should be allowed to do so. They may not be controlled by the Congress policy or *Ahimsa*. They must be given absolute freedom of choice.

Q. Harijans are of opinion that Caste Hindus who are sympathetic to their cause should not use those temples where they are not allowed entry.

A. They are right. It is the bounden duty of Harijan workers not to go where Harijans are not allowed and likewise to dissuade Caste Hindus.

Q. Harijans are legally entitled to send their children to many educational institutions as also to draw water from public wells. But public sentiment still militates against this being put into practice. Should Harijans resort to the law courts for justice in these matters or wait patiently until the Caste Hindus are converted?

A. Where there is no danger of violence being done to them, the Harijans should exercise their legal rights and where necessary, resort to law courts. Harijan workers must continue agitation among Caste Hindus and not rest content with mere legal rights.

Q. Is it not essential to reform the insanitary methods employed by sweepers for cleaning latrines and scavenging?

A. It is not necessary. What is more, until this is done the condition of sweepers will remain pitiable. To this end it is the duty of Harijan workers and Caste Hindus to do sweepers' work themselves. No Caste Hindu will employ the methods used by sweepers. He will do the work scientifically. For example, he will never remove excreta in a basket or carry it on his head; he will cover excreta with dry earth and remove it in a metal vessel. He will avoid touching dirt with his hands as far as possible; he will clean the vessel with water and a rod; he will bathe immediately after doing the work; he will wear special clothes when scavenging. These reforms do not cost much. They require intelligence, hard work, and love of an ideal. We may not relegate sweepers' work to one particular class. Therefore, all should learn it the same way as cooking. Each person should be his own sweeper. If this ideal were to be put into practice in society, the miserable condition of sweepers would at once be rectified.

The Harijan Sevak Sangh was mainly associated with the welfare work. The members were also advised to organize unions or even conduct *hartals*, not from political motives or for such purposes, but for bettering the social or economic position of Harijans. "The *Harijan Sevak Sangh*, however, being a non-political organization should never put expediency before its main duty towards the Harijans."

Some more questions were answered by him in the following manner:

Q. The Communist Party as successfully organized sweepers' unions and helped them to secure their rights through *hartals*, etc. But the *Harijan Sevak Sangh's* activities are confined mostly two welfare work. It cannot, therefore, successfully compete with the Communists for popularity among the Harijans. Don't you think that in view of this, the

Harijan Sevak Sangh ought to alter its policy and method of work?

A. We must be guided in our policy by our sense of right, not by the lure of winning cheap popularity. If the *Harijan Sevak Sangh* is convinced that it is working on the right line, it will keep on to it, regardless of what others might or might not do. Thus, we may organize unions or even induce *hartals*, not from political motives or for such purposes, but for bettering the social or economic position of Harijans.

Q. The feeling is gaining ground among the Harijans that the Congress is showing more solicitude for Muslim demands than for the just rights of the Harijans. What have you to say to it?

A. The Congress being a political organization is likely to be more susceptible to political pressure, which the Muslims are in a far stronger position to exert than the Harijans. If it succumbs to that pressure, it will pay the price for it. The *Harijan Sevak Sangh*, however, being a non-political organization should never put expediency before its primary duty towards the Harijans.

Q. Would you advise the so-called Savarna Hindus to start, even under the present circumstances an agitation in selected places for securing elementary civic and social rights for the Harijans? Would you for this purpose advise the *Harijan Sevak Sangh* to organize Satyagraha against the Savarna Hindus if necessary?

A. I would not advise the Sangh as an organization to offer *Satyagraha* against the *Savarna* Hindus, but I would certainly not only advise but expect members of the Sangh in their individual capacity to organize such Satyagraha in their respective places. I shall certainly support any such move on their part if it is undertaken in the proper spirit. It is their duty.

Q. Would you, in the absence of popular Governments in the provinces, advise the Sangh to carry on a vigorous and energetic programme of temple entry for Harijans?

A. I could. I understand it is being done even at present but at a rather slow pace. I would certainly like its tempo to be stepped up.

Q. Should not the *Harijan Sevak Sangh* try to secure for the Harijans political power by demanding due representation for them on Grama Panchayats, Municipalities and Legislatures?

A. Certainly it ought to. No effort can be too great for it.

Q. Should not the Sangh give instructions in the essentials of Hindu religion in the Harijan hostels and in Harijan gatherings of adults?

A. It ought to be the primary duty of the Sangh to give to Harijan children and adults a grounding in the essentials of Hindu religion. If they were brought up in ignorance of these, they would not continue to remain in the Hindu fold, and the responsibility for it would rest on those who had failed to give them the necessary instructions.

Shri Sitaram Shastri of Vinaya Ashram, Guntur, asked whether the Sangh ought not to specially train a body of missionaries to carry on propaganda work among the Savarna Hindus. He was ready to open a training centre for the purpose in his Ashram if he were given reasonable help.

Gandhiji, however, had grave doubts as to the practicability of the suggestion. In fact the question had also been brought up by Shri Ghanashyamdas Birla many years ago and dropped after full discussion. He would be quite satisfied if at least the members of the Sangh would fully come up to the ideal.

Gandhiji was next asked: "Ought not we to set up a precedent for having Harijan representatives in the Sangh or at least one member in the Executive Committee of the Sangh?" In reply he referred to the history of the birth of the *Harijan Sevak Sangh* at the conclusion of the Poona Pact, which led to the modification of the decision of the MacDonald Government, on the question of the representation of the minorities. It was thought that if the rot was to be effectively stemmed Hinduism ought to be totally rid of the curse of untouchability. This called for a real change of heart and repentance for its past sins on the part of Hindu society. It was to that end that the Harijan Sevak Sangh came into being.

"I am, therefore, opposed to both the propositions", Gandhiji replied, "I know that under the present arrangement some Harijans are included in the Board of the Sangh. But this was a concession to Thakkar Bapa's weakness. I have described the Harijan Sevak Sangh as an organization of penitent sinners. Its object is to call upon the so-called Savarna Hindus to do explain for having harboured untouchability. The inclusion of a Harijan in the Sangh would be mere eye-wash and make-believe, as his would be a mere voice in the wilderness. Before long, he would himself heartily wish to be out of it. I say this from my personal experience of the way in which committees function. I know the Sangh cannot always keep up to the mark. It is, of course, open to the Sangh to alter its scope and give Harijans a majority in its Executive Committee or appoint a competent body of representative Harijans to act as a Board of Advisors and Supervisors and keep the Sangh on the alert and on the right track."

Gandhiji was next questioned to give his views on the recent work in the Gwalior State to enlist the services of the Sadhu community in the cause of Harijan uplift. Gandhiji replying said he had serious doubts to the correctness or advisability of the step. It appeared to him to smack of politics. He would welcome the assistance of true *Sadhus*, if it was available. But he confessed, he looked in vain in the country for *Sadhus* of his conception. Such *Sadhus* as he saw disappointed him. There might be here and there honourable exceptions and their help would be welcome. But he was frankly sceptical of the possibility of making use of *Sadhus* as a body for their work. Even if they tried the experiment, he was afraid they would come to the parting of the ways before long.

Another friend asked whether a portion of the Kasturba

Memorial Trust Fund ought not to be earmarked for Harijan sisters. Gandhiji's reply was that they could have the whole of it provided they could show the ability to utilize it. No special earmarking of a part was, therefore, necessary.

Once, the questions and answers were over, Gandhiji addressed a few general remarks to those assembled to give his diagnosis of the relative sluggishness of the *Harijan Sevak Sangh's* activities and his remedy for the same. "I am responsible for the policy of conducting Harijan uplift work through the agency of the *Savarna* Hindus. They had to do expiation. All of them, I argued to myself, could help with money even if they could not, owing to lack of necessary qualifications, render direct service. For instance, they might not be able themselves to do teaching work, but they could engage a competent teacher to give education to Harijan children. That would be one way of doing expiation. They would be able to penetrate Harijan society and help in its progress." He knew there were sceptical critics, who questioned whether this type of work could lead to the eradication of untouchability. He himself had at one time doubted this. But he had since realized his mistake. He owed a debt of gratitude in this respect to the late Shri Devdhar, at whose activity he had at one time looked askance and which he had even criticized. A year's experience, however, had cured him of his conceit and taught him humility. He felt that if he confined himself exclusively to doing propaganda among the *Savarna* Hindus regarding their conversion, he might have to wait till the Greek Kalends and in the meantime the actual uplift work among the Harijans would remain hopelessly bogged. His own experience has since convinced him that if they could only get sufficient workers with the requisite purity and devotion and spirit of sacrifice to work among Harijans, untouchability would soon become a thing of the past, even if the *Savarna* Hindus were left severely alone. But that would mean that they must become Harijans at heart and live and labour among the Harijans as Harijans. "But can the members of the *Harijan Sevak Sangh* truthfully claim to have eradicated the last trace of untouchability from their own hearts? Are their professions altogether on a par with their practice?" he asked.

A member asked as to what his criterion was in that respect. "Are you married?" questioned Gandhiji in return. "I happen to be," answered the puzzled interlocutor. "Then have you an unmarried daughter?" resumed Gandhiji. "If you have, get for her a Harijan bridegroom not to satisfy her lust but in a purely religious spirit and I shall send you a wire of congratulations at my expense."

"You will now realize," went on Gandhiji, "Why the *Harijan Sevaks* are unable to move the hearts of the *Savarna* Hindus. The reason is that they have not that fire of faith in their hearts, impatient hunger for service which is the first essential for an effective appeal. Let but a handful of *Savarna* Hindus go forth in that true missionary spirit and they will leaven the entire Hindu mass. But not even a whole army of missionaries so-called will produce any effect upon them." It required a Malaviyaji to make such a missionary. He (Gandhiji) could not convert his own sister. And if he could not, argued he, how could he find fault with others? This would show how hard and thorny was that path. It was however, open to them if they thought that they had the requisite qualification, to try the experiment for themselves in their locality.

The reason for this partial failure, Gandhiji further explained was also that the approach of most of the members of the *Harijan Sevak Sangh* to their mission was not unmixed with political motives. If they really desired to penetrate the hearts of *Savarna* Hindus, they ought to be filled with a purely religious spirit. Mere dialectics was a poor weapon for this type of work. As it was, they were too much weighed down by inertia, heedlessness and woodenness of mind.

"The other method is more fierce and not altogether free from danger," continued Gandhiji. "It is the method of fasting." He himself had before condemned fasting when it appeared to him to be wrong or morally unjustified. But to shirk a fast when there was a clear moral indication with a dereliction from duty. Such a fast had to be based on unadulterated Truth and *Ahimsa.*

The creation of Harijan Boards was recommended and the qualifications of members were laid down. Only those who were to show sincerity, keen interest and honesty of purpose were to be enrolled as members. The member should have firm commitment for the removal of untouchability from its roots. He should serve the Harijans in various ways.

What should be the qualifications of members of Harijan Boards and what should be the number constituting them were the questions generally asked. Only those were to be included who are eager to serve the cause and whose presence would promote the usefulness of the Board to which they belong and whose capacity for service would be raised by their being members of a Board.

The Conditions

No one should allow himself or herself to be a member of a Board unless he or she:

(1) believes in the uttermost removal of untouchability;
(2) pays something to the Board as per his or her capacity;
(3) does some kind of definite service for Harijans, e.g., having a Harijan in his or her home as a member of the family, or at least as a domestic servant, or his teaching a Harijan or Harijans, or paying a regular visit to Harijan quarters and cleaning them, or, if he or she is a doctor, treating Harijan patients free of charge, etc.;
(4) sends to the Board of diary showing record of his or her service every month.
(5) If some such conditions are followed no restriction is required to be put on the number of members. The more, the merrier. Such Boards will meet to take notes, exchange experiences and solve mutual difficulties. They will never waste time in useful discussions.

(6) There may be Advisory Committees attached to the Boards. These will lay down for themselves some minimum qualifications. Naturally the qualifications of Advisors will be less stringent than those of members of regular Boards.

Then, the Mahatma posed another question, "What if members with the qualifications I have described cannot be found is the natural question arising from the bare mention of them. I must repeat the answer I have given often enough before now. The persons invited by the Central Board to form Sanghs in their own provinces will, in the absence of members having the necessary qualifications, perform the service through agents. "Act True" must be the motto of every Harijan Board, and there should never be any departure from the wholesome maxim." The sense of unanimity should prevail among the members of the Advisory Committee of Harijans. The factions and divisions should be avoided and let there be no quarrels among you.

Gandhiji had recommended the formation of Advisory Committees of Harijans to help *Harijan Sevak Sangh* Boards consisting of Caste Hindus. When asked for guidance in this regard by a Harijan correspondent, Gandhij replied:

"I should suggest the formation of compact, small representative Committees who would truly represent the opinion of local Harijans. They would frame rules for the conduct of their proceedings and formulate their expectations of Savarna Hindus and generally watch the proceedings of Harijan Boards. These Advisory Committees, wherever they are formed, would advise Harijan Boards of their existence and show their preparedness to help the latter. If the Boards are sincere in their desire to discharge their debt, that is to serve Harijans, they will establish the friendliest contact with the Advisory Committees, and perfect co-operation and harmony will prevail. There may be friction in the beginning because of mutual suspicion. Harijan Boards being naturally better organized and better off in every respect, will have to exercise tact in handling what may appear to be extravagant demands. Advisory Committees would endeavour to be considerate. The more considerate they are, the better able they will be to help themselves. From their ability to conduct themselves in a dignified manner, they will learn the art of asserting themselves if the occasion ever arises. For they should know that Savarna Hindus will never be able to discharge their debt except with the co-operation of Harijans. But the question of asserting themselves does not arise just yet, because the vast mass of Harijans have been rendered so completely helpless that they have no power of resisting injustice, even if they wanted to. Let me explain what I mean. Harijan Boards have three functions, to raise the economic, social and religious status of Harijans, or to put it in another way, to remove the difficulties that Savarna Hindus have for centuries put in the way of Harijans raising their heads in any department of life. Thus the Harijan Boards have to provide wells, scholarships, boarding houses, schools and social amenities, wherever the need arises. In all these, the general body of Harijans simply take the help wherever it is offered. Advisory Committees can therefore, help the cause and themselves by making useful suggestions to the Boards and also rendering such help as they themselves can to those whom they represent. Thus only will they acquire the power of asserting themselves. In short, Advisory Committees will best help the cause by taking up internal reform and causing an awakening among the Harijan masses, so that they may begin to realize that they are men and women entitled to the same rights as are enjoyed by the other members of the society to which they belong."

At Rajahmundry a deputation of Harijans met Gandhiji and had a long discussion with him. They agreed, among other things, that, as they had a reasonable number of men among them who were enlightened and efficient, they should be given the reins of the *Harijan Sevak Sangh*. Caste Hindus, they said, might help in the work, but the office bearers should be all Harijans. Gandhiji gave them the following reply:

"One important question that you have raised is that the Harijan Sevak Sangh should be principally manned and managed by you. That shows that you have not followed the pages of the Harijan. That shows also that you have not understood the origin of the Board. The Board has been formed to enable Savarna Hindus to do repentance and reparation to you. It is thus a Board of Debtors, and you are the creditors. You owe nothing to the debtors, and therefore, so far as this Board is concerned, the initiative has to come from the debtors. You have to certify whether the debtors discharge their obligation or not. What you have to do is to enable and help them to discharge their obligation; that is to say, you can tell them how they can discharge their obligation, you can tell them what in your opinion will satisfy the great body of Harijans. They may or may not accept your advice. If they do not, naturally they run the risk of incurring your displeasure. A debtor may go to a creditor and say to him, "I have brought so much money, will you take it?" The creditor may say, "Off you go; I want full payment or none". Or the creditor may say, What you have brought is not part payment, but worse. All these things you, creditors, can do. And so, when this Board was established and some Harijan friends wrote to me, I told them that Harijans should form themselves into Advisory Boards or Boards of Inspection. I want you to understand this distinction thoroughly. You will please see that there is no desire not to accept your advice or co-operation or help. I am only putting before you the true and logical position. This is a period of grace that God has given to Caste Hindus, and it is during this period of grace that they have to prove their sincerity. And I am moving heaven and earth and am going about from place to place, simply in order that this obligation on the part of Savarna Hindus may be fully discharged."

A member of the deputation then made suggestion that the Board should appoint Advisory Committees of Harijans of its own choice. Gandhiji as a fellow Harijan by choice showed them the danger underlying this suggestion and said, "Do not ask the

Board to select a Committee of Harijans but select your own Committee and say to the Board, you have selected these members and it should carry on correspondence with them. There is another danger in the suggestion. There may be factions and divisions among you. Different committees may be appointed by different factions. The Board may recognize all of them. But that will be unfortunate. Let there be no quarrels among you. Present a united front to the debtors. The debtors may put you against one another, though the Board, if it is worth its name, will not do that. The Congress has been able to present a united front. Today, the Congress is full of simple men like you and me. You should have a body of business like men who will put down with a strong hand all quarrels among you. Then you will dominate the Board without being on it. Do not be easily satisfied. Tell the debtors you are not going to be satisfied with 5 shillings in the pound but that you must have 20 shillings in the pound. This is not a matter for bargaining."

The Mahatma recommended to fix a *Harijan Day* under the auspices of the *Harijan Sevak Sangh*, "It should be a day of sanitation and cleanliness. The poorest could do this by denying themselves a meal or a portion thereof. House to house collection was to be made by the members. The literature should be sold or given away as the exigency of the time might need."

He added further: "The fixing of a special day can only be warranted by extraordinary effort. In a sacred cause like the Harijan cause, a special day should be one of greater dedication, prayer and intensive work. I should divide the day somewhat after this style:

1. I should begin the day from 5 A.M. with prayer and set apart for the cause some money or cloth or grain according to my means. The poorest can do this by denying themselves a meal or meals or a portion thereof without feeling the slightest deprivation. Preferably donations in kind should be converted into cash. Where this is not possible, they should be given to the most deserving and needy Harijans.

2. The work of the family Bhangi, if there is any, should be wholly done by the family or at least shared with him. This will enable one to understand the nature of the service that the Bhangi performs and may also lead to an improved method of performing such services. Not many persons have any consideration for the 'knight of the broom' at the time of using the sanitary convenience. If we had no untouchability in us and if we even occasionally shared the work with the Bhangis, we would have a different method of working the home sanitary system.
3. Having done these two things, we are ready for corporate effort for the day, which should open with house to house collection of donations in cash or kind. This work should be finished by a given hour. The donations should be handed to the local committee, which will in its turn, hand the collection to the superior committee till it reaches the headquarters of the province. Collectors should take with them a judicious selection of literature including leaflets, pamphlets books and even copies of *Harijan*, English or vernacular edition as may be required. The literature should be sold or given away as the exigency of the moment may require. But each committee should bear the cost of the literature ordered by it. If extra copies of the *Harijan* required, previous advice should be given to the publishers so as to enable them to print extra copies.
4. Harijan quarters should be visited in each place and they should be cleaned wherever necessary. Meetings of Harijan should be held and their wants *noted*. They should be advised as to the part they have to play in the removal of untouchability. Dr. Deshmukh's authoritative opinion should be used in support of the plea for the giving up of carrion-eating. Children can arrange meetings and excursions for Harijan children. Possibilities of inauguration of improved methods of

sanitation should be explored. It is neither difficult nor expensive if the people will shoulder the burden willingly. In the end it means a visible addition to the health and wealth of the community.

5. The day should be wound up by a general meeting of both Savarnas and Harijans to pass resolutions, pledging the meeting to the removal of untouchability and emphasising the desirability of permissive legislation regarding temple entry.
6. Where public opinion is favourable, public wells and private temples should be opened to Harijans."

He clarified further, "An accurate report of the work done should be sent to the Central Committee. Hardly had the great central organization of the Servants of Untouchables Society made the commencement, when complaints against it and the provincial organization started cropping up. They came chiefly and naturally from *Harijans.* One of these correspondents sent to me some time ago an able letter undertaking to give details if I wished. I took him at his word and asked him to provide me details; and the letter he has sent me in reply is abler than the first. It will compete with any well written report of an inspector. It contains a summary of reports of every organization claiming to work in the writer's province for the uplift of Harijans and after giving me sufficient details, his one conclusion about all the organizations practically without exception is:

> "They are run principally by Caste men who have their own axes to grind or who are in need of some occupation that would maintain them decently. The utmost that some of these have done is to fung a few scholarships at Harijan boys. Some others have been great at delivering lectures. All have come to us as patrons. Hardly has anyone come as a friend and equal, let alone as a servant. Your provincial organization is no exception. It is difficult for a Harijan to approach its chief man without fear and trembling. He is always in danger of being met with a frown."

"My correspondent is also not without suggestions, which may be summarized thus:

> "If you are to take advantage of the great awakening that has taken place, you must concentrate upon primary education on a mass scale. You will not drive out the ignorance of ages without spreading that education. We shall certainly help, but seeing that Caste Hindus want to remove untouchability and make us one with them, there is no better way of employing their money and their labour than in imparting this education."

"It is necessary to know the Harijan mind in any programme of work that may be taken up. Caste Hindus, for whom removal of untouchability is a matter of penance and purification, have undoubtedly to do much more than open schools everywhere. I have discussed elsewhere where such schools may be opened. The conduct of Caste Hindus would be generally tested by its reaction upon the mass mind of the Harijans. If we have really changed towards them, they will feel the change in a thousand ways. Our activity, I mean that of Caste Hindus, will affect every department of their lives. Even in the remotest village we are interdependent, so much so that this interdependence cannot be dissolved all at once, even if we desired it, without resulting in the greatest harm to the nation in general; and this interdependence, which is today that of slave and master, will never be corrected unless there is absolute religious equality. It is a tremendous task, but as we progress towards the goal, the truth must dawn upon every Caste Hindu that there is no halfway house between abject slavery and perfect religious equality. Hence my humble insistence upon temple entry without losing sight of the other things we must do."

"My correspondent is bitter in discussing what he considers to be the extravagant management of the different organizations that have come under his lash. As an expert organizer that I may claim to be, I have been generally guided by the rule that the cost of administration, that is, overhead charges, should never exceed 10 per cent of the receipts – 5 per cent being the ideal – the balance going to the cause which brought the organization into being. I suggest this test to the Central Board and the Provincial Boards and all other independent Harijan organizations run by Caste Hindus. Let it not be said of us that we spend more on running the organizations than upon Harijans themselves. Let us see to it that, out of every Rs. 100 received as donation for the Harijan cause, Rs. 90 go straight into the pockets of Harijans.Therefore, our officials should be largely volunteers, never highly paid wherever paid service is required. Wherever it is possible, we should get Harijans. We should select candidates and train them. The correspondent says that peons in the organizations inspected by him are not drawn from the Harijan ranks. Let every organization for the service of Harijans introspect itself in the light of the criticism I have condensed and the suggestions I have made."

"I have repeatedly said that this work can be done only by those who sincerely believe untouchability to be a stain on Hinduism. This is a movement requiring the change of heart of millions. It cannot be led to success by any political manoeuvres. It can be done only through self purification. This is a great sacrificial fire in which we have to burn our load of sins and come out purified. Those who do not take to this work with faith and spirit will fail to move the hearts of millions. We shall be nowhere if we deceive ourselves or the Harijans. The success or failure of this movement depends on our getting the right type of workers. We are on our trial today. If we miss today the opportunity that God has given us, we may never hope to get the opportunity again in this generation. What we refuse to do voluntarily today we shall have to do in future perforce, and we shall repent for having lost this opportunity. I pray to God that we may come out successful from this trial and save Hinduism and ourselves from destruction."

Gandhiji writes further on untouchables, "Injustice is being done all the world over, but we have given to it the sanction of religion. These distinctions have not been created by God. The Harijans are on the lowest rung of the ladder not because of any inherent defects but only because they have been kept down by the so-called higher castes. God had bestowed on them the same talents that He had given us, but we deny them the opportunities for using them. They should surely have the same rights and privileges and the same opportunities of growth that we enjoy."

"We are now awake to the wrong we have done to them, and the least we can do by way of penance now is to contribute money for their uplift and to share with them all the amenities of life that we have created for ourselves. We are all creatures of the same God and, therefore, equal in His eyes."

"From the money that you give for this cause, you will reap a hundred-fold, for it is like grain sown in good, manured soil. The money spent after luxury and lust is, on the other hand, wasted like grain sown in barren soil."

"I am told you have suffered heavily. But you should know that no nation has ever come to its own without having passed through the severest fire of suffering. Voluntary suffering only adds of our strength. I, therefore, congratulate you for having suffered. But I should also like to remind you that one of the causes that add to our sufferings is this curse of untouchability. We have oppressed the weak. We reap as we have sown. It is for us now to undo the wrong we have done to the Harijans and remove the yoke of serfdom from their shoulders."

"Caste Hindus must first ask you to forgive the wrongs they have done to you. But I should also tell you, as a Harijan by choice, that you should give up your evil habits, especially carrion and beef-eating. The whole world looks upon carrion with abhorrence. And beef-eating should be given up because that is a *sine qua non* for a Hindu. The cow is the giver of plenty, and by killing her we kill ourselves. Then I would urge you not to accept leavings. And above all, you should abolish the distinctions of high and low that have crept in among yourselves. And these things you should do, not in a bargaining spirit but because they are good in themselves. I would therefore, ask you also to give up drink, irrespective of the fact that many other Hindus drink. A friend writes:

> "I observe that there are some people in the Harijan service organizations not working in the spirit in which you want them to, that is, merely for the sake of serving Harijans. They are seeking its shelter in order to satisfy other ambitions.... I know that you do not desire civil resistance to be mixed up with Harijan service organizations. If you propose to make any public use of the letter you may emphasize this last point and make it clearer...."

"I am thankful to the friend for giving me the benefit of his experience. It is a most difficult task to keep a big organization like the Servants of Untouchables Society with branches all over India free of all self-seekers and time-servers. I have discussed the subject fully with Seth Ghanshyamdas and Thakkar Bapa. I know that they are both anxious to keep the organization as pure as possible. Personally I can do no more. It was because of my utter helplessness that I undertook the fast of 21 days. On discovering impurities amongst Harijan Servants, I saw that it was no use merely writing about impurities. I was searching for a way out of the difficulty. The reader should believe me when I tell him that the fast was the last thing in the world that I was thinking of, but as I have described in these pages, it came to me all of a sudden and gave me great relief. I know that it did much good. But, how far could the fast of a single mortal go? Hence it was that I developed the idea of a chain of such purificatory fasts. The idea has by no means been dropped. It comes to me again and again. But it does not admit of a mechanical organization. Several co-workers are ready to inaugurate or take part in the chain after it is inaugurated, but I have not yet found the way to begin it. The proper way will have to come to me or to the co-workers before the chain can be begun. Meanwhile I can only reiterate my conviction that untouchability will not be removed root and branch except through the service of men and women who take it up for its own sake and in a religious spirit. Unless we have a fair number of such servants throughout the length and breadth of India, we will never succeed in changing the hearts of millions of human beings. The *Savarna* Hindus are at one end, Harijans at the other, and the evil custom of ages, which has assumed the dignity of religious tenet, will not be uprooted without penance and purification. Whilst it gladdens my heart that thousands of people flock to the meetings that are being held in towns and villages and that they willingly give their pices as a token of their approval of the movement. I am painfully conscious of the fact that, if the thousands were suddenly called upon to enforce in their own lives what they seem to approve by their attendance at these meetings, they would fail to respond, not from want of will, but from sheer inability. I have discovered this again and again amongst my closest associates who have frankly confessed their inability to enforce immediately in their conduct what they knew was the right thing and what they knew had to be done immediately. They had to put up a brave fight against their traditional repugnance. The mere intellectual grasp that untouchability is an evil, corroding Hinduism, and that belief in it is tantamount to disbelief in God, His goodness and His Fatherhood, is not enough to destroy the monster. The vicarious penance of the comparatively pure is needed to bring about a change in the hearts of both Savarnas and Harijans."

"A movement, so grand and so pure, so religious and so humanitarian, must not be exploited by anybody for his own end. Certainly, not for its political consequences. It will be discovered, as the movement progresses, that the political approach can only end in accentuating the strife. It can only add to the confusion already existing and add one more, if not many more warring parties, to the existing ones. May God save us and save the movement from such a calamity!"

"So far as the connection of civil resistance with the movement is concerned, I am as emphatic as ever that Congressmen who desire to offer active civil resistance should not accept office in the various organizations, and much less can they be used for serving the purpose of civil resistance. Civil resistance is a unique weapon, it does not admit of alloy. It is the weapon of the fearless and, therefore, needs no shelter; but it has to be wielded in the open daylight. Therefore, whilst Congressmen who are also civil resisters on active service may do, as they are bound to do, such service to the cause as they can, they may not belong to the Servants of Untouchables Society or any of its branches. By holding office in the organizations they will harm both civil resistance and the Harijan cause. It would be like a man going to a temple to pray and using the act of worship for advancing civil resistance. Neither God nor man will be cheated in that manner and, as I have said often enough in these columns, the great reformation of Hinduism will not be brought about, if it is to depend purely upon Congressmen. For, much as I would like to think that every Indian is a Congressman, I know that such is not the case. Nor is every Hindu a Congressmen, if only because every Harijan is not a Congressman. Therefore, a Harijan organization must in the very nature of things be strictly non-political and non-party and should contain in it both Congressmen and non-Congressmen, office-holding being restricted to those who are not active civil resisters and who will not exploit the office secretly or openly to advance the cause of civil resistance."

Further, he stated, "A correspondent sends me the following questions for answering:

1. In the propaganda against untouchability, should a worker make use of the Hindu Shastras and religious texts to show that Hinduism does not sanction untouchability as we practice it today?

2. Should a Harijan sevak, even in his private capacity, take part in inter-dining functions?
3. Should a Harijan who is employed as a domestic servant sit at meals alongside all the members of the family?

"These three questions, the correspondent says, have been seriously discussed in the columns of a newspaper and the readers have been advised that Harijan workers should serve with all seriousness, I, therefore, beseech you, to purify your hearts of the sin of untouchability, to treat Harijan boys and girls as if they are your own children, brothers and sisters. We have for long ages suppressed Harijans and today if we sacrifices our all for their sake we shall be only making some slight and tardy reparation for all the wrongs inflicted upon them in the name of religion. Therefore, whatever you give, whether it is a trinket or heavy piece of jewellery or silver, I want you to give as merely as a token of your determination to rid yourselves of this taint of untouchability, the idea that you are high and somebody else is low. May God give you wisdom to see this very simple truth and enforce it in your life. Now you can give the things, whether jewellery, or silver or paper, whatever you want to give."

In an address presented to him at a public meeting held at Calicut on 13 January, 1934, Gandhi replied:

"I am much obliged to you for these addresses that have been presented to me this evening and I thank you for the self-restraint you have imposed upon yourselves by not desiring to read those addresses to me. Only you have thereby appreciated the fact that I have been going from one place to another from day to day, now for over two months, and at the end of the day I am, therefore, fatigued. You, wise men that you are, have appreciated this fact and absolved me from the duty of having to listen to these addresses. You having exercised this self-restraint, naturally it was up to me to read those addresses and be prepared. But I must say to you that I had no notion whatsoever that I was to have all these addresses nor have I been given copies of these addresses. Had I been given copies I would certainly have read them. However, I have no doubt whatsoever that these addresses contain nothing more than what I have noticed in the numerous addresses that I have been receiving throughout these two months or more. Almost without exception they have expressed to me great joy, not only their sympathy with the cause that I am espousing for the time being but they have in these addresses signified their intention, nay their determination, of doing everything that these various bodies of gentlemen or ladies could possibly do in their own sphere to advance the Harijans' cause.

"It has given me a great deal of satisfaction and joy to discover that there is consensus of opinion on the part of the intelligentsia. I would have been painfully surprised if it had been otherwise. Not only has it been so with reference to the intelligentsia but as far as mere assent goes, I have found to my great delight the masses also are equally with this movement. I am not easily self-deluded. I have no doubt that I have, must have, my due share of self-dilusion or else life perhaps would be a positive burden to most of us if not to all of us. But due allowance having been made for self-delusion I can say that all these scenes that I witness every day cannot possibly be a matter of masses or classes coming to me to signify their praise or their satisfaction for services that I might have performed in a previous life or in days gone by. This life has rushed and with me it has rushed with such rapidity that it is impossible for me to have a photography of the events that have happened and, that being the case, I should be intensely surprised and also disappointed that these classes and masses had signified not only their satisfaction and their sympathy by their presence at these meetings but also give me donations more or less and had done certain acts also as a consideration for those services. I would let that pass by. I am assuming that all your addresses contain a serious and solemn pledge that you are determined to do everything that is humanly possible for you to do to render the reparation that is overdue to the Harijans. Malabar, if one were to draw the untouchability map of the whole of India, I suppose will easily wear the black crown and Malabar would be the blackest spot so far as untouchability is concerned. It is a matter of regret but it is no use ignoring the fact. I would turn this blackness to good account and I would invite you to gird up your loins and make such Herculean effort that at the end of the struggle it may be possible to say of Malabar that Malabar had been in the vanguard of progress in this battle against the monster of untouchability. Let it be said of Malabar that Malabar counted no sacrifices too great for removing this evil of untouchability. And what could be a better and more sacred reminder for this meeting than the portrait of Mr. K. Madhavan Nair?

"I had the pleasure of knowing him long ago. When I first visited Calicut I had the honour of being introduced to him but I must confess that I did not know him so intimately as I came to know him when he paid me a visit at Yeravda. I came into very intimate touch with him, and when Mr. C. Rajagopalacharia was here and the Guruvayur referendum was going on, naturally I was corresponding with him as with other friends almost from day to day. Then Smt. Urmila Devi and my wife came into close contact with Mr. K. Madhavan Nair. My wife is a simple woman. She knows nothing, she does not know the English language, certainly she does not know Malayalam, but she was able to tell me in her very simple language that she was very much struck by the simplicity of his character. She merely strengthened the impression that Mr. Madhavan had left on my mind and that impression is still indelible. I have the most vivid recollection of my contact with him and what struck me most was his transparent humility. This is his faithful picture and I congratulate the artist on presenting the citizens of Calicut with this picture. I think there you can easily see humility written in his features. I don't think that the artist has enhanced the transparence of his humility. I think the artist is incapable of doing that. To look at Mr. Madhavan Nair and look at the living eye would give you a better illustration of that humility. The whole of his behaviour is on the picture. Mr. Madhavan Nair is in front of me today as I saw him in Yeravda. He stands vividly before me and this is one peculiar impression that he left on me.

"I discovered also that he was a man of very few words. You do not find many people who are economical in the use of language of their words. In his contact with me Mr. Madhavan Nair showed this quality in a supreme degree. His letters were compact, nice, neat and the briefest possible. Whatever he had to say he expressed a few words and he had finished.That was the man. If you were to recall the men who had died in body but are even now still living, you will discover that they are living not because of their intellectual gifts but because of virtues which you and I and every one of us can cultivate if we have the will and if we will make the necessary effort in order to cultivate them. Therefore, I would say you will be doing wrong to the memory of the man whom I have described as I have known him, if you think that you have performed your duty by calling upon me to unveil his portrait and for having witnessed this ceremony and having heard a few words in praise of his memory; nay, you will be doing wrong. But you will be doing the right thing if you will treasure this as a perpetual reminder to you that you also would like to be if not wholly at least somewhat like Mr. Madhavan Nair. At the end, to put a finishing touch, Mr. Madhavan Nair died in harness so far as the Harijan cause in concerned. He was a true co-worker in the Harijan cause which is a matter of self-purification, repentance and reparation. I give you my evidence that Mr. Madhavan Nair, when he took up this cause had the spirit in him, for every act that he did in connection with the Harijan cause was an act of sacrifice, repentance and reparation. There was no meanness about anything that he did. May his memory ever remain in my heart and in your own hearts.

"I thank you once more for having presented me with addresses. Since I think that this is not the proper time for auctioning these addresses, I hope that tomorrow you will help me to realize some money from these addresses because I know that Calicut will not send me away with disappointment."

Some time after the end of his fast, Gandhi disclosed in *Harijan* of July 8, 1933, that although he believed God to be without any form, he went on the fast as God ordained him to do so. "I have always believed God to be without form. But what I did hear was like a voice from afar and yet near. For me he continued "the voice of God, of Conscience, of Truth or the inner Voice, or the still small voice mean one and the same thing. The sceptic, he added, was free to say that it was self-delusion or hallucination, but not the unanimous verdict of the whole world against him could shake him out of the belief that "what I heard was the Voice of God".

"The hearing of the voice," Gandhi told the world, "was preceded by a terrible struggle within me. Suddenly the voice came upon me. I listened, made certain that it was the voice, and the struggle ceased. I was calm. The date and the hour of the fast were fixed. Joy came over me."

And God came to his succour and asked him to go on a fast for the uplift of the Untouchables, and though he held that it was for purification of self and a penance it was also for the misbehaviour of his disciples. The civil disobedience movement after a hard extensive struggle, had nearly failed for want of leadership. The suspension of the struggle was criticized harshly by some leaders. Vithalbhai Patel and Subhas Bose, who were in Vienna, became angry and issued a statement on May 9, 1933, declaring that Gandhi as a political leader had failed. They added that his method of warfare working on the principle of maximum suffering for Indians and minimum suffering for the enemy could not possibly lead to success. Gandhi never forgave Subhas Bose for this angry and violent attack on his leadership. Vithalbhai Patel died of heart-trouble on October 22, 1933, in a Swiss clinic near Geneva. Hearing the news, Gandhi wrote to the Sardar that Vithalbhai Patel's death caused him much pain and he had written to Subhas showing praise on him for his devoted service to Patel during his illness and asked the Sardar to write to him about it.

On his release, Gandhi was welcomed at many places in Poona. On June 12, 13 and 14, 1933, a conference was held there and Congress leaders from all provinces attended it. Gandhi made a small speech, asking the delegates to put forward their opinions frankly. While reviewing the situation, the majority of them said that the movement should be suspended. In the end Gandhi was authorized to seek an unconditional interview with the Viceroy. Gandhi telegraphically requested the Viceroy to grant him an interview, but the Viceroy declined his request, stating that nothing was possible unless the movement was withdrawn. Sir Samuel Hoare declared that Gandhi could not be a negotiator while keeping in reserve the unconditional weapon of civil disobedience. On July 13, Gandhi made another appeal for an interview but the Private Secretary to the Viceroy informed him that there was no chance of holding conversations with the representative of an association which had not abandoned the movement.

On July 19, Gandhi came back to Ahmedabad where he visited Mirabehn in Sabarmati Jail. He announced his desire to disband the Sabarmati Ashram and asked the Bombay Government to take possession of it. Later, on September 30, 1933, Gandhi offered the Sabarmati Ashram for Harijan work to the Servants of Untouchables Society which was the new name given in July 1933, to the All-India Anti-untouchability League. Much later on September 5, 1939, the property of the Sabarmati Ashram was vested in the Trust for the uplift of Harijans and it became officially known as *Harijan Ashram.*

On July 26, Gandhi issued his famous statement on the methods of secrecy adopted by Congressmen during the movement. A few days earlier he had appreciated the bravery and sacrifice of the numerous civil resisters but had asked them to give up secrecy if the movement was to be continued.

To those who implored him not to stick to the Harijan movement alone, Gandhi replied that he could not give twenty-four hours of the day to Harijan work, and he could not give up a life principle for the sake of Harijan work. It would be pertinent to note here what Aurobindo, philosopher and spiritualist, had to say on Gandhi's opinions on secrecy. He said, "Gandhi talked about secrecy being a sin, but that is one of his many extravagances."

Gandhi felt deeply humiliated at the Viceroy's refusal of an unconditional interview and so on July 30, he announced his intention at Ahmedabad to march with thirty-three companions, the first halt being at Ras. This time there were nearly as many women as there were men with him, and he informed the Government accordingly. The Government refused to take possession of the Ashram, but Gandhi's offer showed how great men are often out to sacrifice everything for their principles, even the organizations they have set up.

Gandhi, Kasturba, Mahadev Desai and thirty inmates of the Sabarmati Ashram were arrested on the morning of August 1. Gandhi was taken to Sabarmati Jail and from there to Yeravda jail. This was his sixth arrest in India. On August 4, he was released at 9 a.m. with orders for him to leave Poona by 9.30 A.M., but he expressed his desire to disobey the orders and was arrested for the seventh time, tried in Yeravda jail by a magistrate and sentenced to one year's imprisonment. When the magistrate asked him about his occupation, he answered that he was a spinner, weaver and farmer, and his residence was "Yeravda Jail now". Mahadev Desai and Kasturba were also sent to prison. After Gandhi's arrest, the campaign of civil disobedience picked its thread again and hundreds of Congressmen were arrested in the first week of August 1933.

In jail, Gandhi wanted all the facilities of doing Harijan work that he had been given during his earlier incarceration. If he did not get permission to do so, he would deny himself all nourishment except salt and water. "Life," he wrote to Government, "ceases to interest me, if I may not do Harijan work without let or hindrance". The Government replied that Gandhi courted imprisonment on a purely political purpose and so would not be given any special treatment, not given to other `A' class prisoners. If Gandhi, stated the Government on August 18, abandoned civil disobedience activities and incitements, he would be freed at once so that he could devote himself wholly and without restriction to the cause of social reform. But Gandhi refused this offer of conditional release. His health deteriorated rapidly. He was removed to Sassoon Hospital, Poona and the end appeared near. On August 23, his health became critical. He even disposed of the few articles he had with him among the members of the nursing staff, but he was released on the same day. He secured his release by observing a fast, a weapon he invariably used against the Government which was afraid of events resulting from his possible death in prison.

Yet Gandhi described his release as an unexpected event which had taken place through the unscrutable ways of God! Among the prominent leaders who bitterly criticized Gandhi's retreat was K.F. Nariman.

Gandhi decided to devote himself to Harijan work till August 3, 1934, as the period of sentence would have finished on that date. "Up to the 3rd of August next," he observed, "I must not court imprisonment by offering aggressive civil resistance." On September 9 and 10, 1933, Jawaharlal Nehru met him in Poona. They discussed the aims and policy and goal of the Congress. They reiterated that the goal was Independence. Nehru was of the view that without a material change in the vested interests the condition of the masses could never be improved. He also told the Mahatma that the problem of India's independence could not be separated from the vital international problems of the world and so they must range themselves with the progressive force of the world. He plainly told Gandhi that their movement was essentially an open one, but in corresponding with each other a measure of secrecy might be required, but secrecy was hardly the word for it and privacy was much better.

Gandhi replied that though he might not go as far as Nehru, he agreed that without a material revision of the vested interests the lot of the masses could not be improved. He could not seek to coerce anyone; he sought to convert the vested interests. In a press statement in December 1933, Nehru said: "There is no middle road between fascism and communism, one has to choose between the two and I choose the communist ideal."

These differences in the two leaders' outlook began to manifest themselves from this time. They aroused from fundamental as well as temperamental attitudes and principles. Gandhi, who was not ready to allow Nehru an opportunity to break from the Congress and his own ideology, later said in a reply to a note by the editor of *Madras Mail* in December 1933 that they should not be disturbed at the opinions of a same and honest man like Jawaharlal Nehru who did not stand for Russian Communism. It would be Indian Socialism with a different colouring. "As regards the tenants," Gandhi went on, "they also had a right to the land, they must have a just share of the produce of their labour, and the actual holder of the land must be one who worked by the sweat of his brow." Yet Gandhi came to the defence of the system of *zamindars* and taluks and talked of trusteeship.

On September 20, 1933, Dr. Annie Besant expired at Adyar, but Gandhi, who was in Bombay did not utter a word of condolence for the great and fearless friend of Indian independence.

In the last week of September 1933, Gandhi moved to the *Satyagraha Ashram* at Wardha. It took some time for him to get well again. His weight had gone down to 90 pounds. But he kept worrying about Sardar Patel's nose and Jamnalal Bajaj's ear!

After taking a rest for six weeks, Gandhi raised his weight to 108 pounds. Now aged sixty-five, he started on a whirlwind Harijan tour of nine months on November 7, 1933, from Wardha, declaring open some private temples to Harijans, collecting money for the Harijan Fund and telling people that it was blasphemy to say that God resided in a temple from which a particular class of the same faith was excluded. He was glad that he had begun his Harijan tour from Wardha, the geographical centre of India. He pleaded that the untouchable Hindus should have access to all public institutions, such as schools, roads and public wells which had been thrown open by the Bombay Government in the Bombay presidency in pursance of a resolution moved by S.K. Bole, a social reformer, and adopted by the Bombay Legislative Council on August 4, 1923. Dr. N.B. Khare was in charge of his Berar tour, and Gandhi praised him on the smooth arrangements he had made for it. Gandhi appealed to the masses to support the Temple Entry Bill of Ranga Iyer which, according to him, wanted to legalize the view of a majority.

At Nagpur Gandhi auctioned a cowrie donated by a poor man and it fetched Rs. 111. He sold caskets. He announced that about Rs. 20,00,000 had been spent for the removal of untouchability and the uplift of the Harijans. He had personally spent a sum of nearly five lakhs of rupees. At the Nagpur meeting eggs were thrown at Gandhi by *Sanatanists.* Pandit Lalnath, a Sanatanist leader, and his fanatic followers from north India along with other Sanatanist workers made abortive efforts to hold up Gandhi's car at Dhamangaon and Amraoti, and at Akola by even lying prostrate before it. On November 20, Gandhi rested for a day at Chikalda which is a hill station.

Then visiting Raipur, Itarsi and Anantpuri, Gandhi reached Jubbulpore where on December 8, Dr. Ansari found that the continuous strain of his tour had led to a rise in Gandhi's blood pressure and so advised him to take the utmost precautions. Gandhiji requested to the people to take no more than four hours work from him a day. In one of his letters from Raipur; Gandhi wrote to Sardar Patel, 'The crowds are as large as before, perhaps larger, and as crazy as ever.' This implied that the suspension of the civil disobedience movement had not affected his popularity. But Gandhi's health, it appears, was failing him. He wrote to Patel on December 25, 1933: "I cannot even recall what has to be written to whom, may be on account of old age." He visited Delhi and spent five days giving a fillip to Harijan work.

On December 16, 1933, Gandhi started his Harijan tour in southern India by addressing a meeting of the Harijan workers in Andhra. He told them that their purity and suffering would not fail to touch the hearts of the orthodox. If they missed this god-given opportunity to purge themselves of the curse of untouchability, they would have to pay for it with bitter tears. During his three-day visit to Madras, he addressed meetings of women, students and workers appealing them not to make distinctions of high and low between man and man, and that labour at least should have no distinctions of high and low.

While giving an interview to a Harijan deputation on the eve of his departure, Gandhiji said, "Untouchability is a dead thing but being a monster, it still appears to be taking breath. But it is the last breath." So optimistic Gandhi was and confident of his success in this great venture and mission!

Gandhi continued his Andhra tour, visiting Guntur, Ellore, Rajahmundry, Vizagapatnam and other places. He addressed the Andhra villagers sitting on the hood of his motor-car and shouted out, 'a bangle for an autograph.' If we fail in this trial, he declared, "Hinduism and Hindus will perish." On January 4, 1934, he entered the Mysore State. On his begging mission, he went to Bangalore, Mysore and Badanwala and then took three days' rest from January 6. Mahadev Desai and Kasturba were in jail and their absence, he said, affected him deeply. At Bangalore he put up at Kumar Park, the palace belonging to the Maharaja of Mysore. The Viceroy was displeased with the Maharaja at this.

On January 10, 1934, Gandhi started his tour of Malabar, the blackest spot on the "untouchability map" of India. Swami Vivekanand had described the Malabaris as lunatics. Gandhi told them that they should clean up the shame of untouchability from Malabar. The face of the Nayadis (unapproachables) would always haunt him. At a Guruvayur meeting, some men were wounded in the scuffle that took place between the supporters of Gandhi and the volunteers sent by the Varnashram Sangh from north India. The Sanatanists attempted to break Gandhi's meetings, obstructed his movements and staged blackflag demonstrations at almost all prominent places. During the tour some women gave him bangles, some necklaces and Gandhi's *Harijan* showed his gratitude for and delight at these gifts. On January 16, 1934, Gandhi left for a tour of Travancore and Cochin. He visited Kottayam and Alleppey. He said that some men there defended the sin of untouchability as if it had divine sanction! If untouchability, he said, were removed, it must result in uniting all Indians together, and all humanity nearer to them.

During the tour Untouchables told him at some places that nothing was done in villages to remove untouchability, and temples were again closed for them. Gandhi agreed to their suggestion that caste Hindus should employ Harijans as domestic servants. They also told him that the temple entry movement had come to a dead stop though Gandhi believed that it was moving forward.

On January 20, 1934, when he entered Trivandrum, he was glad to see that the Travancore State had already declared open public roads, wells and *chatrams* to all classes of people. Gandhi congratulated the State on the reform it had recently initiated. Everywhere Gandhi heard the walls and woes of those who were affected by social tyranny. He said he had become a Harijan and he would like to suffer with Harijans. The Maharaja was indifferent to Gandhi, and Sir C.P. Ramaswamy Aiyer the Dewan, did not bother to meet Gandhi. "Kelappan" Gandhi wrote to Patel, "will probably marry a Christian lady," and so his connection with the Harijan Sevak Sangh will come to an end."

When Gandhi was at Calicut on the night of January 15, 1934, the terrible calamity of earthquake overtook Bihar, destroying thousands of lives and lakhs of houses and about 6 million wells up to a distance of thousand miles. The daily life of the people was totally shattered and paralysed. The Bihar Government freed Rajendra Prasad on January 17, to help the earthquake sufferers. Gandhi was seeking God's advice but he said: "I am being crushed to pieces still I talk, laugh and seem to enjoy, for I have to do that. But I am thinking of it all the twenty-four hours and made a public appeal for funds for the stricken Bihar."

Gandhi wrote in a statement in *Harijan* of February 2, 1934: "Let the anti-untouchability reformers regard the earthquake as a nemesis for the sin of untouchability. I share the belief with the whole world, civilized and uncivilized, the calamities such as the Bihar one come to mankind as a chastisement for their sins. I regard untouchability as such a grave sin as to warrant divine chastisement." He must have shuddered at his own superstitious interpretation and so he extended the cause of the calamity to a wider range and whispered, "I do not interpret chastisement as an exclusive punishment for the sin of untouchability".

Gandhi did not cancel his tour programme and go to Bihar. He thought there was no immediate requirement for him to go there. He toured Karnataka and Orissa and from there he went to Bihar.

Tagore and Savarkar held up Gandhi's interpretation of the earthquake to ridicule. Tagore denounced it as an unscientific view of things. He claimed that physical catastrophes have their inevitable and exclusive origin in certain combinations of physical facts. "If," he proceeded, "we associate ethical principles with cosmic phenomena, we shall have to admit that human nature is morally superior. We are perfectly secure in the faith that our own sins and errors, however enormous, have not enough force to bring down the structure of creation to ruins." Tagore was sorry that Gandhi's views stressed "the elements of unreason which is a fundamental source of all blind powers that drive us against freedom and self-respect".

Savarkar was sorry that superstition should hold its sway in India even during the twentieth century. The Britisher, he observed, crushed everything that was with the Indians, but not their precious possession of credulous superstition. It was, he added, quite okay when Indians did not know the causes of such things as an earthquake, a disease or a pestilence, but to stick to prayer and sacrifice of animals even when science had found out the causes of physical calamities was simply absurd. Savarkar appealed to the Hindus to follow the cause and effect theory that is never disturbed by the thought of divine pleasure or displeasure. Later Savarkar issued a booklet in Marathi condemning the irrational outlook of Gandhi and called it *Gandhi Gondhal*—Gandhian confusion.

About Tagore's criticism of his unscientific and superstitious views, Gandhi said that Tagore wrote such things in a hurry and then corrected himself. But in *Harijan* of February 16, 1934, replying to Tagore, he wrote: "I early discovered certain differences of outlook between us. God rules me in tiniest detail of my life. I believe literally that not a leaf moves but by His will."

But the philosophical basis of Gandhism is further disclosed when he noted: "Visitations like draughts, floods, earthquakes and the like, though they seem to have only physical origins, are, for me, somehow connected with man's morals. Therefore, I instinctively felt that the earthquake was a visitation for the sin of untouchability." "I admit," he continued, "my utter ignorance of the working of the laws of Nature. But even as I cannot help believing in God though I am unable to prove His existence to the sceptics, in like manner, I cannot prove the connection of sin of untouchability with Bihar visitation even though the connection is instinctively felt by me". "With me," he concluded, "the cosmic phenomena and human behaviour is a living faith."

In this regard Gandhi was indeed the spokesman for the ignorant masses, reason and science were not his strong points. In his view God poured His anger on the people of Bihar for the sins of untouchability committed by Hindus all over India. They deserved to suffer, he thought, even the innocent children, non-Hindus and animals in that region for no sin of untouchability on their part. And if God was omniscient, kind, all-prevading, why did He punish in the earthquake persons who were linked with the sin of untouchability? Sometimes men of God turn their back upon science and reason. And Gandhi, who believed that not a leaf moved without God's will, did just that.

The Christian Harijans in Malabar and Tamilnad, who had changed their faith to escape the hardships inflicted upon them by caste Hindus, had, they told Gandhi, fared no better in the Christian fold. Gandhi consoled them by saying that they would get indirect benefits in future.

In February 1934, Gandhi used the good offices of his European emissary Muriel Lester to see the Governer of Bengal. But nothing came out of it. On the eve of Gandhi's visit to Pondicherry on February 17, 1934, Gandhi had urged to Aurobindo Ghose for an interview. But he courteously refused to see him.

Aurobindo granted an audience to his visitors thrice a year. Aurobindo had criticized Gandhi's opinions on the *Gita*, Hindu-Muslim unity, non-violence and secrecy in politics. It was about this time that the American Journal *Christian Century* suggested that Gandhi should be given the Nobel Prize.

Gandhi finished his tour of Malabar and Karnataka and reached Allahabad on March 11, 1934. He called on Kamala Nehru and Swarup Rani Nehru as Jawaharlal had been sentenced to two years' imprisonment on February 16 for the three provocative speeches he had made at Calcutta in January 1934. Then Gandhi visited Patna and toured Bihar from March 11 to April 9, 1934, supervising the relief work, cheering the grief-stricken people and giving them detailed instructions. He fervently appealed to them to abolish untouchability and to abolish distinctions between man and man. He then toured Assam on foot from April 10 to May 3. There he told the people that no human being could be unclean born and he only was pure who had the fear of God and His creatures.

Gandhi had sensed the eagerness of some of the Congressmen to enter Legislative Councils. Dr. B.C. Roy, Dr. Ansari and other Congress leaders of their persuasion had met in Delhi on March 31, 1934, and had decided to revive the Swaraj Party and fight elections to the Legislative Assembly and Councils which were scheduled to be held in November 1934. But before this Delhi conference the Democratic Swaraj Party Conference under N.C. Kelkar and Jamnadas Mehta had resolved to fight the ensuing elections. Gandhi had sensed the change of political climate. So after "an intense introspection and heart searching and waiting upon God", Gandhi on Monday, April 2, his silence day, drafted a statement at an out-of-the-way place called Saharsa, without having any knowledge of what had happened in Delhi, and passed it on to Rajendra Prasad. It underwent considerable revision and was abridged. Meanwhile, Dr. Ansari and Bhulabhai Desai met him at Patna. Gandhi issued his statement on April 6 and made room for the council-goers, himself remaining the sole representative of civil resistance in action.

On May 1, and 2, the Congress leaders, Bhulabhai Desai, B.C. Roy, Deepnarayan Singh, K.F. Narainan and K.M. Munshi, met Gandhi at Ranchi and talked with him over his statement of April 6. Gandhi was told by them that they were not disowning him, but that he should release the Congress from civil disobedience. Gandhi agreed that his words had lost their power, but he knew, he added, he would give a good account of himself when the time came to do so. The Swaraj Party met in conference at Ranchi on May 3, 1934, he accepted their demand and decided to enter the Councils to effect reforms in matters as labour, currency, exchange, agriculture and the constructive programme of the Congress. As the civil disobedience movement was suspended, the office of Acting President M.S. Aney terminated and in his place Jamnalal Bajaj was nominated to act as President.

On May 4, Gandhi left for a tour of Orissa and from May 5 he took to touring on foot. He was protected by the police and he said he felt ashamed that they had to defend him against possible mischief. At some places Harijans showered flowers on him and welcomed him with conch shells while the orthodox howled and staged black flag processions against him. On May 16 he went to Patna by train to attend meeting of the AICC meeting there.

The AICC, which had not been banned by the Government, met under the presidentship of Pandit Malaviya at Patna on May 18 and 19, and Gandhi officially suspended the civil disobedience movement. He allowed Congressmen to enter the Councils but the AICC, instead of permitting the Swaraj Party to function, appointed a Board to conduct the affairs of elections of members to the legislatures on behalf of the Congress. Gandhi then completed his Orissa walking tour on June 7, 1934.

On June 12, 1934, the Government lifted the ban on Congress organizations which resumed their work freely. Thus the civil disobedience campaign rose and fell. But just at this moment an important event took place in the history of India and India declared her will to march forward with the progressive forces of the world. India stood once again at the cross-roads like it did in 1907 at Surat and in 1920 at Calcutta. On May 17, 1934, at Patna Congress leaders of the socialist persuasion first met in conference under Acharya Narendra Dev, Principal, Kashi Vidyapith, and decided to organize an All-India Congress Socialist Party.

The Socialists doubted the efficacy of Gandhian economic policy and methods of warfare. They were now disillusioned with Gandhi. According to them, Gandhism was a system of clemancy and charity and not a system of social justice. Yet they kept their association with the Congress. Some leaders, who had opposed individual satyagraha at Poona in June 1933, had decided to start a separate Socialist Party independent of those who had taken a similar decision in Nasik Jail. The

Nasik group was led by Jayaprakash Narayan who was one of the founders of the Bihar Socialist Party. The spirit of the Socialist Party was Jayaprakash Narayan, and the godfather was Jawaharlal Nehru, who often made efforts to rationalize Gandhism. He was in jail at this time.

The Congress Socialist Party was opposed to entry into Council and in order to ward off the danger that might come from it, the Congress Working Committee resolved: "It was necessary in view of all the loose talk about confiscation of private property and the necessity of class war to remind Congressmen that such ideas were contrary to the Congress creed of non-violence." The Congress Socialists observed that this was a further retreat from the Karachi resolution.

Gandhi came back to Wardha on June 9, 1934. His disciples, Mirabehn and Muriel Lester, left for England. Miss Agatha Harrison, who had come to India, also left for England. These British emissaries of Gandhi, Mirabehn and Muriel Lester, were doing political work according to their lights, meeting leaders like Lloyd George. The Congress Working Committee met at Wardha on June 12 and 13 and again at Bombay on June 17 and 18. It passed a resolution condemning the White Paper and another on the Communal Award. Aney and Malaviya wished the Congress to denounce both the White Paper and the Communal Award. But under the pressure of its National Muslim members, it resolved "that the Congress in view of the division of opinion can neither accept nor reject the Communal Award as long as the division of opinion lasts." Bose later said in his *Indian Struggle* that the Muslim leaders in the Congress held a pistol at the Working Committee and due to their insistence, the Congress was forced to take up this ridiculous attitude of neither accepting nor rejecting the Communal Award. Nehru opined that the Communal Award was just a problem created by the middle and upper classes for the sake of a few seats in the legislature or appointments in Government service or to get ministerial positions. Subhas Bose was in Europe and Nehru was in Naini Central Jail.

This equivocal and nefarious neither accept-nor-reject policy showed how a cancerous growth was developing in the body of India's leading political party under the leadership of Gandhi. The Congress Party in the Central Assembly later yielded to Jinnah to compel the Central Assembly to endorse the Communal Award which was against all democratic and secular ideals! Gandhi communicated to Sardar Patel that the "Congressmen will loyally support the policy enunciated in the resolution of the Working Committee regarding the Communal Award."

Gandhi went to Poona on June 19 and remained there for a week. He went to various Harijan localities, the Women's University and the Christ Seva Sangha, addressing meetings and holding discussions. While he was on his way to attend a meeting at Vishrambag Wada on the evening of June 25, 1934, to receive a municipal address, a bomb was thrown at a motor-car which, the bomb thrower identified as one carrying Gandhi. But Gandhi was following in another motor-car and was thus saved.

Seven persons including the Chief Officer and two constables who were in that car were injured. The bomb fell at the feet of L.B. Bhopatkar, a municipal member, a prominent leader in Maharashtra and an ex-President of the Maharashtra Provincial Congress Committee. Bhopatkar was seriously injured.

Gandhi released a statement on the bomb explosion and said that he could not believe any sane *Sanatanist* could ever encourage the insane act that was perpetrated that evening. This sorrowful incident, he observed, advanced the Harijan cause. But Gandhi did not say about the suffering of Bhopatkar. His heart had no compassion for him as he differed from him in politics. Bhopatkar was a man of broader sympathies. Writing about the bomb explosion, Gandhi said to Sardar Patel that something of the kind was only to be expected. But he added, "not a sparrow falls without God's will." It is said that the bomb-thrower was a fanatic devotee of *Sanatana Dharma* which treated a section of their co-religionists as worse than dogs.

Writing on the bomb incident, Gandhi stated in *Harijan* of June 26, 1934: "I am not aching for martydrom, but if it comes in my way in the prosecution of what I consider to be the supreme duty in defence of the faith I hold in common with millions of Hindus. I shall have well earned it, and it will be possible for the historian of the future to say that the vow I had taken before Harijans that I would, if need be, die in the attempt to remove untouchability literally fulfilled."

Gandhi told the Socialists in Poona that he claimed to be a socialist due to his belief and conduct and added: "Jawaharlal is my heir and successor so far as my hold on the Congress is concerned. I am discharging his stewardship."

Gandhi then visited Ahmedabad, Bhavnagar, Karachi, Ajmer and Lahore. Everywhere the *Sanatanists* greeted him with black flags. Pandit Lalnath did not shed a grain of his inhumanity. His religion breathed hatred. He attempted to break Gandhi's meetings and once received a lathi blow. Gandhi chastised his audience who thought a word to the wise would not be enough and so had given a blow to the insensate, unsympathetic and unenlightened pundit. At Karachi a man with an axe called on Gandhi but was caught by the police.

Gandhi then went to Lahore, Calcutta, Kanpur and Lucknow. He faced the Sanatanists; but he was mightily happy to see the crowds more than ever before in Lahore and elsewhere. He told the Bihar *Zamindars* that class war was foreign to the essential genius of India and "*Ramrajya* of my dream ensures rights alike of prince and pauper". Supposing that there was an effort to unjustly deprive them of their property, they would find him fighting on their side. Nehru, he added did indeed talk of nationalization of property, but it should not frighten them.

Gandhi completed his Harijan tour at Benares on July 29, 1934, where the *Sanatanists* led by the infamous Pandit Lalnath publicly burnt Gandhi's portrait and released inflammatory leaflets against him. The police and the social workers of the town were anxious about Gandhi's safety. Baba Kalbhairav, a rabid Sanatanist, was there at the root of this trouble.

Gandhi travelled and trudged about 12,500 miles for his Harijan work and raised about eight lakhs of rupees. He concluded his tour with a press statement in which he enthusiastically announced that the impression left on my mind is that untouchability is on its last legs. And he shared the belief of many that untouchability would soon become a thing of the past.

On August 5, 1934, Gandhi came back to Wardha, undertook a fast and concluded it on August 14. Though the fast was primarily and nominally intended for the hurt caused to Pandit Lalnath, he wanted the Harijan workers to assist the Harijan movement with greater personal purification and greater concentration. He wanted congress workers to use clean truthful and non-violent means in elections and to observe the rule about the use of *khaddar*. He was filled with horror and anguish at their deceit and manipulations. He concluded that "no fast was ever proved an insurance against human frailties. We can only mount to success through failures."

What was the result of the Harijan tour in which Gandhi canvassed support for Ranga Iyer's Bill? With the connivance of the Congress members in the Central Assembly and due to lack of sympathy on the part of the Government which thought the Bill to be impracticable and is likely to lead to a serious invasion of private rights, the orthodox leaders smothered it by resorting to dilatory tactics. Ranga Iyer withdrew the Bill on August 23, 1934.

The Depressed Classes rightly said that if Gandhi was the uncrowned King of India, why did he need the sanction of the British Government to abolish untouchability and why could he not succeed in his object? In the temple entry movement the Depressed Classes themselves did not take part; they were just onlookers. They knew that most of the Congress Hindus were opposed to social equality, had spent little out of the Tilak Swaraj Fund on their welfare, and that

Gandhi's movement was basically semi-reformist. It lacked the real urge for a social revolution. Gandhi looked at the problem from the angle of a humanitarian and not that of a social revolutionary. Dr. Ambedkar had already captivated their minds and had become their saviour. That is why the applause, purses and propaganda emanating from Gandhian Harijan movement did not prove largely beneficial to them.

While taking a rest in Wardha, Gandhi proffered advice to village workers regarding spinning, tanning, the rearing of cows, and the use of buffaloes which Gandhi desired to discourage.

At this time Gandhi had a serious problem to solve. Kaka Kalelkar resigned the trusteeship of the Gujarat Vidyapith and Gandhi wrote to Patel, who had been released, that if anyone could keep Kaka in Gujarat, it would be Sardar's approval and blessings. So he sought Sardar's approval. Gandhi wrote again to Patel: "I have decided that even in order to get over this bitterness Kaka should not leave Gujarat for the present." Gandhi, who once said that Patel had his protecting eye on him, was totally dominated by him. He could not do anything in Gujarat without his consent!

Gandhi received a shock from Jawaharlal Nehru who had been freed temporarily on August 11, 1934 on account of his wife's illness. Nehru revolted against the suspension of the civil disobedience movement. The decision gave Nehru, he said the biggest shock he had ever had, and he felt absolutely alone, left high and dry on a deserted island! He was indignant at the thought that those who were entrusted with the flag of Indian freedom with pomp had actually pulled it down at the height of the national struggle at the bidding of the enemy! The resolution of the Working Committee on the subject, Nehru added, showed such an outstanding neglect of the elements of socialism that it was painful to read it and to realize that it might be read outside India. It was, he added, hardly becoming for a reasoned argument to be replied by sentimental appeals or by the cheap remark that the conditions in India were different and the economic laws that applied elsewhere could not be applied in India. In passing, Nehru reminded Gandhi that political aims were the special province of the Congress. By this he indirectly showed his disapproval of Gandhi's Harijan movement.

On August 17, Gandhi answered that there was not enough reason for all the grief and disappointment Nehru had felt. He wanted complete freedom in the full English sense of the term. As for socialism, he said that the Socialists as a body were in a hurry. He said he had seen the dictionary meaning of socialism, but it took him no further than where he was before. However, he brought to the notice of Nehru that the latter had been tough on the members of the Working Committee. They were also his colleagues, and after an explosion he wanted construction. But on August 19 he wrote to Sardar Patel that Jawaharlal's explosion was not as dangerous as it appeared. "He only exercised his right to let off steam. I believe he is now quiet," he added.

Gandhi was now about to retire from the Congress and his statements and sad utterances were an indication of this. In a statement he issued from Wardha on September 17, 1934 he listed the reasons for his retirement. It was his impression that a very large body of the Congress intelligentsia were tired of his methods and opinions that he was an obstacle rather than a help to the natural growth of the Congress and as the Congress was dominated by his personality it could not remain the most democratic and representative organization. "Many Congressmen," he observed, "have despaired of resisting me."

After fourteen years of experiment, non-violence still remained a policy with the majority of the Congress. His method for the removal of untouchability was different. "I cannot remain," he proceeded, in the Congress. And to be in active opposition was beyond thinking. Regarding civil resistance, there need not be any wonder that it should have been limited only to him. Besides many Congressmen believed that the end justified the means. He had his programme:

untouchability, Hindu-Muslim unity cent per cent swadeshi in the sense of revival of village industries. He would, he concluded, love to serve the Congress in his own humble way, whether he was in it or outside.

Srinivas Sastri said at a meeting in Bombay: "The Congress is not meant for saints and sages. It is meant for the common man and woman." Aney and Malaviya, who differed from the Congress over the Communal Award, resigned their membership of the Congress Parliamentary Board, and on July 31, 1934, they established the Nationalist Party to combat the Communal Award and the White Paper.

As the last resort, Gandhi placed for the consideration of the ensuing Congress four amendments to the Congress creed. The first aimed at changing the words "legitimate and peaceful" by "truthful and non-violent". The second was about four anna franchise, to be substituted by the delivery of 2,000 rounds of a prescribed quality of yarn every month and the third was about the right of vote in the Congress elections.

Meanwhile elections were held to the Central Legislative Assembly and Gandhi said the election results were very satisfying. The Working Committee appointed on October 20, 1934, a sub-committee of Gandhi, Bhulabhai Desai, K.M. Munshi, Pattabhi Sitaramayya and Jairamdas Daulatram with power to co-opt and to report on Gandhi's amendments by the next day. The sub-committee studied the whole constitution and submitted its report to the Working Committee, but the amendment of the creed, as proposed by Gandhi, was not acceptable to the Subjects Committee on the Congress. The words signifying the reasonable attitude of a political party "legitimate" and "peaceful" were not replaced by the spiritual pair "truthful and non-violent". This was a signal defeat for Gandhi although his other amendments were accepted in one form or another.

Three and a half years after its Karachi session, the Congress met on October 27 and 28, 1934, at Ghaffar Nagar in Bombay under the presidentship of Dr. Rajendra Prasad. The neither-accept-nor-reject policy of the Working Committee was confirmed. The Congress rejected the White Paper on which the British Government's proposals were based. The most significant issue before the Bombay Congress was the change Gandhi sought to effect in the creed of the Congress; and on that issue he was well and truly defeated. The Congress remained a political organization belonging to the matter of fact world.

The last day of the Congress witnessed a heart-breaking scene when Gandhi in his sixty-sixth year broke his official connection with the Congress. The Congress shed tears over it, reiterating its confidence in the leadership of Gandhi. In his farewell speech Gandhi hoped that the Congress would soon give effect to the khaddar clause and the labour franchise, and said that his interest in the Congress organization would thenceforth be limited to observing from a distance the enforcement of the principles for which the Congress stood. He vouched for the correctness of the Congress programme which had progressive social, moral and economic goals.

Gandhi thus was concerned with the issues of Dalits no less than any other leader. His heart went out to them and he worked very hard and sincerely for their uplift.

FIVE

Babasaheb's Crusade

Apart from being an academician, thinker and scholar, Dr. B.R. Ambedkar was a man of action. He studied deeply the social history of India. The interest that he had in this study as a student of sociology and history led him to analyse the origin of some of the social evils existing in this country. Ambedkar's whole life was shaped and influenced by his personal experiences, bitter and degrading, those of other Untouchables whom he had come to observe and also those his forefathers had suffered in the past when Untouchability as a social practice was initially being observed by the Hindu society and become institutionalised and embedded in the Hindu social system. He therefore wished to enquire into the origin, growth, spread and perpetuation of Caste and Untouchability, their utility or otherwise, if any, and also the justification in continuing them in this era. This urge might have led him to enquire into and write his books like *Who were the Shudras and How They Came to be The fourth Varna in Indo-Aryan Society", The Untouchables, who were They; Castes in India, Their Origin, Genesis and Mechanism and; Annihilation of Caste.*

This leads us to discussion of Ambedkar's views upon Chaturvarnya, origin of the Shudras, Caste-System and Untouchability.

Social organization of the Indo-Aryans was based on Chaturvarnya is the generally accepted theory. Chaturvarnya meant the division of society into four classes—*Brahmins, Kshatriyas, Vaishyas*, and *Shudras*, based on division of labour and heredity. In the Rig-Vedic period, descent or heredity was not a criterion of belonging to a particular Varna. Gradually the Varnas became distinguished, marked off and separated from one another leading to immobility between the four Varnas and created disabilities for the fourth *Varna*, the *Shudras*. Ambedkar opposed this system as being unscientific, inhibitive and degrading. He strongly criticized it.

Ambedkar levels harsh criticism against Chaturvarnya, as a basis of social organization. According to him it is not just based on division of labour, but also a division of labourer, into water-tight compartments... Chaturvarnya presupposes classification of people into four definite classes. Ambedkar strongly raises objections against this. In this respect according to Ambedkar, the ideal of Chaturvarnya has a closely resemble of the Platonic ideal of division of society into three classes, i.e. Philosopher King, Soldiers and Artisans. Therefore, he subjects both to the same criticism. According to him, modern science has shown that lumping together of individuals into a few sharply marked off classes is unnatural man and not worthy of serious consideration. In his opinion both Plato and the propounders of *Chaturvarnya* have failed to recognize the infinite diversities of the active tendencies and the uniqueness which an individual is capable of. Ambedkar stresses that it is impossible to classify people accurately into four definite classes. That is the reason why the original four classes have now become four thousand castes, he notes, apart from leading to the caste-system, Ambedkar points to some other defects in the *Chaturvarnya* scheme. Its defenders offer that in it the Shudras are looked upon as the wards and the three other Varnas as their guardians.

Even if it is accepted to be so, this system is not fool-proof. He points out that there is no provision in the scheme of *Chaturvarnya* to safeguard the interests of the wards from the misdeeds of their so-called guardian. He also points out how in India the upper three *Varnas* had combined together to beat down the Shudra. The latter was not allowed to acquire wealth, lest he should be independent of the three *Varnas*. He was barred from gaining knowledge lest he should keep a steady vigil regarding his interests. He was prohibited from bearing arms lest he should have the means to protest against their authority. "That this is the way, the Shudras were treated by the *Trya-Varnikas* is evidenced by the Laws of Manu," he says "...There is no other code of laws more infamous regarding social rights than the laws of Manu. Any instances from anywhere of social injustice must pale before it." Ambedkar indignantly observes.

Ambedkar further makes a pertinent enquiring why one person should depend upon another in the matter of his vital needs ? Education and means of defence are needed by everyone for his self-preservation. The *Chaturvarnya* scheme denied both these things to the Shudras. Ambedkar tries to look for the reasons of the disability of the Shudras' deprivation. The above constitutes the reason why the Shudras have not rebelled against the system, and there has not been a social revolution in India, he explains. The lower classes in India have been completely denied for direct action on account of the system of Chaturvarnya. Ambedkar points out that social war has been raging between the strong and the weak far more violently in Europe than it has ever been in India. Yet, the weak in Europe has had, according to Ambedkar; In his freedom of military service his physical weapon, in suffrage his political weapon and in education his moral weapon. These three weapons for emancipation were never withheld by the strong from the weak in Europe. All these weapons were, however, denied to the masses in India by *Chaturvarnya*. It is the system which deadens, paralyses and cripples the people from helpful activity.

Thus, he has examined the case of *Chaturvarnya*, and finding it very harmful denounced it totally. He finds no hope for the emancipation of the Shudras in it, which was the chief aim of his life.

Ambedkar has himself tried to search for the origin of the Shudras. He completely disagrees with the explanation offered in the *Purusa Sukta* that they were born from the feet of the

Brahma. His own thesis for the same is contained in his book: *Who Were The Shudras And How They Came To Be the Fourth Varna In Indo-Aryan Society?*

Incidentally, while justifying the inordinate length of quotations given in the book, he has explained the purpose of writing this book. He states, "The book is written for the ignorant and the uninformed Shudras who do not know how they came to be what they are... When one remembers that it is the Shudras who have largely been instrumental in sustaining the infamous system of *Chaturvarnya,* though it has been the primary cause of their degradation and that only the Shudras can destroy the *Chaturvarnya* it would be easy to realize why I allow the necessity of educating and thereby preparing the Shudras fully for such a sacred task to outweigh all other considerations which favoured the deletion or if not deletion the abridgement of the quotations."

Without doubt Ambedkar wants to give an uplift to the morale of Shudras in their fight against caste-system and practice of Untouchability. Ambedkar tries to clarify that in writing about the problem of the Shudras in this book he had in his mind no other consideraion than that of pure history. According to him "It is true that there is a non-Brahmin movement in this country which is a political movement of the Shudras. It is also well known that I have been connected with it. But I am sure the reader will find that I have not made this book a preface to non-Brahmin politics."

Ambedkar claims a deeper purpose behind his study, i.e. to prepare the ground for social reform. According to him, even an ardent Hindu politician, will admit that the problems are arising out of the malignant form of communalism which is inherent in the Hindu social organisation and which the politically motivated Hindus choose to ignore or postpone. These problems invariably return to plague those very politicians at every turn. These problems are our permanent difficulties and an attempt must be made to repair them at the earliest.

Ambedkar has put forth two questions in this book—(1) Who were the Shudras ? (2) How they came to be the fourth Varna of Indo-Aryan society? As a result of his research and investigations he came to the following conclusions:

Earlier, there was a time when the Aryan society recognised only three varnas – *Brahmins, Ksatriyas,* and *Vaisyas.* The Shudras were not a separate Varna but a part of the Ksatriya *Varnas.* There was continuous feud between the Shudra kings and the Brahmins, in which the latter were subjected to many tyrannies and indignities. Consequent to their hatred towards the Shudras, the Brahmins refused to invest the Shudras with the sacred thread. Due to this loss of sacred thread, the Shudras became socially degraded, fell below the rank of the Vaisyas and came to form the fourth *Varna.* But it has been generally believed that originally there were four *Varnas,* Brahmins, Ksatriyas,Vaisyas and Shudras. This belief gets its support from the *Purus-Sukta* of the Rig Veda. The constitution of society as prescribed by the *Purusa Sukta* is known as the *Chaturvarnya,* i.e. there were to be four *Varnas;* Brahmins, Ksatriyas, Vaisyas and Shudras. Based on his research, Ambedkar rejected this theory, and believed that originally there were only three *Varnas* and not four. In support of this contention Ambedkar offers two arguments. He observes that the Rig Veda excluding the *Purusa sukta,* mentions Brahmins, Kshatriyas and Vaishyas many times but does not mention Shudra as a separate *Varna.* Therefore, there were only three *Varnas* according to Ambedkar. His second argument is that the *Satpath* and the *Taittiriya Brahmans* speak of the creation of three *Varnas* only and not of the fourth *Varna* as a separate one. And the *Brahmans* are equal in point of authority. Ambedkar argues, since both are *Shrutis.* On the basis of these two evidences, Ambedkar writes that originally there were only three Varnas and that the Shudras belonged to the second, i.e. Kshatriya *Varna.*

Regarding the *Purusa sukta* with its theory of *Chaturvarnya* Ambedkar opines that it is a latter production interpolated into the Rig Veda. He quotes several scholars on the subject in support of this theory. He gives the opinion of Professor Colebrooke, according to whom the language, metre and style of the *Purusa sukta* are quite different from the prayers of the rest of the Rig Veda. It has a decidedly a more modern tone, and must, therefore, have been composed after the Sanskrit language had been refined and its grammer and rhythm perfected. He also quotes from Max Muller and Weber in support of his view. Therefore, Ambedkar finally concluded that there were originally only three *Varnas.*

Ambedkar stresses on the importance of *Upanayana* ceremony. A boy was initiated into the class of the 'Twice-Born' and was made eligible for the study of the Vedas only after his *Upanayana* ceremony was performed. Ambedkar holds that there was a time when Shudras had a right to *Upanayana.* According to him, if Sudas was a king and if Sudas was a Shudra; if his coronation ceremony was performed by Vashistha and if he performed the *Rajsuya Yaga,* then there can be no denying the fact that the Shudras did at one time wear the sacred thread and that later they were deprived of it. Ambedkar further explains how the deprivation of the *Upanayana* resulted in the general degradation of the Shudras.

As per Ambedkar's findings when *Upanayana* was open to everyone, Aryan or non-Aryan, it was not a matter of great social significance. It was only after it was denied to the Shudras that its possession became a matter of honour and its denial a badge of servility. This introduced a new factor in Indo-Aryan society. It made the Shudras look up to the higher classes as their superiors and is made possible that the three higher classes looked down upon the Shudras as their inferiors. Ambedkar quotes from *Purva Mimansa* where there was a rule that all property was meant primarily for the purpose of providing a person with the means of performing sacrifice. The right to property depended upon the capacity to sacrifice, which depends upon *Upanayana.* Thus, those not entitled to *Upanayana* lost the right to have property, Ambedkar reasoned.

In the same way Ambedkar mentions that the Shudras as well as the women of Indo-Aryan society did not held property not because they were women and Shudras, but because they were debarred from performing sacrifices.

According to the second rule of *Purva Mimansa*, sacrifice must be accompanied by *Ved Mantras*, Ambedkar points out. Since the study of Vedas is open only to those persons who had undergone the *Upanayana* ceremony, the right and road to knowledge were closed to everyone else. Thus without *Upanayana* the Shudras were driven to degradation; ignorance and proverty. He states that "the stoppage of *Upanayana* was a most deadly weapon discovered by the Brahmins to avenge themselves against the Shudras. It had the effect of an atomic bomb, it did make the Shudra as in the language of the Brahmins, a graveyard."

The next question that Ambedkar takes up is "what power did the Brahmins have to deny *Upanayana* to the Shudras?" Ambedkar urges that the Brahmins did have powers to deprive the Shudra of his right of *Upanayana*. He offered two reasons to prove what he had to say. First, the Brahmins' exclusive right to officiate at an *Upanayana* and secondly penalties to which he is made liable for performing an unauthorized *Upanayana*. Their combined effect according to Ambedkar, was to vest in the Brahmins the power of performing as well as denying of *Upanayana*. Though this power was not expressly bestowed yet it had an indirect effect.

According to Ambedkar, there is nothing unnatural in assuming that in these conflicts with the Brahmins, the whole Shudra community not merely a few Shudra kings, was involved. Ambedkar pointed out to the fact that this conflict had taken place in the hoary past when life was tribal in thought and action. He stated that:

> In all ancient societies the unit was the tribe or the community and not the individual with the result that the guilt of the individual was the guilt of the community and the guilt of the community was the

guilt of every individual belonging to it. If this fact is borne in mind then it would be quite natural to say that the Brahmins did not confine their hatred to the offending kings, but extended to the whole of the Shudras community and applied the ban against *Upanayana* to all Shudras.

The next question that Ambedkar goes on to answer is, why a section of the Kshatriyas became degraded to Shudras and not all those belonging to the Kshatriya *Varna*. According to his finding most of Kshatriyas involved in conflict with the Brahmins belonged to the Solar line. They were higher than the Kshatriyas belonging to the Lunar line in martial spirit, learning and pride. It was they who challenged the Brahmins while the latter submitted to the Brahmins and became their slaves. Ambedkar's next contention is, that there could be no reconciliation between the Brahmins and the Shudras. The Brahmins not only did not forgive the Shudras, they pursued, even the progency of the Shudras with the same spirit of relentless revenge. This he says, would become clear from the black laws that the Brahmins enacted against the Shudras. Therefore Ambedkar's conclusion is that Manu provided the social ideal of *Chaturvarnya* contained in the *Purusasukta* a degree of divinity and infinity which it did not have before.

Another contention of Ambedkar is that the Shudras of the Indo-Aryan society are entirely different from the Shudras of the modern Hindu society. Ambedkar notes that in the Indo-Aryan society the word Shudra was the name of the people who belonged to particular race. The word Shudra as used in the Hindu society. Later is an epithet for a low uncultured class of people, who are a miscellaneous and heterogeneous collection of tribes having nothing much in common except that they are similar to the original Shudras but on a lower plane of culture. Ambedkar stated ".... it is a pity that these backward people of later days have been rolled up with the original Shudras and subjected to the same penalties for which they had given no cause.

In this fashion, Ambedkar accounts for the degradation of the Shudras. One cannot help noticing in this connection that the conclusions that he has drawn fitted well with the aim he had in view, i.e., the uplift of the Shudras. Since the degradation of the Shudras was a result of the religious texts of Hinduism, he uses the same authority to prove that originally they were not a degraded fourth *Varna* but *Kshatriyas*. Ambedkar, it appears, is inclined to provide a higher and more respectable lineage to the original Shudras than is given in the theory of the *Purusha Sukta*, i.e., origin from the feet of the Brahmin. And for those who are not original Shudras but 'a low uncultured class of people' there is no need to feel degraded for reasons already offered.

Ambedkar's analysis proves that the theory of *Chaturvanya* and the caste-system in India are closely interrelated.

The people of India, according to Ambedkar composed of Aryans, Dravidians, Seythians and Mongolians, in due course of time and after some inevitable conflict settled down as peaceful neighbours.Through constant contact and mutual interaction they evolved a common culture that superseded their distinctive cultures. Thus there is cultural homogeneity though ethnically the Indians are found to be heterogenous. It is because of this fundamental cultural unity and harmony that caste becomes a difficult problem. "If the Hindu society were a mere federation of mutually exclusive units, the matter would be simple enough. But caste is the parcelling of an already homogeneous unit and the explanation of the genesis of caste is an explanation of this process of parcelling."

Ambedkar starts his enquiry with an examination of the definitions of caste. Senart, according to Ambedkar, has drawn attention to the idea of pollution, as a characteristic of caste, but Ambedkar does not regard it as a peculiarity of caste. Ambedkar states that it usually originates in priestly ceremonialism and is a particular case of the general belief in purity. The 'ideas of pollution' has been attached to the institution of caste that suits the highest rank, i.e. the priestly class, as we know that the priest and purity are old associates. We can conclude that the 'idea of pollution' is a characteristic of caste only in so far as caste has a religious flavour. Nesfield, according to Ambedkar, dwells on the absence of messing with those outside the caste as one of its characteristics. Ambedkar accepts the newness of his point. Still he stresses that Nesfield here has mistaken the effect for the cause. According to Ambedkar:

> "Caste being a self-enclosed unit naturally limits social intercourse including messing, etc., to members within it. Consequently this absence of messing with outsiders is not due to positive prohibitions, but is a natural result of caste, i.e., exclusiveness. No doubt this absence of messing, originally due to exclusiveness, acquired the prohibitory character of a religious injunction, but it may be regarded as a later growth."

Ambedkar states that Ketkar speaks of prohibition of inter-marriage and membership by autogeny as being the two characteristics of caste. Ambedkar agrees with this as being the essence of caste, i.e., absence of intermarriage and endogamy. Endogamy is the clue for Ambedkar to solve the puzzle of the genesis of caste. He insists that "Caste in India means an artificial chopping off of the population into fixed and definite units, each one prevented from fusing into another through the custom of endogamy." Thus he regards endogamy not only to be a characteristic peculiar to caste but also a key to the understanding of its genesis and mechanism.

According to Ambedkar, "No civilized society of today presents more survivals of primitive times as does the Indian Society. One of these primitive survivals is the custom of exogamy.... Regarding the people of India, the law of exogamy is a positive injunction even today." He refers to the law of matrimony in India, which revolves round the principles of exogamy, for it is not only that *Sapindas* (bloodkins) cannot marry but a marriage even between the *Sagotras* is regarded as a sacrilege. The various *gotras* of India are and have been exogamous, and same is the case the other groups with totemic organisation. So for the people of India, in Ambedkar's opinion, exogamy is a creed and not many dare infringe it, so much so that in spite of the endogamy of the castes within them, exogamy has come to be strictly observed. Moreover, there are more rigorous penalties for violating exogamy than for endogamy. Thus Ambedkar concludes that:

> ...With exogamy as the rule there could be no castes, for exogamy means fusion. But we have castes, consequently in the final analysis the creation of castes, so far as India is concerned, means the super imposition of endogamy over exogamy.

The maintenance of caste, Ambedkar proceeds further, is done by preventing marriage from outside the group. That means that a group willing to make itself into a caste must have the maintenance of numerical equality between marriageable units of the two sexes as the ultimate goal as in the absence of this, according to Ambedkar, endogamy can no longer subsist.With the death of one of the partners, a surplus man or a surplus woman will be created, which according to Ambedkar is a menace to caste. If they are not disposed of within the caste otherwise by finding suitable partners they will get married outside and important offspring that is foreign to caste. The required numerical equality is, attained by forcible means the customs of *sati*, enforced widowhood and early marriage of girls. Thus while looking for the mechanism of caste, Ambedkar has also stumbled on the social evil of early marriage of girls and the prohibition of widow-remarriage in India. All in all women's downfall according to him was due to the caste-system.

Ambedkar goes on to explain how new castes were created and this process continued. According to him the sub-division of a society is quite natural. What is unnatural thing about these sub-divisions is that they have lost the open door character of the class system and have become self-enclosed units called 'castes'. The question is, were they compelled to close their doors and become endogamous, or did they close them of their own accord? He submits that there is a double line of answer. Some closed the door, others found it closed against them. The first is a psychological interpretation and the other one is mechanistic but they are complementary and both are necessary to explain the phenomena of caste-formation in its entirety. Ambedkar gives his theory as follows:

> "I will first take up the psychological interpretation. The question we have to answer in this connection is, why did these sub-divisions or classes, industrial, religious or otherwise, become self-enclosed or endogamous? My answer is because the Brahmins were so. Endogamy or the closed-door system, was a fashion in the Hindu society. As it had originated from the Brahmin caste, it was whole-heartedly initiated by all the non-Brahmin sub-divisions or classes, who, in their turn became endogamous castes. It was "the insertion of imitation" that caught all these sub-divisions on their onward march of differentiation and has turned them into castes."

Ambedkar examines the reasons that led to the further and further sub-division of caste. He notes that castes have no mercy for a sinner who courages to violate the code. As a result of the penalty, in the shape of ex-communication for him a new caste is born. The ex-communicated may be quite willing to be humble member of some already existent caste (preferably higher) but they find it impossible due to the clear conspiracy of other castes which have enclosed themselves not to allow entry or re-entry. They are shut out. The logic behind this abdurate circumstances, he states, is merciless, as a result of which new group, (formed on any basis abnoxious to the caste-rules) by a mechanical law are constantly being converted into castes to a bewildering multiplicity. Thus is told the tale in the process of caste formation in India.

Ambedkar offers the following conclusions:

(a) That although composite make up of the Hindu population, yet there is a deep cultural unity

(b) that caste is a parcelling into bits of a larger cultural unit
(c) that there was one caste to start with, and
(d) that classes have come to become castes via imitation and ex-communication.

The burden of starting the practice of caste falls on the Brahmins according to Dr. Ambedkar's logical analysis. It will be remembered that he held the denial of *Upanayana* by the Brahmins to be responsible for the origin of Shudradom. Untouchability, he maintained originated due to the Brahmins declaring beef-eating an offence and not touching the Buddhist converts.

No wonder then, that Ambedkar came out in his career as an anti-Brahmanist. He held the Brahmins responsible for Untouchability and caste system and also indirectly for downfall of women, viz. Sati-practice, Child-marriage, prohibition of widow-remarriage and female infanticide.

According to Ambedkar, *Chaturvarnya* got degenerated into the caste-system. The caste-system influenced the Hindus lives in the past and continues doing so even today. Ambedkar strongly rejects the system. He analyses and explains the features, characteristic evils and the all-round impact of the caste-system on Indian society, simultaneously taking into account the injustice done to the Dalits.

Ambedkar gives in detail the features of the caste-system in India as follows :

Hierarchy: The four classes are hierarchically graded. Being based on birth, there is no spontaneity on duals part in the hierarchical gradations. Individuals practically can do nothing to change their castes.

Lack of Efficiency: Tasks are appointed to individuals not on the basis of training or original capacity but based on birth and social status of their parents, leading to inefficiency.

Social Immobility: Individuals cannot change their occupations which belong to them by heredity. Ambedkar, therefore, brands the caste-system as positively pernicious.

Industry, he points out, is never static but undergoes rapid and sometimes abrupt changes. With such changes, individuals must have freedom to change their occupations, he contends. This is the reason much of the unemployment seen in the country, according to Ambedkar.

Reason for Disruptive Tendencies: Ambedkar states that each caste is conscious of its existence. "Its survival is the be-all and end-all of its existence." A caste has no feeling of affiliation to other castes under normal circumstance and endeavours to distinguish itself from other castes. There is lack of national consciousness in the average Hindu and as such Hindu society does not exist, he says, because the caste system prevents common activity and by preventing common activity, it has prevented the Hindus from becoming a society with a unified life and a consciousness of its own being." Thus, segmental divisions in society are created on account of caste.

Excommunication: A caste has an unquestionable right to excommunicate any individual guilty of breaking the rules of caste.

Endogamy: Castes are endogamous or self-enclosed, as a result of which defaulters were forced out and this leads to formation of new caste. They imitated endogamy of the Brahmins and thus the closed door system continued. Endogamy or restriction about inter-marriage is practiced even as an essential characteristic of caste.

Anti-Social Spirit: The worst feature of the caste system is the anti-social spirit, Ambedkar said. Castes enjoy singing the hymns of hate against one another which spoiling their mutual relations.

Ambedkar spoke so

Prevents assimilation: In Ambedkar's opinion the Hindu religion was once a missionary one but it ceased to be so with the advent of caste system among the Hindus. Caste is inconsistent with conversion. Unlike the club, the membership of the caste is not open to all. The law of caste limits its membership to persons born in the caste. Castes are autonomous and there is no authority to compel a caste to admit a newcomer into its social life. Hindu society is a collection of castes and each caste a close corporation which has no place for a convert. Caste has restricted the Hindus from expanding and absorbing other religious communities, Ambedkar points out.

Creates indifferentism and inactivity among the Hindus: Caste consciousness prevents fellow-feeling. The reason, why the average Hindu behaves like a coward and is timid, is because of the fact that he does not feel assured that another Hindu will come to his rescue if he is in danger, Ambedkar states. Unlike the Sikhs and the Muslims there is no social cement amongst the Hindus to make them feel like brothers is his lament. According to him "... Indifferentism is the worst kind of disease that can infect a person" and this is the result for caste system and has made organisation and even cooperation for a good cause impossible.

Ambedkar laments that there were thirteen million aborigines of India, who "have remained uncivilized in a land which boasts of a civilization, thousands of years old, "but there have no efforts to civilize them." Civilizing the aborigines means adopting them as your own, living with them and cultivating fellow-feeling; in short, loving them, Ambedkar points out. It is not possible for a Hindu to do this as his whole life is one anxious effort to preserve his caste. Caste is his precious possession which he must save at any cost. He cannot afford to lose it by having close contact with the aborigines, the remnants of the hateful *Anaryas* of the Vedic days. Not that a Hindu could not be taught the sense of duty toward fallen humanity but the problem is that no amount of sense of duty is likely to enable him to overcome his duty to preserve his caste, Ambedkar thinks. Caste is, therefore, the real reason as to why the Hindu has let the savage remain a savage in the midst of his civilization without feeling any sense of remorse or repentance, according to him. The Hindu has not realized that these aborigines are a source of potential danger. If these savages remain savages they may not do any harm to the Hindus. But if they are reclaimed by non-Hindus and converted to other faiths they will swell the ranks of the enemies of the Hindus. If this happens the Hindu will have to thank himself and his caste-system for this, Ambedkar issues a timely warning.

The Hindus according to Ambedkar deliberately try to prevent the lower castes, within the pale of Hinduism from rising to the cultural level of the higher castes. He holds an opinion opposite to one held by Professor M.N. Srinivas. According to the latter, the caste-system is far from a rigid system, in which the position of each component caste is fixed for all time. Movement has always been possible and specially so in the middle-regions of the hierarchy. A low caste was able in a generation or two to rise to a higher position in the hierarchy by adopting vegetarianism and tetotalism and by Sanskritizing its rituals and pantheons.

Ambedkar cites examples of the cases of the *Sonars* and the *Pathare Prabhus* of Maharashtra who tried to improve their status by adopting some of the ways and habits of the Brahmins. The Sonars were styling themselves as *Daivadnya* Brahmins. They were wearing their dhotis with folds on and using the word *Namaskar* for salutation. The Brahmins did not like the imitation and this attempt by Sonars to pass off as Brahmins. Under the authority of the Peshwas the Brahmins successfully put down this attempt on the part of the Sonars to pass off as Brahmins, and they even got the President of the Council of the East India Company's settlement in Bombay to issue a prohibitary order against the *Sonars* residing in Bombay. This meanness was entirely because of the strict rules of caste and the exclusiveness that they breed, Ambedkar notes.

The Brahmin's main worry is to protect "his interests" against those of the non-Brahmins, Ambedkar states. Moreover, "...the existence of caste and caste consciousness has served to keep the memory of past feuds between castes green and has prevented solidarity." This seriously destroys national patriotism and a feeling of all-India unity, in Ambedkar's opinion.

According to Ambedkar, the overall effect of caste on the ethics of the Hindus has been simply deplorable. Caste has killed public spirit, damaged the sense of public charity, and made public opinion impossible. Virtue has become caste-ridden and morality has become caste-bound. There is no sympathy for those deserving it. The capacity to appreciate merits in a man apart from his caste have lost existence in a Hindu. Virtue is appreciated but only when the man is a fellow caste-man. "... The whole morality is as bad as tribal morality. My casteman, right or wrong, my casteman good or bad..." The evil effects of caste have been brought out in totality by Ambedkar, in the above assessment by him.

Therefore, we find that Ambedkar was disgusted with the evil effects of the caste system on the Hindus and their social life. But there are people who do not agree that the caste system is all that bad, Ambedkar laments. Such people put up defences in favour of the system. Ambedkar does not spare them. Putting forward his strong arguments he tries to bring them round to his point of view, namely that caste-system has been the bane of India and the Hindus. Let us examine his argument against defence of caste system.

The defenders of caste hold that it is based on the economic principle of division of labour which promotes efficiency and fosters specialization. However, Ambedkar levels strong criticism against this view. Firstly, he states that it is not just the division of labour but also a division of labourers graded into watertight compartments. Secondly, it is based on birth, and not on natural aptitude. Thirdly, the caste-system does not encourage the Hindus to take upto occupations where they are wanted but do not belong to them by heredity. It gives rise to lot of inefficiency and unemployment. Ambedkar points out that there are many occupations in India which because of the fact that they are regarded as degraded by the Hindus provoke those who are engaged in it, to aversion, ill-will and the desire to evade. However, they are not changeable. "What efficiency can there be in a system under which neither men's hearts nor their minds are in their work. As an economic organisation, caste is therefore a harmful institution, in as much as, it involves the sub-ordination of man's natural powers and inclinations to the exigencies of social rules."

Those who put forth the biological defence of caste opine that the object of the caste is to preserve purity of race and blood. Ambedkar is unable to accept this proposition.

Ambedkar states that the ethnologists are of the view that men of pure race do not exist any where and there has been a mixture of all races all over the world. In support of his argument he quotes D.R. Bhandarkar from the latter's paper "Foreign Elements in Hindu Population" as follows:

> There is hardly a class or caste in India which has not a foreign strain in it. There is an admixture of alien blood not only among the warrior classes—the Rajputs and the Marathas but also among the Brahmins who are under the happy illusion that they are free from all foreign elements.

Ambedkar's second contention is that the caste system cannot be stated to have grown as a means of maintaining purity of blood as castes came into being long after the different races of India had inter-mingled in blood and culture. To hold that distinctions of caste are really distinctions of race and to treat different castes as though they were so many different races is a gross distortion of fact, according to Ambedkar. Caste system, he asserts, does not demarcate racial division. Caste system is a social division of the people of the same race, Ambedkar firmly holds. He advances yet another argument to support his view. Caste system cannot be there for preserving purity of race and blood, since caste system is a negative thing. It just prohibits persons belonging to different castes from inter-marrying. It is not method of selecting which two among a given caste should marry. He, further states that if caste means race then differences of sub-castes cannot mean differences of race because sub-castes become ex-hypothesia sub-divisions of one and the same race. As a result Ambedkar argues, the bar against inter-dining and inter-marrying cannot mean to be for the purpose of maintaining purity of race and blood. He stresses that caste has no scientific origin and those who are attempting to give it an eugenic basis are trying to support it what is grossly unscientific.

Whether caste-system has preserved purity of race and blood can be judged by the race of men it has produced in past. What sort of men has it produced, Ambedkar puts the blunt question and then gives his own answer to it as follows:

> "Physically speaking, the Hindus are a C^3 people. They are a race of pygmies and dwarfs stunted in stature and wanting in stamina. It is a nation, 9/10th of which is declared to be unfit for military service. This shows that the caste system does not embody the eugenics of modern scientists. It is a social system which embodies the arrogance and selfishness of a perverse section of the Hindus who were superior enough in social status to set it in fashion and who had authority to force it on their inferiors."

Thus according to Ambedkar, the eugenic defence of caste fails to stand.

Those who defend caste on the basis of social consciousness are bitterly criticised by Ambedkar. Ambedkar considers that Hindu society is a myth. There is no Hindu consciousness but only caste consciousness. It has given rise to evils like anti-social spirit, created segregation and exclusiveness, prevented fellow-feeling and common consciousness. Therefore, caste cannot be defended this way either, according to Ambedkar. It is no use finding comfort by saying thaı caste is found among non-Hindus also, Ambedkar says. He explains his point by making a comparison of castes among non-Hindus.

Ambedkar agrees that everywhere in the world, the human society is a plural society. At the same time, he stresses that the ties which hold the Hindus together are non-existent, while among the non-Hindus, there are many ties that hold them together. The organic filaments or points of contact are missing among the Hindus, in his opinion. Thus he holds that there is an absence of integrating force to bind the different groups together in Hindu society. Ambedkar further observes the second differences. He states that caste does not have the same social significance for the non-Hindus as it has for the Hindus. If, after asking, you get a reply from a person that he is a Sikh or a Mohammedan, you are satisfied, says Ambedkar, but if the reply is from a Hindu, you immediately proceeded further to inquire about his caste. Why ? Ambedkar poses the question. He himself answers that without knowing it, you do not feel sure of what sort of a being he is. This is not the case with the non-Hindus. Thirdly, the ex-communication that follows breach of caste-rules as a punishment among the Hindus is not found among the non-Hindus, Ambedkar points out. The individual concerned in the latter will not be out-casted, if he makes a breach of caste as is the case among the Hindus.

The fourth point of difference, according to Ambedkar is that among the non-Hindus, caste is only a practice and not a sacred institution. They do not regard caste as a religious dogma. Religion compels the Hindus to treat isolation and segregation of caste as a virtue. If the Hindus wish to break free from caste, their religion will come in their way. His conclusion is, "It is, therefore, a dangerous delusion to take comfort in the mere existence of caste among non-Hindus, without caring to know what place caste occupies in their life and whether there are other 'organic filaments', which subordinate the feeling of caste to the feeling of community."

Ambedkar thus examines the utility of caste, if any, from all but finds none. He deals with it in detail and with emphasis because he has realized that while *Chaturvarnya* in its original form has disappeared, it has left behind caste-system which is still very much alive, influential and pervading ; but having impact towards the worse.

After discussing Ambedkar's views on *Chaturvarna* and caste, we now pass on to his thesis on the origin of untouchability.

Ambedkar himself remarks that his thesis is an altogether novel one. He puts forth the following propositions:

1. There are no racial differences between the untouchables and the Hindus.
2. The distinction between the Hindus and the Untouchables in its original shape before the advent of Untouchability, was a distinction between 'Tribesmen' and 'Broken Men' from alien tribes. These 'Broken Men' later came to be treated as untouchables.
3. Just as Untouchability has no social basis same way it has no occupational basis.
4. There are two roots from which Untouchability has come up.
   (a) Contempt and hatred of the "Broken Men" as of Buddhists by the Brahmins.
   (b) Continuation of beef-eating by the "Broken-Men" after it had been given up by others.

Ambedkar raises some questions, while discussing the origin of Untouchability and he offers own answers.

Ambedkar dealt at some length with the process of the growth and development of primitive societies. He gives his own theory of the Broken Men. He considers it to be the result of the continuous tribal warfare which was the normal way of life of the tribes in their primitive condition. In a tribal war it so happened that a tribe instead of being completely annihilated was defeated and routed. In many cases a defeated tribe was broken to bits. As a result of this, there always existed in primitive times a floating population comprising of groups of Broken tribesmen roaming in all directions. To understand what gave rise to the problem of the Broken Men it is necessary to realize that primitive society was basically tribal in its organization, Ambedkar points out. It meant two things. First, every individual in primitive society belonged to a tribe and no individual had any existence outside the tribe. Secondly, tribal organization being based on common blood and common kinship, an individual born in one tribe could not join another. The "Borken Men" had, therefore, to live as stray persons. In primitive society where a tribe was fighting against tribe, a stray collection of "Broken Men" was always in danger of being attacked. They did not know where to go for shelter. They did not know who would attack them and from whom they could seek protection. Shelter and protection thus became the problem of the Broken Men.

There was a time in the life of primitive society, Ambedkar points out when there existed two groups. One group consisted of "Settled Tribes"and faced the problem of finding a body of men who would do the work of watch and ward against the raiders belonging to Nomadic Tribes and the other group was of the "Broken Men" from defeated tribes with the problem of finding patrons who could offer them food and shelter.

The next question arises how did these two groups came to solve their problems ? "...Although we have no written text of a contract coming down to us from antiquity we can say that the two struck a bargain whereby the "Broken Men" agreed to do the work of watch and ward for the "Settled Tribes" and the "Settled Tribes" agreed to give them food and shelter. Indeed, it would have been unnatural if such an arrangment had not been made between the two, specially when the interest of the one required the co-operation of the other, Ambedkar wrote.

One difficulty, however, must have arisen in the completion of the bargain, according to him. It is that of shelter. Where were the "Broken Men" to live ? In the midst of the settled community or outside the settled community? In deciding this question two considerations must have played an important part. One that of blood relationship and second, that of strategy. According to primitive notions only persons of the same tribe, i.e. of the same blood line, could live together. An outsider could not be admitted inside the area occupied by the homesteads belonging to the tribe. The "Broken Men" were outsider. They belonged to the tribes which were different from the "Settled Tribes". Accordingly they could not be permitted to live in the midst of the "Settled Tribes". From the strategic point of view also it was required that these "Broken Men" should live on the border of the village so as to meet the raids of the hostile tribes. Both these considerations decided how these Broken Man came to live says Ambedkar.

Ambedkar concludes by saying that in the case of India, the same processes must have taken place when the Hindu society was transform from nomadic life to the life of a settled village community. The Hindu society must have had the "Settled Tribes" and "Broken Men". The "Settled Tribes", according to Ambedkar, founded the village and formed the village community and the "Broken Men" lived outside "for the reason that they belonged to a different tribes and therefore to a different blood. To put it definitely, the Untouchables were originally only "Broken Men". It is because they were "Broken Men" that they came to live outside the village.

Ambedkar then goes on to point out that the word *Antya, Antyaja* and *Antyavasin* given to certain communities by the Hindus Shastras are derivative in meaning. He points out to a section of opinion which supports that the word *Antya* means one who is born last in the divine order to creation. Ambedkar notes that this argument is absurd and does not conform to the Hindu theory of the order of creation, according to which the Shudra is born last. But "the Untouchables", Ambedkar points out, "is outside the scheme of creation. The Shudra is *Savarna*. As against him the Untouchable is *Avarana*, i.e. outside the Varna system. The Hindu theory of priority in creation does not and cannot apply to the Untouchable."

In Ambedkar's view the word *Antya* means not the end of creation but the end of the village where the Broken Men had to live. The use of the words *Antya, Antyaja* and *Antyavasin* has dual significance he says. It depicts that living in separate quarters was such a peculiar phenomenon that a new terminology had to be evolved to give expression to it and secondly the words chosen express in exact terms the conditions of the people to whom it applied namely, that they were aliens. The second set of facts, Ambedkar says shows that the Untouchables were Broken Men relates to the Mahar Community, a major Untouchable community of Maharashtra. Ambedkar then states a number of facts to show the relation between the Mahars and touchable Hindus: (1) The Mahars are found in every village, (2) Every village in Maharashtra has a wall and the Mahars have their quarters outside the wall, (3) The Mahars by turn do the watch and ward duty on behalf of the village and (4) The Mahars claim 52 rights against the Hindu villagers. Among the 52 rights, the some important ones are:

(i) The right to collect food from the villagers;
(ii) The right to collect corn from each villager at the harvest season; and
(iii) The right to appropriate the dead animal belonging to the villagers.

Thus the question, why do the Untouchables live outside the village was convincingly answered by Ambedkar. However, Ambedkar has to agree that the evidence arising from the position of the Mahars is confined only to Maharashtra. Whether similar cases exist in other parts of India is remains to be investigated he says. But the Mahars can be taken as typical example he says, because that explains the conditions of Untouchables living outside the village all over India.

Ambedkar observes that the Mahars have a tradition that the fifty-two rights as claimed by them against the villagers were accorded to them by the Muslim Kings of Bedar. According to Ambedkar, this can only mean that these rights were very ancient and that the Kings of Bedar only confirmed them. Ambedkar agrees that these facts are very meagre but they do substantiate some evidence in support of the theory that the Untouchables lived outside the village since the very beginning. They were not departed and made to live outside the village because they were declared Untouchables. There may be some difficulty he says, in accepting this explanation but that arises from the notion that the Untouchables were always Untouchables. But this was not the case, Ambedkar states. Initially, they were not Untouchables but only "Broken Men", living outside the village because they belonged to a tribe different from the one to which the "Settle Tribe" of village community belonged.

If this is accepted, the next question that arises is when, why, and how did Untouchability originate? Ambedkar first discusses the theory of "Racial difference as the origin of Untouchability" and "The occupational theory of Untouchability" and finds both of them untenable. He then gives his own theory, "Contempt of the Buddhists and beef-eating are the roots of Untouchability."

Ambedkar states that the Census Reports of 1910 reveal certain facts. He gives them as follows:

(1) The Untouchables are not offered the *Mantras* from a Brahmin.

(2) They donot get served by good *Brahmin* priests at all.

(3) They have their own priests reared from amongst themselves.

According to Ambedkar the Census Commissioners of all Provinces are unanimous on these facts.

Ambedkar says that people got so much accustomed to thinking that the Brahmin is superior to the Untouchable and that the Untouchable accepts himself to be inferior, that the statement that Untouchables look upon the Brahmin as an impure person is sure to come to them as a great surprise. He opines that this has been noted by authors who have observed the social customs of the Untouchables. What is the reason of this strange phenomenon, is Ambedkar's question. To answer it, he begins from the point when the Untouchables were not Untouchables but only "Broken Men." He poses certain questions, whether the Brahmins refused to officiate or the "Broken Men" themselves refused to invite them to their religious ceremonies ? Why did the "Broken Men" regard the Brahmins as impure, or vice-versa. What is the root cause of this antipathy?

Ambedkar advances his hypothesis for his antipathy saying that the "Broken Men" were Buddhists. They did not rever the Brahmins and considered them as impure. According to Ambedkar's conclusion, ..." the Brahmin also disliked the "Broken Men" because they were Buddhists and preached against them contempt and hatred. As a result the Broken Men came to be regarded as Untouchables.

He further holds that these existed hatred and abhorrence against the Buddhists in the minds of the Hindus and that this feeling was created by the Brahmins is not without support. Ambedkar says that if we accept that the "Broken Men" were the followers of Buddhism and did not wish to return to Brahminism when it became triumphant over Buddhism we get an explanation for this antipathy.

Ambedkar goes on to say that this hatred between Brahminism and Buddhism can not be taken to be the only cause for the "Broken Men" becoming Untouchables. This is because the hatred and contempt preached by the Brahmins were directed against Buddhists in general and not so much against the Broken Men in particular. Since, Untouchability got struck to "Broken Men" only, what could be the reason ? This leads him to further inquiry.

According to Ambedkar it is a fact that the meat of dead cows forms a part of the food of Untouchable communities of India. In support of this fact he quotes the Census reports. On the other hand he says that no Hindu community, however low, is against touching cow's meat. Now, the question that naturally came in Ambedkar's mind in the above context was

"Had beef-eating any relation to the origin of Untouchability? Or is it merely an incident in the economic life of the Untouchables?" He answers the first question in the affirmative and proceeds to present his case for it.

Ambedkar quotes from the Hindu Shastras to prove his theory. According to Ambedkar the theory of beef-eating as a cause of Untouchability has raised the question, did the Hindus never eat beef ? Ambedkar has given many quotations from the *Dharma-Shastras* and other ancient literature to prove that "... Once upon a time Hindus, both Brahmins and non-Brahmins ate not only flesh but also beef."

Having established this, what remains unanswered is as to why a person who is flesh-eater should object to cow's flesh. Why did the non-Brahmins give up meat eating?

After examining the two evidences he relies upon—what he calls the Law of Manu and the Law of Ashoka, he comes to the conclusion that it was because of their desire to imitate the Brahmins that the non-Brahmins gave up beef-eating. According to him it may be a novel theory but certainly not an impossible theory because he thinks that the lower classes always tend to imitate the ways and manners of superior classes in an effort to raise their status. Apart from this, he says, there was extensive propaganda in favour of cow-worship by the Brahmins. The *Gayatri-Purana,* according to him is a piece of this propaganda. Ambedkar, thinks it to be the result of the natural law of imitation. The next question that comes in his mind is why did the Brahmins give up beef-eating?

According to Ambedkar, once the Brahmins were great beef-eaters, once upon a time. The *Yagna* of the Brahmins was nothing, Ambedkar says, but the killing of innocent animals sacrificed in the name of religion with pomp and ceremony, in an effort to enshroud it with mystery with a view to conceal their appetite for beef. He quotes from the *Atreya Brahman* regarding sacrifice. Ambedkar quotes thus:

"To my mind, it was strategy which made the Brahmins give up beef-eating and start worshipping the cow. The clue to the worship of the cow is to be found in the struggle between Buddhism and Brahmanism and the means adopted by Brahmanism to establish its supremacy over Buddhism. The strife between Buddhism and Brahmanism is a crucial fact in Indian history. Without the realisation of this fact, it is impossible to explain some of the features of Hinduism. Unfortunately, students of Indian history have entirely missed the importance of this strife. They knew there was Brahmanism, but they seem to be entirely unaware of the struggle for supremacy in which these creeds were engaged and that their struggle which extended for 400 years has left some indelible marks on the religion, society and politics of India."

Ambedkar opines that Buddhism was at one time the religion of the majority of the people of India. It continued to be the religion of the masses for centuries. It attacked Brahmanism on all sides as no religion had done before. Brahmanism was put on the defensive, he comments. As a result of the spread of Buddhism, the Brahmanism had lost all power and prestige at the Royal Court and among the people. They were smarting under the defeat they had suffered at the hands of Buddhism and were trying all means to regain their power and prestige. Buddhism had made so deep an impression on the minds of the masses and had taken such a hold of them that it was absolutely not possible for the Brahmins to fight the Buddhists except by accepting their ways and means and practising the Buddhist creed in its extreme form. After the death of Buddha his followers began setting up the images of the Buddha and building *stupas*. The Brahmins in retaliation, built temples and installed in them images of Shiva, Vishnu, Ram and Krishna all with the object of drawing away the crowd that was attracted towards the image worship of Buddha. That is how temples and images which earlier had no place in Brahmanism came into Hinduism. The Buddhists rejected the Brahmanic religion which consisted of *Yajna* and animal sacrifice, particularly of the cow. The objection to the sacrifice of the cow had taken a very strong hold of the minds of the masses specially as they were an agricultural population and the cow was a very useful animal. The Brahmins in all probability had come to be hated as the killers of the cow. Ambedkar points out :

> ... In this connection, it must be remembered that there was one aspect in which Brahmanism suffered in public esteem as compared to Buddhism. It was the practice of animal sacrifice which was the essence of Brahmanism and to which Buddhism was deadly opposed. That in an agricultural population there should be respect for Buddhism and revulsion against Brahmanism which involved slaughter of animals including cows and bullocks is only natural. What could be Brahmins do to recover the lost ground ? To go even better than the Buddhist Bhikshus—not only to give up meat-eating but to become vegetarians—which they did. That this was the object of the Brahmins in becoming vegetarians can be proved in various ways.

Had Brahmins acted from the conviction that animal sacrifice was bad, all that was necessary for them to do was to give up killing of animals for sacrifice. It was unnecessary for them to be vegetarians. That they did go in for vegetarianism shows that their motive was far-reaching. Secondly, why was it necessary for them to become vegetarians while the Buddhist *Bhikshus* were not vegetarians. He states that it was due to the fact that they did not want to put themselves merely on the same footing in the eyes of the public as the Buddhists *Bhikshus*, but attain a higher status and to oust the Buddhists.

He advances another reason, for the above. It is the date when cow-killing became a moral sin. It is well known that killing of cow was not made an offence by Ashoka. Many people expect him to have come forward to prohibit the killing of the cow. Prof. Vincent Smith regards it as surprising. But there is nothing surprising in it, says Ambedkar. Buddhism was against animal sacrifice in general and had no particular affection for the cow. Ashoka, therefore saw no particular reason to make a law to save the cow. It is astonishing that cow-killing was made a *Mahapataka*, a mortal sin or a capital offence by the Gupta Kings who were champions of Hinduism that recognised and sanctioned the killing of the cow for sacrificial purposes. Thus follows Ambedkar's conclusion:

> The question is why should a Hindu king have to come forward to make a law against cow-killing, that is to say, against the Laws of Manu? The answer is that the Brahmins had to suspend or abrogate a requirement of their Vedic religion in order to overcome the supremacy of the Buddhist Bhikshus. If the analysis is correct then it is obvious that the worship of the cow is the result of the struggle between Buddhism and Brahminism. It was a means adopted by the Brahmins to regain their lost position.

He then tries to find out answers next logical question - why should beef-eating make "Broken Men" Untouchables?

The answer to this question according to Ambedkar is, that if beef-eating had remained a secular affair and not a religious one, a mere matter of individual taste—such a bar between those who ate beef and those who did not would not have arisen. Unfortunately, beef-eating was made a matter of religion as the cow was made a sacred animal. This made beef-eating a sacrilege, he says. The "Broken-Men", therefore being guilty of sacrilege, came to be placed beyond the pale of society.

The question arises "if the Brahmins gave up beef-eating and the non-Brahmins imitated them why did the "Broken-Men" not do the same?" Ambedkar's answered to this is that during the period when beef-eating was common to both the "Settled Tribesmen" and the "Broken-Men" a system had grown up whereby the "Settled Community" ate fresh beef, whereas the "Broken-Men" ate the flesh of the dead cow. We have no positive evidence to show that members of the "Settled Community" never ate the flesh of the dead cow. But we do have negative evidence which shows that the dead cow had become an exclusive possession and perquisite of the "Broken-Men". The evidence consists of facts that relates to the Mahars of Maharashtra who had the right to take the dead animal, against every Hindu in the village. This means that no Hindu can eat the flesh of his own animal once it dies. Ambedkar points out. He has to give it to the Mahar. This is just another way of stating that when eating beef was a common practice the Mahars ate dead beef and the Hindus ate fresh beef. Two questions that arise are, whether what is true today was also true in the ancient past? Can this fact which is true of Maharashtra be taken as typical of the arrangement between the "Settled Tribes" and the "Broken Men" throughout India.

Ambedkar makes reference to the tradition according to which the Mahars claim fifty two rights from the Kings of Bedar. Ambedkar stresses that it would have been quite natural for the "Settled-Community" to have agreed to the "Broken Men" its dead animals as parts of their wages of watch and ward. It can therefore be taken for granted that in the ancient past when both the "Settled Community" and the "Broken Men" had common practice of eating beef the former ate fresh beef and the latter of the dead cow and that this system was universal throughout India and not confined to Maharashtra alone. This is the origin of Untouchability according to Ambedkar.

Discussed below are some important events involving Ambedkar aimed at uplift of Dalits.

At Mahad in 1927, a conference attended by 10,000 Depressed Classes people was held to discuss action. It was led by Dr. Ambedkar, and the main topic of discussion was the refusal of caste-Hindus to allow Untouchables to take water from the communal wells even though they had the legal right to do so since 1924. It was a peculiar type of religious descrimination : Hindus allowed Christians and Muslims to draw water and it was only the presence of Untouchable Hindus that offended their co-religionists. Led by Dr. Ambedkar nearly 10,000 delegates marched to Chowdar Tank and ceremonially exercised their civic rights to use the water—

probably the first Untouchables to participate in this form of social activity for 1000 years.

This peaceful protest was followed by wide repercussions. It showed Untouchables that their strength lay in their very numbers. It was the first of many similar actions which later followed. It also drew attention to the nature of the Untouchables complaints—the refusal to allow them any civil rights at all.

The protest caused great concern to many orthodox Hindus. Chowdar Tank was ritually purified by priests using a mixture compounded of cowdung, urine and curds. The Mahad Municipality revoked its 1924 decision, and declared that the Tank was no more open to Dalits.

The purification of the Tank particularly embittered Ambedkar, and the Untouchable communities planned a satyagraha campaign. However, they decided not to antagonise the Government whose support they need and they refrained from illegality in their actions. In the year 1929, the promised Temple-entry campaign began and many Temples were closed down for long periods rather than allow in Untouchables. Negotiations with Hindu leaders led to opening of a few Temples. Later on the campaign became more earnest. For Ambedkar, "The question of whether we belong to the Hindu religion is to be decided by us once and for all."

Untouchables, 15000 in numbers, tried to gain entry to the major Temple at Nasik in order to worship Shree Rama, and sat down in front of the gates when permission was not given. An agreement between the communities led to riots when it was broken, and so the satyagraha-direct action-campaign continued into the next year, leading to complete closure of Temple. Gandhi objected to the use of *satyagraha* (his own weapon) against fellow-countrymen but he supported the aims of the Temple-entry campaign and appealed all Temples to throw open their doors to Untouchables. This powerful plea of Gandhi proved to be a very damp squib as no temple was thrown open following his request.

Although the Temple entry campaign did not produce sweeping reforms for Untouchables, it had important effects in India and the outside world. Untouchables beame extremely loyal to Dr. Ambedkar; they were increasingly driven together by common cause a community feeling was being developed; they showed that the caste system could be successfully broken; and world opinion to know about the plight of India's Untouchables.

Meanwhile Ambedkar got elected as a member of the Bombay Legislative Council which gave him some official standing in the community as well as further opportunities to better the conditions of his fellow Untouchables. For example, Ambedkar exposed the hidden discrimination against Untouchables in the Police Force, and also tried to abolish hereditary serfdom.

Dr. Ambedkar became increasingly involved in the political problems of Untouchables, which he believed were crucial and could spare less and less time for the satyagraha campaign. Ambedkar became the official representative for the Untouchables. When the Simon Commission came to India in 1928 to examine and report on the government system, the Congress Party boycotted it. Ambedkar, however, used the occassion to explain the grievances of the Dalits and suggested some ways of improving their position, e.g., by having a cabinet post reserved for them and seats in the Legislature. In spite of Dr. Ambedkar's strong plea, the eventual Simon Report (1930) rejected this. Even though it awarded separate electorates to the Sikhs, Moslems, and Christians, it included the Dalits with the Hindus.

Dr. Ambedkar went on to represent the Untouchables at the Prime Minister's Round Table Conference in London (1930). Although much of the Congress Party was boycotting this Conference, most of the Indian representatives were demanding Dominion status for their country. Ambedkar was not opposed to this but insisted on guarantees for Untouchables as a pre-condition of self-rule. Ambedkar used the Conference as an opportunity for influencing public opinion. Many labour M.P.s took up the Untouchable's cause and it was heard by an even wider audience. The Conference itself was inconclusive, however, although Dr. Ambedkar managed to come to an agreement with the other minority leaders for a joint stand.

The next Round Table Conference held in 1931, turned out to be more authoritative, if only because the British authorities had expediently released from prison the leaders of the Congress party to enable them to attend. Gandhi was sympathetic to the problems of Untouchables but was completely opposed to their separation from the rest of the Hindu population. Dr. Ambedkar stood up against emotional, political and spiritual pressure of Gandhi; he refused to be dominated and stood his ground. He threw in the lot of the Untouchables with the rest of the Minorities, and they each agreed to recommend separate electorates for each community—much to Gandhi's disliking. This was a great achievement for Ambedkar. Up to then, the Untouchables had been regarded as part of the property of the Hindu community; now they had made their case for separate treatment.

The Communal award in 1932 consented the Depressed Classes and Minorities most of their requests. The Dalits were awarded two votes—one to elect their representatives to separate seats in the Provincial Assemblies, and the other to vote with Hindus in general constituencies. Other Minorities were given separate electorates.

Although Gandhi had earlier agreed to allow the British Prime Minister to arbitrate between the communities and decide the basis of representation, he now began a fast-unto-death protesting against the Communal Award. Gandhi was not opposed to separate electorates as such, but only the granting of them to the Dalits, thus creating a division among Hindus. Gandhi believed that Untouchability was more of a moral problem and not one that could, or ought, to be tackled by constitutional formulae.

In initial stage, Dr. Ambedkar showed elaborate

unconcern over Gandhi's fast. Eventually though in response to the urgent pleas of the Congress Party leaders, who were fearing that Gandhi would die, he concluded an agreement with Gandhi's followers which came to be known as the Poona Pact. In some ways this was very similar to the Communal Award. More seats were reserved for the Dalits, but the candidates had to be chosen by joint electorates of both Hindus and Untouchables. But in practical terms, even though Untouchables now had more representatives, they had less direct power—and this has been true right up to the present day. Most of the Untouchable representatives are Untouchable in their origin, but are creatures of a political machine; they are not very forceful in putting forward their people's case. Ambedkar once said : "A foreigner reviewing the work of the Parliament might well draw the conclusion that the Untouchables are subject to no sort of persecution, that they have no grievances of any sort".

This is the consequence of having no independent power-base and allowing the majority to choose the representatives of the minority. There were of course some offsetting advantages for the Dalits—for example, they now had direct access to the Central Assembly—but at Poona, Ambedkar and the Untouchable castes were blackmailed to save Gandhi's life. As a result of Poona Pact, the Congress Party made a good gesture, they adopted in their policy the elimination of Untouchability. Gandhi formed his Anti-Untouchability League, probably one of the most lethargic organizations ever set up ; its achievements were minimal, and there was not even a token Untouchable on its Executive Body.

In 1934 after a period of inactivity, Ambedkar became Professor and then Principal of the Government Law College of Bombay. The climax to a long series of personal worries happened in 1935 when his wife died of tuberculosis. Four of his children had earlier died and now his wife. By 1935, Ambedkar was preparing his people for a change in strategy. At the Yeola Conference he asked them to leave Hinduism and join some other religious group. At this time, he was thinking of joining Sikhism. But many of the Dalit leaders were against this, and so he committed them to wait for five years before officially changing his religion. Ambedkar also suggested that they give up the Temple-entry Campaign, because it was unlikely to succeed and a change of religion made it irrelevant.

Dr. Ambedkar's book, 'Annihilation of Caste' gives insight into the various reasons why he had rejected Hinduism. He believed that Hinduism was based on the caste system and the real method of breaking up the caste system was "to destroy the religious notions on which caste is founded." The idea of the Untouchable leader daring to embrace some other religion, and the chances of his leading his sixty million followers out of the Hindu fold caused some panic amongst Hindu leaders. The traditional role of the Untouchables, like that of Victorian children, was to be seen and not heard—to suffer and be silent. The title of Ambedkar's first newspaper expressed this well—"Mook Nayak". Leader of the Dumb. Now the dumb masses, about whose welfare the religious leaders had so far been indifferent, were in danger of repudiating Hinduism, and completely tilting the religious balance of power in India. *Annihilation of Caste* is a powerful book written with considerable authority, based on Ambedkar's personal experience of the problems. He discusses all the arguments in favour of caste, and then dissects each one. Does the caste system give a feeling of community? He replies, "A caste has no feeling that it is related to other castes except when there is a Hindu-Moslem riot. Indians are not a nation, they are an amorphous mass of people." He returns the inward-looking nature of Hinduism upon itself, and discusses the reluctance of Hindus to civilize the 13 million aboriginal tribesmen in India.

> "Who is more worthy of our respect-the Mohammedans and Christians who attempted to thrust down the throats of unwilling persons what they

regarded as necessary for their salvation, or the Hindu who would not spread the light, who would endeavour to keep others in darkness, who would not consent to share his intellectual and social inheritance with those who were ready and willing to make it part of their own make-up ? If the Mohammedan has been cruel, the Hindu has been mean, and meanness is worse than cruelty."

If they showed disinterest in aboriginals, they had shown an equal lack of interest about Untouchables. Gandhi opposed Untouchability, but thought the caste system was a valuable means of social restraint. His ideas changed slightly with passage of time, perhaps due to the restlessness of Untouchables, but even so he was able to declare. "The Law of Varna teaches us that we have each one of us to earn our bread by following the ancestral calling... The callings of a Brahmin and a scavenger are equal, and their due performance carries equal merit before God." As Ambedkar remarked, "this was a very innocuous proposition which nobody can find difficult to preach of dangerous to believe in."

Ambedkar had never been much affected by the cult of Gandhism. He pointed out that out of Gandhi's twenty-one fasts- unto-death, none had been against Untouchability. Gandhi's main aim was home rule. He believed that all other reforms would automatically stem from this; and meanwhile he tried to keep the different coalitions of Hindus together in the Congress fold and this entailed avoiding any attack on urgent social evils in Indian society. Ambedkar, however, thought that home rule would be a step towards slavery, unless the conditions of Untouchables were rapidly improved beforehand. So Ambedkar and Gandhi were set on a collision course.

Rejecting Hinduism was not only a religious change : it was intended to have impact on political results also. As long as the Untouchables were Hindus, it was possible to lump them together with the caste Hindus, and overlook the fact that they had any problems as Untouchables. This would be impossible if Untouchables adopted some other religion. The threat of conversion itself began producing some results. Every religious minority in India courted Ambedkar; and in a number of states, Temples were thrown open to Untouchables and they were permitted to take part in religious festivals.

For the moment though, Ambedkar agreed to postpone the religious conversions.

The centre of attention returned to the political field, when Ambedkar formed the Independent Labour Party in 1936. In the 1937 elections for Provincial Councils it did well although the Congress Party won most of seats. Ambedkar was elected and used his position to win rights for Dalits, and indeed for all ordinary people. Many of his suggestions which were turned down at some point of time, later reappeared as Congress Party legislation—for example, the principles contained in his land tenure bill became the basis of legislation in the 1959 Act, some twenty-two years after he had introduced it.

At this time he became involved with trade union organization helping to organize strikes against a Congress Party Industrial Regulations Act in 1938. He also helped worker organizations of peasants, railway workers and textile operatives. Dalits in these occupations generally had the worst jobs reserved for them and Ambedkar tried to bring about change this state of affairs.

In 1942, Ambedkar founded the All India Scheduled Castes Federation, a political organization for the Dalits. In the 1945 election it was completely routed and failed to win a seat. This was very poor repayment for Ambedkar's services to India. It was something he was to later experience again, for the record of Ambedkar's last few years was that of a fruitless campaign for proper political representation for Dalits.

The S.C.F. started a Civil Disobedience campaign to get better representation of Dalits in the Cabinet. The Untouchable representation was soon doubled when the Muslim League used their right to appoint the Law Minister by choosing a Dalit. The Muslim League also appointed Ambedkar as one of their representatives at the Constituent Assembly. The outlook became somewhat less depressing.

In 1947, the Constituent Assembly 'abolished' Untouchability—"Untouchabilty in any form is abolished and the imposition of any disability on that account shall be an offence". This clause has certainly not legislated discrimination out of existence, but it was a beginning : the problem was recognised at last.

Later in that year Ambedkar became Law Minister in the Congress Government. He decided to co-operate with Congress as much as he could, wanting to use his abilities for the nation. Thus he became the person who is responsible to draft the Indian Constitution. He was proud of his achievement, although he would have preferred a completely free hand in framing it. India owes to him adept as a result of this great Constitution.

What drove him out of the Cabinet was the failure of the Government to take speedy action about improving the lot of the Dalits. In addition, the bill which he introduced as Law Minister to amend certain traditional aspects of Indian society seemed to gather no support, even though it was a Congress Party policy. The Hindu Code bill would, for example, have granted female children inheritance rights; permitted and regulated divorce and marriage; and established property rights for women. Ambedkar's concern was not only for Dalits, he felt the genuine grievances of all the people.

Though, Ambedkar had tasted political power, he was not so seduced by it that he could repudiate all his previous career and beliefs in order to stay in office 'The Times of India' then wrote:

> "The Cabinet is not overburdened with talents, and the departure of this discerning scholar and illustrious student of public affairs cannot but dim its limited lustre."

In the following elections the Scheduled Castes Federation allied itself with the Socialists. Ambedkar lost his seat and his party was defeated. The new legislature was sufficiently influenced by Ambedkar however to pass the "Untouchability Offences bill", which provided more severe penalties for discriminating against Untouchables and was a further step forward on the road to freedom for Untouchables. Ambedkar, however, was later selected to represent Bombay in the Council of States (the upper chamber of the legislature), where he could play a small part in the future of India.

The unwillingness of India to give recognition to one of its great men meant that Ambedkar, who had been denied office for so long, was now deprived of it for ever.

Ambedkar spent the few remaining years of his life laying substantial foundations for the further advancement of Dalits. Following are some of them:

1. He devoted himself to another civil disobedience campaign this time with the objective of redistributing surplus and wasteland to Untouchables. This was called off after receiving an encouraging response from states and landowners.
2. Ambedkar's People's Education Society, founded around this time, set up a number of colleges and schools with intention to provide Untouchables with a basic non-discriminatory education.
3. He also intended to form a new political party, to be named the Republican Party of India. This had to wait until his death; obedient to his wishes, his followers set up the Republican Party.
4. He changed his religion embracing Buddhism.

By 1956, it became clear that Ambedkar was going to change his religion. In "Buddha and his Dhamma" he had argued that only Buddhism provided a religion which was acceptable to him and would be worthwhile for Dalits. It was not based on caste; it could be earlier amended by the believer;

it did not believe in a personal God or miracles; it did not provide its spiritual leaders with superstitious powers; and above all, it was a religion that would produce "a religious revolution that is today necessary for a political revolution."

In 1935 he had declared "I will not die a Hindu." So, in the last few months of his life he publicly entered into the Buddhist faith at Nagpur, bringing with him one and a half million of his supporters. A campaign was immediately begun to bring all other Dalits into the Buddhist faith.

PART THREE

Problems and Issues

SIX

Role of Society

It has been found usually that each Scheduled Caste tries hard to claim higher than the others in the relative social scale of the Scheduled Castes. Each thinks that he is superior than the other and therefore is not ready to grant right superiority to the others. They all try to prove their superiority by tracing their relationship with some saint or king and elaborating some myths by exaggerating behind the origins of their own castes (unfortunately such materials could not be collected due to lack of time at the disposal of our investigators).

At present setting of the Scheduled Castes are not so rigid about untouchability among themselves. Though one tends to bring down the other member of a Scheduled Caste who is inferior to his own caste, yet it is not so apparent since they have been recorded as getting together and passing their apparent free time in each others' company together in the same place, the only exception being that they do not eat together. They all participate in the social or religious functions of each other.

Practically in all societies people stay together in groups by various kinds, or bonds. The most universally accepted and the most basic of all such bonds is that which is based on reproduction, on inherent human chain, and it is called kinship.

Among the Scheduled Castes both types of kinships are found, a kin of the same blood, consanguineous kinship and affinal (which arises out of a socially-defined marital relationship). The kinship relationship is not very strong and at any of social occassion the presence of all the relatives is essential. On the birth, marriage and death ceremonies they have to be rightly invited. The members of the lineage support one another at times of need and in various economic operations.

Society is patriarchal or in the other words male is head of family or tribe among the Scheduled Castes of this area. He is the supreme authority. A girl after marriage goes to her husband's house but some very amazing incidents that have been recorded when the husband comes to reside in his wife's house. The reason being quite simple. The husband of the girl is either too poor or the wife's father has no male issue. This category of husbands who live in the father-in-law's house are called "Ghar Jamai" (Literally, House-son-in-law) in Indian society.

In a patriarchal society the son adopts the title of his father or father's ancestors and this is a common practice.

After the demise of the father, the son is entitled to inherit the property. If a man has no son to inhent this property then it is his own option to give or donate his property to any kinsman or to any institution, his daughter or daughters have also the right to inherit the property, but generally the property of a childless man is given to his nearest relations like his brother's children.

The joking and avoidance relationship is also found among the Scheduled Castes. The joking relationship is found among the husband's brother, wife's younger sister, maternal aunt, and husband's sisters. It may be explained under the few following headings:

1. *Dever and Bhabhi (Bhouji)*

A younger brother of a man cuts jokes with his sister-in-law (*Bhabhi*) and her younger sisters. Naturally a *Bhabhi* cuts joke with him.

2. *Bhabhi and Nand (Husband's Sister)*

The wife of a persons has joking relationship with husband's sisters and obviously *Nand* in return also cuts joke with her *Bhabhi*.

3. *Wife's Younger Sister or Brother and Jija*

Jija (sister's husband) has joking relationship with his *Sala* (wife's younger brother) and *Sali* (wife's younger sister).

4. *Maternal Aunt and Husband's Sister's Son or Daughter*

This type of joking relationship is a common scence among the Scheduled Caste people.

Our informants among the Scheduled Castes were unable to give the reasons behind these joking relationships.

The avoidance relationship is prevalent among the Scheduled Castes. It is found between the younger brother's wife and husband's elder brother, daughter-in-law and husband's father or uncle or grand-father between wife's father and mother and son-in-law, wife's elder brother's wife and sister and younger sister's husband.

The daughter-in-law, while seeing her father-in-law, mother-in-law or brother-in-law covers her body fully with the sari. She is not likely to touch the hand or any part of her husband's elder brother. The same is the case with the husband's elder brother who also keeps a distance from his younger brother's wife. He makes some sound as a signal before entering into the house if his younger brother's wife is there. When the question was put by the investigator "Why do you behave like this?", they answered that it is a signal to alert them and in this way hearing the signal if the wife of his younger brother is there she will cover herself and give way to him to enter into the house.

Looking into other types of avoidance they informed us that it was a mark of regard which was paid by the younger members of the household, like son-in-law, sister-in-law (younger brother's wife), brother-in-law (younger) etc.

The inhabitants belonging to the Scheduled Castes feel that marriage is an essential function of life. The majority of them believe that marriage is essentially as an act of generation. Six types of marriage are in practice among the Scheduled Castes. They are viz. monogamy, polygamy, levirate and sororate, widow and re-marriage with the divorced.

Monogamy and Polygamy

Monogamy in simple words means marriage of man with only a single woman and he devotes his whole life with only one life partner, whereas polygamy means marriage with more than one person.Two forms of polygamy may be differentiated: Polygamy is the marriage of a man to several women and Polyandry is the marriage of one woman with couple of men.

The scheduled castes mostly go after monogamous marriage and in several cases polygamy type of marriage has been recorded as well.

When two or more sisters are simultaneously, or potentially the wives of the same man the practice is called Sororate. The practice of becoming an actual or potential spouse to one's deceased husband's brother is called Levirate.

These types of marriages although permitted by Scheduled Castes society are rarely seen in practice.

These types of marriages are usually performed only in view of inter-families binding agreement. If one family does not wish to break off relations with the family of the deceased then the younger brother or sister of the deceased is generally married to maintain the family relationships going in proper manner.

When a divorced man or woman marriages again it is called *Chhora Chhori* or divorce-marriage among the Scheduled Castes. Widow remarriage is also a common practice.

They hold the opinion that this type of marriage is important for the betterment of society as well as for that of a young divorced widow or widower. All the people who are member of this very Scheduled Castes were in favour of widow marriage.

There are basically two ways of obtaining mates among the Scheduled Castes. In the first form of marriage the bride is taken by the bridegroom's father or guardian about a week before the marriage and the rituals of marriages are performed in the house of the bridegroom. The day of marriage is usually fixed by a Brahmin or Pandit. On the particular day of the marriage, the bridegroom's father alongwith some of his relatives and caste-men come to the bride's house. When the *Muhurat* of marriage as suggested by the Brahmin comes, both the bride and the bridegroom in new dresses sit on the place where the marriage ceremony is to be performed. The musicians begin to play on *Shehnais*. A Brahmin officiates at the marriage rituals. The Brahmin starts uttering his *mantras* and then he advises the bridegroom to put some vermillion on the forehead of the bride. The *Vedic* rites of marriage is not strictly followed by them looking into the minute details. Then they worship their respective deities and after giving a *bhoj*, a ritual feast, in which meat and drink are most essential, except among the *Kabir-panthis*, the marriage ceremony comes to an end.

The second type of marriage is similar to a marriage of the Hindus of the higher castes in all respects but the *Vedic* rituals are also not severely followed by them in this type of marriage. In this type of marriage the traditional rites are performed in both the houses but the final ceremony is performed only at the bridegroom's house.

The bride and the bride's relatives as well as her father or guardian arrive at bridegroom's house on a day fixed by the Pandit after the negotiations for the marriage have been finalized. The Brahmin of the bridegroom's house has to performs all the ceremonies like the *Karotma* marriage. All performances are exactly the same as those of the *Karotma* marriage. The marriage ceremony usually ends with a *bhoj* or ritual feast. After the marriage the bridegroom takes away the bride to his house. After a day or two after (the parting) she is returned to her father's house. If the girl is still a child, she is allowed to live in her father's house till she is of the marriageable age. Then a day is fixed for her farewell and the bridegroom with his relatives comes to receive her. It is called *Gawna*, and thus she is sent to her father-in-law's house.

The people who are poor prefer first type of marriage,

i.e., *Karotma* and those who can afford it, go for the second type, i.e., *Charotma*.

It is seen that among the Musahars the *Katorma* type of marriage is generally celebrated, while among the Dusadhs, the Chamars and the Rajwars, both the types are in practice. In all the four castes; however, mostly the *Karotma* marriage is prevalent.

It is observed that within the Scheduled Castes widow marriage and re-marriage of the divorced are a common practice. A widow or widower or a divorced spouse goes for remarriage. In case of widow-remarriage, the first preference is given to the younger brother of the family of the deceased if he is unmarried and is willing to marry her. It is similar in the case of widowers. The first preference is given to the younger unmarried sister of the deceased but both are independent on this matter.

Either the guardian of the widow or widower is in search of a male or the widow or widower himself selects a mate and then informs his guardian. It has been recorded that a young virgin and unmarried girl is given to a young widower. Similarly, a young widow can get a young and unmarried boy. In case of an old widow or widower, generally an old widower or widow or a divorced mate is selected. Age factor is generally looked after.

For this type of marriages no formal ceremonies are performed, the widower's father goes to the house of the widow or the divorced woman with his nearest relatives. In fact musical instruments, are not played. No Pandit is required for this sort of marriage. This type of marriage is also celebrated in the Kavowha manner. The barber is call for by the family. In the night the barber paints the nails of the feet of the bride and the bridegroom with a red coloured paste which is locally known as *alta.* The Thakur (barber) takes the ends of the *sari* and *dhoti* and the bridegroom puts *sindur* on the forehead of the bride. Here they worship some local deities and this *sindhur* plays a very signifiant role throughout the marriage life of a woman.

The cause of divorce suggested by the Scheduled Castes may be grouped under the following categories: 1. If one of them is not trustworthy. 2. If the married life is not happy.

Among the Scheduled Castes, sex maladjustments are the main reason of divorce. When a man or woman is frustrated by his/her sexual life and tries for extramarital sex-relations, Scheduled Castes society consider it as unethical and immoral. Divorce, therefore, follows.

Another reason is the unhappy and disturbed family-life. The conjugal quarrels and misunderstandings are very important in this context. The two following causes of the family quarrels were recorded during the interview of the informants : (i) Behavioural differencs and (ii) Differences in age.

One of the main factor for the unhappy family life which has been suggested by people belonging to the Scheduled Castes, is difference in age. There are a number of marriages in their society between couple unmatched from the point of view of age. Though it has a wide circle yet it has been put here to indicate age differences. These differences give rise to so many sexual as well as social problems. This age gap not only effects basic sexual desires but it stands in the way of understanding the sentiments of each other. It is the problem of the generation gap which leads to misunderstandings.

Local Assembly: The term Caste in this context refers to the community and the *Panchayat* denotes an assembly of the Panchas or five elderly members. It means a pure society which is formed to settle the disputes or to punish a social-transgression or wrong-doing within a community according to its code of conduct. In fact it is found in all the four Scheduled Castes under detailed study.

The Head of the Caste Panchayat is called *Matha* or *Mukhiya*. The office of the *Mukhiya* is usually hereditary but in some cases he is also chosen by vote. This election has got nothing to do with the popular election system. It is just a type of selection. The following are the criteria when an election or selection can take place : (i) if the head-man has no male child, (ii) if the successor of the headman is not a man of sound health, and (iii) if the son of a headman is not a man of respect.

The selection can be made only under the above mentioned circumstances.

Normally, the eldest son of the headman takes his place but if he has no essential qualification which are noted below, he cannot be the successor of his father. If a *Mukhiya* does not have to be a successor. The election or selection is open for all belonging to the same caste. However, 1. The candidate has to be a member of the same caste. 2. The candidate must be a respected person. 3. The candidate must be an active member. 4. The candidate must be a male member.

In some cases the most powerful man is also selected, but in the selection of a candidate it does not come into consideration whether one is old and young, rich and poor, strong and weak. Any man can be selected, if he is a respected, active and an able man.

The other office-bearers are selected at the time of proceedings of the Panchayat. This is actually similar to the Gram Panchayat in all respects. All elderly people of the community is involved in the proceedings. Although the *Matha* or *Choudhry* or *Headman* is the head of the *Panchayat,* has to be discuss the matter with the members of the caste present at the Panchayat meeting. They all have the right to give their advice and suggestions. After discussion with the elders, he gives the final judgement.

There is no fixed tenure as such for the office. Although the tenure is life-long, he can be replaced in the following cases: (i) If the headman is not physically fit, (ii) If the headman does not communicate well and (iii) If the headman has lost his self-esteem.

A caste forms a *Panchayat* for its own betterment as well as to prevent itself from the evil elements of other castes. In this way, its jurisdiction is limited by the members of the same caste. Thus it can only settle the disputes arising within the caste. It cannot poke its nose in the affairs of the other castes but all the same it can indulge in inter-caste disputes. In such a case, heads of both the parties or caste panchayats meet together and the proceedings are drawn up in a joint *Panchayat*. They make an effort to reach a final agreement based on mutual understanding.

The *Caste Panchayat* gives the judgement in accordance with the code of conduct, which is drawn up by the community itself and is actually based on tradition. It cannot cross the limit. Because it is for the safeguarding of the rules and regulations of a community, a caste or community is lead by its *Caste Panchayat* which maintains Caste discipline and good order prevalent in a community the consequence of which is caste solidarity.

This is why it can neither disregard its member's attitudes nor can it go beyond the rules and regulations of the community.

The *Caste Panchayat* can be compared as a pivot around which the whole social machinery revolves. It takes possession of a dominating position both in the social and religious fields. It is responsible for some regulatory functions as well as the welfare of the community which falls within its purview. Its duties can be categorised as follows: 1. It settles the disputes within the caste. 2. It can inflict penalty on any member, who violates the social laws approved by the community. 3. It is a godfather of the community. 4. It settles inter-caste quarrels also. 5. It also tries for the betterment of the socio-economic conditions of the caste.

The Head of the *Caste Panchayat* tries to settle disputes arising within the castes. He tries to effect a compromise between the two disputing groups. The decision of the *Panchayat* Head is the ultimate one and must be accepted by both the parties. If it is not approved by any party, that party may produce counter proposals and the *Panchayat* contemplates the same with its members again and again till a final agreement is reached. In this way a *Caste Panchayat* tries to make them united.

The most vital function of a *Caste Panchayat* is to punish the social transgressor. A social violater has to play heavy penalty in cash, kind or by a feast.

In the first case, if the mother does not like to pay the fine he will be ostracized. This is a severe punishment for a man who after all cannot live without society. The person, who is ex-communicated, cannot take part in any social or religious functions of the community. Neither can he attend any functions nor can any member of his society or community attend any function in his own house. He is in a way treated as untouchable. It may even be said that the position of a transgressor is for more inferior than that of any untouchable. The other members of his society do not accept food or water from an ex-communicated person.

It has been stated previously that in the long run even the strongest transgressor has to give up before the verdict of the *Caste Panchayat* and if he wants to be re-admitted into his society, he has to pay the fine. Generally the fine is to give a feast for the community and during the feast he has to touch the feet of all the elderly members of his caste. A poor or weak man in fact has nothing very much to lose has a better position than an ex-communicated strong and rich man. After he pays the fine and arranges a community feast and touches the feet of all in token of deep sorrow and submission he is re-admitted again to his own society.

As the guarding of the caste, the duty of the *Caste Panchayat* is to look after and care the entire caste and maintain discipline and the rule. Its main duty is to watch the community closely so that no rift or violence takes place.

In inter-castes disputes both the *Heads* of the *Panchayats* of the disputing castes gather at a point and try a settlement through compromise.

The following three merits of a *Caste Panchayat* have been related to us by the members of the Scheduled Castes: (i) It unites all the members of the caste together, (ii) the disputes of a caste or village are settled within the caste or village itself i.e.

it is given first priority, and (iii) No chance is given for friction within the caste.

We need not go deep into the first factor which has already been explained above in some detail. The second factor which is also not less valuable, is that the disputes of caste or village are settled within the caste or village. This factor has two-fold benefits as such. On the one hand it saves time as well as money and on the other certain private matters of the Caste concerns are also not leaked. The punishment is so severe that one cannot dare to violate the social rules and regulations and it also creates castes cohesion.

There is a little fear of partiality or of injustice because the proposals and counter-proposals are thrashed out and discussed threadbare till point of compromise is reached ultimately.

To display a balanced picture of the *Caste Panchayat*, just as we have discussed above its advantages, so now we must also examine its disadvantages. So many disadvantages have come into our notice that have pointed out by the informants. The increasing groupism now and then is making it weaker. At present it is not so strong. So its verdicts are not beyond all doubts of partiality. The strong man influences the *Panchayat*, and his wrong doing be turned into noble deeds. This is the reason why its judgement is not always reasonable. It is subject to various pulls and pressures exerted by those who are powerful, rich and strong at the expense of the poor and the needy.

Majority of the people belonging to Scheduled Castes have reported that the Caste Panchayat of this is slowly nothing like anything. It is exclusively so among the castes like the Musahars, the Rajwars, the Dusadhs and the Chamars.

It is partial towards the stronger party to a dispute and that is why it is unable to give a fair judgement, because a strong man can easily influence even the Headman of the *Panchayat*.

It is also stated that the intense emotion for groupism has

weakened the society, which is also an important ground for its failure. Everybody has developed superiority can plan or nobody is ready to accept a man as his *Matha* or *Mukhiya*. Even the political parties have played a major role in weakening the *Caste Panchayats* in their own interest.

The increasing percentage of literacy among the Scheduled Castes is the factor responsible for making the *Caste Panchayat* weaker. The literate people of the Scheduled Castes dislike the *Caste Panchayats* because the latter are rigid and circumscribed and no room for manoeuvre. The young people today like to be confined within narrow walls and frustrating limitations placed on their different activities. The urban impact is also much strongly felt. The people who go to work in the town mix up with other people there and thereby they learn various mix up new things. A person influenced by modernity dislikes traditional boundations. The people who are working outside the State in big cities like Calcutta are least bothered about it. An ex-M.L.A. belonging to the Rajwar caste told our investigator that there was no *Caste Panchayat* in the Rajwar caste, while the other people of this caste gave the shadowy glimpse and innactive existence of the *Caste Panchayat*. A similar case was seen among the Musahars. Although the *Caste Panchayats* among the Dusadhs and the Ravidas are somewhat more active than those of the Musahars and the Rajwars they are also not in their natural form.

Most of the people of the Scheduled Castes have approved that the *Caste Panchayat* is a useful institution. Although it has lost its originality and is now in its decaying stage, yet it may still be useful, if the two main evils, i.e., favouritism and groupism are completely extracted from this institution. It cannot be a helpful or useful institution for all the people, till these pernicious growths are eradicated from this institution. These twin evils try to break up the disunity among the members of the various castes instead of fostering unity among them. It is precisely because of these evils that a *Caste Panchayat* is considered to be an institution good for nothing.

Dr. Srinivas is of the view that the inter-dependence of castes within the village is one of the factors for village unity. Every caste has some form of occupations. For example, the Bhumihars, the Kurmis, the Koiris are agriculturists. The Brahmins officiate at rituals, the Kumhars make potteries, the Barhis supply agricultural and domestic equipments, the Telis make oil etc. and so the various castes are interdependent in some form or other. This can be observed in day to day matters and is very prominent on ceremonial and other auspicious occasions. In any village social functions need the independent and cooperation of various castemen. There are five castes whose cooperation is very essential, they are called *Panch Paunia*. Among them come the Brahmin, the Barber (Naua), the Kumhar, the Chamar and the Barhi. Actually the assistance of the three castes the Brahmin, the Kumhar (potter), the Hajjam (barber) plays a vital role from birth to death. They serve the villagers or outsiders and in return they get their remuneration in kind or cash. So the first group whom they usually serve is called the *Jajmans* and the one who serves is called a *Kamin* and the system of working for others is called the *Jajmani* system or *Gamaity*.

Only a single caste among the four castes under study comes under the professional group. This is the Chamars of the Garor village. And it is also a remarkable thing that not all but only women belonging to 15 families among them are engaged in the profession of midwifery. This profession is generally taken care of by the females. The Chamar midwife is always with the expectant woman. At once after the birth of child the midwife cuts the umbilical cord then separating the mother from the newborn. And then she cleans the room. She gets 5 seers of paddy or any food grain and sari and other clothes as well as food on such an occasion.

The *Jajmani* system is a legacy. After the death of the parents, the *Jajmans* are divided among the sons equally. They can either divide it on the basis of villages or tolas or castes or individual *Jajmans*. Actually the fate of the *Paunia* is dependent on the fate of the *Jajman* and thus are co-related.

In fact it is a medium of unity. Their interdependence makes the villagers united and this is very natural. The Jajmani system not only helps them in uniting but it also makes them skilled in a particular trade of which they are the pioneers. The agriculturist group which is the richest group cannot ignore the *Kamin* because without the latter's cooperation and help they cannot celebrate any social or religious function. So the foundations of the Jajmani system are based on mutual understanding and cooperation.

As it has been stated earlier the relationship between two families or person in a village is not only based on terms of business but on various factors as well.

For instance, although the Chamars are the attendants of the other Scheduled Castes, the latter are also expected to help them in every possible manner. Besides their remuneration at the time of birth, the villagers give them crops at the time of harvesting though the quantity is not fixed and keeps on changing according to ones' need. In fact it is not a rule but a convention. They provide them clothes, food etc. at the time of any ceremony. The *Jajmans* help the *Paunias* during crises as well as on auspicious occasions. After marriage the son of a Chamar alone with his wife visits the house of his *Jajmans* and in return the *Jajmans* give him something in cash or kind as *Ashirbadi* (token of blessing). Similarly, when the son-in-law of a Chamar comes to his father-in-law's house he visits the house of the *Jajmans* and gets the *Ashirbadi*. Thus the *Jajmani* system is an interrelated one.

SEVEN

Role of Economy

Like political factors, the economic factor of human life is also important. It acts as the regulator of different aspects of our life and this is why it is commonly mentioned that to be dependent economically amounts to being dependent in all other respects.

In India around 80 per cent of our population is still found in villages. The Scheduled Caste people are mostly landless agricultural labourers. Only a small percentage of schedule caste people is having one bigha to ten bighas of land.

It is evident from the preceding details that the Scheduled Castes people are mainly engaged as agricultural labourers. Though they may have other supplementary works like agriculture, service, skinning of carcases, basketry, collection of wood and herbs, from the hills. Yet agricultural labour is their main occupation since 77.08 per cent of the total number of families are mainly dependent on agricultural labour. 15.83 per cent families are engaged in agriculture, 2.05 per cent families are engaged in service, 3.33 per cent families are engaged in labour other than agricultural and 1.25 per cent are engaged in other types of work.

Although there have been made attempts to divide the Schedule Castes into the categories described above, yet most of the families follow a mixed occupation. Their occupations can be arranged as follows: 1. Agriculture and other types of work. 2. Agriculture and service. 3. Agriculture and agricultural labour. 4. Agriculture and general labour. 5. Service and agricultural labour. 6. Service and general labour. 7. Service and other types of work. 8. Agricultural labour and general labour. 9.Agricultural labour and other types of work. 10. General labour and other types of work.

For the rural folk the year may be divided into two parts i.e. the busy agricultural season and the slack period. The former period is the busiest one, when intense activity is seen, but the latter period is a period of little activity, we can describe it as 'off period'. As this is the most important occupation and the family budget of Scheduled Castes depends on it, all the villagers irrespective of age and sex engage themselves in the fields in this period. They live in the village upto the harvesting of the crops. It has been very commonly observed that in agricultural operations are found in its peak on the eve of transplantation, weeding and harvesting but excluding these there is little agricultural activity that we see during the slack season which in turn leads to seasonal unemployment.

Agricultural labour is a hereditary occupation. The mode of payment of the wages is still in its traditional form with minor changes. The payment is made on a daily basis as labour is hired only for one day.

There are no fixed working hours of duty. The labourers start working on fields of the farmers early in the morning and return home in the evening only. Only in the case of unfavourable weather conditions he may come back earlier but he will get the usual wages. The work of an agricultural labourer can be divided into three phases: 1. To plough the fields, to sow the seeds, to irrigate the lands. 2. Transplantation of the paddy plants. 3. Harvesting of ripe crops, threshing and winnowing.

In the first phase of work they get three kg. (*kachchi*) of grain and 700 gm. of *sattu* (grampower) and a 100 gm. of *Chabana* (fried gram and maize) for their *Nashta* (breakfast). This is all they get as his daily wage.

In the second phase of work they get five seers (*kacchhi*) of grain per day. In this phase both male and female labourers are engaged. Those who replant get three kg. of grain and 700 gm. of *sattu*.

In the third phase of work, when agricultural labourers engaged in harvesting, get one bundle of paddy (*anti*) for collecting eleven to fifteen *antis*. Earlier a labourer received one *anti* in daily wages against fifteen *antis* collected but nowadays he gets slight better one *anti* for collecting eleven *antis*. This rate has been approved by the Labour Officers of the Bihar Government also. Thus their daily wages depend on their skill and efficiency.

In addition to wages, an agricultural labourer may get 10 to 15 Kathas of land from his peasant-employer for his personal use and he is free to sow and harvest any crop in this plot. The peasant-employer have no share in the crop of that land. Besides giving wages, the peasants arranges some social function to their agricultural labourers. Although labour is the key element of production yet for the following considerations it does not get proper wages: 1. The pressure of some dominant caste. 2.They are afraid of unemployment so they are fully dependent on it. 3. They do not want to go outside the village or the locality where they reside. 4. They work under some compulsion, because their ancestors owned some loan to the peasants. 5. The 'ad hoc' help given by the peasants from time to time.

Being uneducated, poor and unskilled the agricultural labourer face number of limitations. They have limited options. They know that if they leave their village go outside in search of a job and fail to get it, their family will suffer badly. But still during the hard months of seasonal unemployment they are forced to go outside to save them from starvation and this naturally results in a seasonal migration which is described in the following paragraphs.

As it is a known fact that opportunities of securing jobs are not equal all the year round in agricultural operations and the agricultural labourers have not enough savings to sustain them during the hard months of unemployment. This compels them during the off period to go outside or to do some other work to support their families. Those who were unable to go outside the village, adopt some other jobs in the village itself like non-agricultural labour, collection of wood and herbs from the hills of Rajgir, for example fishing and other physical work. Some of them work as coolies, Rickshaw-pullers, in Rajgir town. Some of them have migrated to Calcutta where they are engaged as dock-labour in Calcutta Port. Few of them are employed in the coal-fields of South Bihar and West Bengal, but during the sowing season most of them return to their own villages and do the traditional work.

The women and children also support the family during the slack season. The women grind *Chura*, making foodstuffs (but only the women of Dusadh and Rajwar castes), some of them prepare cow-dung cakes for the purpose of sale. The children also assist their father or elder brother in collecting dry wood or herbs.

For instance, a few young boys and youths get engaged as servants in different hotels in Rajgir (Maharashtra). Most of them are of the Rajwar caste. Some women of the Rajwar caste are also engaged in the hotels as maid-servants.

In this way the seasonal unemployment and the insufficient wages compel them to seek jobs other than agricultural during the slack season to support their families.

The labourers in general are homesick and do not want to go outside. They have obligations to their peasant employers who are kind and helpful on occasions like marriages and *Shradhs* etc. and this prevents them from migrating 'en bloc'.

Although a movement against the low wage was insisted in 1971, yet this has failed to unite them and get full support of the labourers of all castes. The movement against the low wages is generally seen as a direct confrontation between the upper caste people and the people of the labour class like the Musahars and the Rajwars. This has failed to take the form of mass agitation.

According to the old system of the *Varnashrama Dharma* the caste was determined and so there was specific prescribed occupation associated with a particular caste. This had prevented people from giving time and money to search for another job of pursue formal education as it has no bearing on their traditional or hereditary occupation. That, of course, hindered social mobility as everybody was fixed in his grove.

The traditional occupations being hereditary, there is a tendency on the part of those following these to persists in the same. However, circumstances may sometimes compel one to leave one's own traditional occupations, no matter people are not willing to give up their traditional occupations under normal circumstances. This explains why some 50 families out of 240 odd families of the Scheduled Castes have changed their traditional occupations. It covers about 20 per cent of the total number of families.

As has been mentioned earlier that people are resistant to change their traditional occupation which is so dear to them and where they feel thoroughly at home and a sense of belonging, but either due to some better propsects or compulsions to change under certain pressures as due to some other reasons in all societies people have opted for a change in due course of time. This change has been termed as a deviation from the traditional occupation which is the norm.

The data collected in the field give us the conclusive results that the agricultural communities have deviated from their normal occupation either because most of them have lost their landed property or had insufficient land to support them. It is very obvious, they were forced by these harsh circumstances to deviate in order to avoid starvation.

The economic policies of the Government have also been responsible for these deviations. For example, the Zamindari Abolition Act compelled a large number of those employed by the Zamindars to change their occupation because the entire system was seen in different track. Some of them who were once labourers or rendered services purchased lands from the Zamindars and started cultivation on their own and hence they finally deviated from their traditional occupations.

The Chamars who had once a monopoly in the trade of

shoe-making lost their trade because of their outdated technique. They produced only shoes of the old pattern which could not be competed with mass-produced shoes. Hence the deviation from leather work to labour or service was seen among them.

The majority of the people belonging to the Scheduled Castes are landless. Most of the people from the Scheduled Castes have *kachcha* houses made of mud. Roof is generally made of straws.

All the Scheduled Castes are found using earthenware pots and aluminium utensils. In addition to these, about 50 per cent of them used brass utensils also. Only few of them had a few pots of China-clay. The people belonging to the Scheduled Castes are seen dressed with *dhoti, kurta,* shirts, trousers, saris, blouses and frocks. The older men of the Scheduled Castes generally used to *dhotis* and *kurtas,* but the young men and male children have been seen wearing both types of dresses. It has been recorded that the boys of 11-12 years of age are generally fond of loin-cloth.

Girls upto 7-8 years age wore a small underwear only. After that if their economic condition allowed them, they were seen in frocks or saris. The women wore saris and blouses.

Among all the different types of dresses the percentage of rough and coarse cotton clothes is the highest. Families which could afford silk or terene or nylon were very few in number.

Thus it is clear that most of the families of the Scheduled Castes cannot afford expensive clothes. Even those who can afford do not wear silk or terene or nylone clothes daily. However, they put on such dresses on some festive or some special occasion like marriage etc.

To study the economic condition of community it is required to have some elementary knowledge about its income and expenditure. The Scheduled Castes which are one of the weakest and most vernerable sections of the Indian population are generally seen far below the poverty line.

It has been said that the Indian peasant is born in debt, is brought up in debt and dies in debt. This holds ideally good in the case of the Scheduled Castes under study. They found themselves in the grip of our money-lenders and usurers. Although a few families have escaped out of their grip, yet a large number of them are still suffering from this social evil of chronic indebtedness.

As has been mentioned earlier, the Scheduled Caste men never get themselves make able to fulfil their need. If and when they get loans at whatever exorbitant rate of interest they rush headlong for the same. The *Mahajans* (ususers and money-lenders) are opportunistics. They charge a very exorbitant rate of interest. In most of the cases the amount of interest multiplies the principal amount. Thus the famous *cheer* of Draupdi can be the only analogy for the interest of the *Mahajans.* It is sometimes rather amazing to note that a person is still paying the interst for the last three generations for a loan of Rs. 50 only advanced to his grandfather.

The people belonging to the Scheduled Castes repay their loans in the following ways: 1. From crops. 2. From wages. 3. From selling land or ornaments.

Regarding the repayment of loans from various sources it has already been mentioned that a large majority of the Scheduled Castes belong to the class of agricultural labourers whose earning is in the form of daily wages. It is interesting to note that even the payment of wages to an agricultural labourer in our country is very low. There were only a limited number of families among the Scheduled Castes which paid back the debt from sale of land. As the majority of them are landless labourers, hence the cases of the sale of land to pay back loans are very few.

While evaluating the effects of indebtedness on the Scheduled Castes, we should always keep this important fact in mind that they are too backward economically. Most of them are landless people. They are lacking behind both politically and educationally. Most of them lead wretched live and their standard of living is very low. They work very hard for their existence from the little income that they have earned from their daily wages or earnings. They have no money left for future saving and hence they are pressed by dire circumstances to borrow. Therefore, they fall an easy prey to opportunistic and merciless money-lenders from whose clutches they find it virtually impossible to escape. The loan like a mill-stone round their needs persists through their life-time and is transmitted to their hiers, to the next and subsequent generations. Hence once a debtor, always a debtor and a debtor has to face various humiliations and threats from his creditor, consequents, he leads a demoralised life crushed by the weight of the debt and the hopelessness of the situation. Even knowing all these very well, they have no other option.

The Scheduled Castes are mostly illiterate hence generally no one maintains any written family-budget. They gave our investigators an oral account of income and expenditure. They calculate their annual income on the basis of the prevailing prices of the crops. Only a limited number of people working in Rajgir town or at other places earn in cash. Their annual income depends upon their nature of work and the number of physically fit and adult members of the family. Their expenditure depends on their habits, nature and circumstances of the jobs they do and also the income they have.

A family budget of a person belonging to the Scheduled Castes contains expenditure on food, cloth, medicines, health and sanitation, drink, tobacco, tea, lighting and fuel. This is a common type of family budget which is found in 93 per cent of the Scheduled Caste families. In most of the cases people do not include education as they feel that it is worthless. Ultimately they have to adopt their traditional occupation. There are only 2 per cent families out of 240 families which include education in their family budget. About 3 to 4 per cent families include transportation in their family budget.

A family budget of a Kabir Panthi does not include intoxicants i.e. drink, tobacco, smoking etc. They lead their lives very simply. They are non-vegetarian and they keep themselves away from having any drink or smoke or any intoxicants.

A common family budget includes 65.70 per cent expenditure on food and 6-7 per cent on other items. These relate to their major expenditure. As regards to minor expenses, a commonly used family budget consists of 1.5 per cent expenditure on tobacco, one per cent on each item on tea, medicine, health and sanitation. Their are only a few number of families that include transportation and education which are only one per cent and 5 per cent respectively in their budget.

In fact the major portion of income is spent over food, the second item cloth gets only 6.7 per cent while liquor and other items gets 6-7 per cent each. The other items include social and religious functions and festivals and other inescapable occasions. As many of them are also indebted, their family budget as such includes also repayment of loans.

Except a few, majority of them spend whatever they earn. Although some of them do save some money, while some others maintain the equilibrium of income and expenditure, most of them are in deficit every year and do struggle whole life.

The standard of living gives the picture of the economic status of person's life. However, wealth is not the only important factor in contributing to a high or low standard of living of an individual or of a castes, but other factors are there that counts. There may be a persons who may attach more importance of saving at the cost of a decent standard of living. They are satisfied if they are having handsome bank balance or cash reserve.

The interaction from these schedule caste people to more affluent urban life plays an important role in this connection also. The people who have not visited from their native village or have not came in contact with other people of more economically sound, have a low standard of living, but the standard of living of the families, whose members are working in urban cities like Calcutta, Dhanbad, etc., is better. As has been stated some members of the Scheduled Castes like the Chamars, the Dusadhs, and the Rajwars are working outside their own villages.

Some of them have lost the hope and they do not like to raise their standard of living as they believe that it is better to live in the manner of their ancestors but most of them are unable to raise their standard of living as their financial condition does not allow them to do so.

The living condition of an agricultural labourer and especially of one belonging to the Scheduled Castes was the worst before independence. Neither did they get proper wages nor were they found themselves able to leave the field of a landlord. As in Feudal Society, they were all for practical purposes 'adscripted' to the land on which they worked. They are mostly landless and compelled to plough the lands of their owners as long as they lived. In most of the cases whole families were considered to be slaves of a landlord. After the death of the head of the family, one of the sons of the deceased labourer had to work in the landlord's fields. They work under no fixed system. The wages were completely dependent on the mercy of the landlord. It was virtually like serfdom in a feudal society.

After cultivation they might be recalled to do other jobs also. They were the 24 hours attendants of a Zamindar. At the time of social or religious functions they had to perform the menial and other tasks assigned to them. They could not utter a single word of complaint against the orders. The tenant was well acquainted with the results of disobedience. Any negligence of work or duty caused heavy fines either in cash or could even lead to physical torture. The poor people were always under pressure of the Zamindars.

The yesmen and the functionaries of the *Zamindars* were having full authority. In fact, they had persecuted and suppressed the poor agricultural labourers, more than even the *Zamindars*. They were the *Patwaris* the *Gumastas* and the *Piyadas*. They were the pillars of the *Zamindari* system. The Zamindar was the supreme authority but the field officials were the Patwaris, the *Gumastas* and the *Piyadas*. They considered themselves in no way less than the Zamindars while dealing with labourers.

With the social campaign of Mahatma Gandhi a new life and in other words new era began for the Untouchables. He called them Harijans, i.e., the Children of God. It was the struggle of Mahatma Gandhi on their behalf which gave a modicum of self-respect to the Scheduled Castes. He treated them the human being equals to other.

With the downfall of the Zamindari system in 1951-52 the oppression and miseries attendent on that stenile and obnoxious system tended. Now a member belonging to the Scheduled Castes could breathe in the open air of Independent India. As Mahatma Gandhi was in favour of improving the social and economic conditions of the Harijans and other weaker sections of society, the Constitution of the India has given special status to them and provided them with adequate safeguards. Due to Gandhiji's moral influence on the members of the Constituent Assembly, the Constitution of Independent India provides several safeguards for them.

But the 'Neo-Zamindars, the landowners and Mahajans are still found in rural areas. So the Scheduled Castes started an agitation against them in the year 1971. It was led by Sri Himour, M.L.A. They were getting the wages fixed by the Government.

The peasant-proprietors or employers agreed to pay them the wages, prescribed by the Government but later they felt that the wages given by the peasant-employers according to the new rates were less than the older ones and again they are the loosers, this created unsatisfaction among workers. It then turned into very serious matter. They adopted violent means. Several people were killed and a number injured. Although the agitation was suppressed due to severe reasons like non-cooperation of all the Scheduled Castes and other castes as well as the agricultural labourers, illiteracy, poverty, lack of good leadership etc. yet the fire is still unquenched in their hearts.

The village of Pilkhi was most affected by this agitation. The Rajwars of the village Pilkhi and of some other nearby villages were compelled to leave the villages. Most of them left their villages and took shelter on the hills or in the Dalit colony established by the Government in Rajgir town.

Other Scheduled Castes left to participate in the struggle at a later stage and in the eleventh hour it became a direct fight between the Rajwars, the Musahars etc. and the upper-caste people. This agitation also not succeeded.

Later on a new movement of land-grabbing and forcible harvesting of crop started. The protagonists tried to make it successful but it has owned with a little effect.

They have not tried to protest against the *Mahajans*. Although the Musahars and the Rajwars have stopped repaying the loans which they took from their landowners and employers, yet the other agencies such as the moneylenders and users are still unaffected.

Apparently it seems that the fire, which has been lit by the leaders has been extinguished, but in fact, it is still burning in the hearts of every member of the Scheduled Castes and they are always in search of a chance to right their wrongs.

In fact, the economic condition of the Scheduled Castes is still very deplorable. They pass their whole life either having one meal a day or keeping enforced fast, living in the houses which are unable to protect them from cold and rains and wearing old and torn clothes, which are insufficient to cover their body. They get insufficient wages for hard labour, which are not enough to support their family throughout the year. The insufficient wages and the burden of loan make them so weak and emanciated that they become old prematurely. They lead a very low standard of living. It cannot be raised so long as they are dependent, and it is also a fact that they cannot be independent as long as they are upto their necks in debts. The government of India has given them some Constitutional safeguards by reserving some seats in jobs but that by itself is not sufficient.

EIGHT

Role of Religion

Although, the basic pattern of religious ceremonies among all sections of the Hindus is same, yet there is an unavoidable difference in minor details of the rituals in practice among different castes.

The Scheduled Castes worship two types of deities. The general ones, like Durga in three forms, Siva, Mahavir, Vishnu, Ballava and Yama and their own particular deities also, belonging perhaps to a pre-Aryan or aboriginal part. Among these deities also many are common to all the Scheduled Castes of this area except few, who are worshipped only by the caste concerned. For instance, *Ram Deo* is a deity who is worshipped by the Dusadhs only. The change is in the elaboration of the rituals. Articles like sweets, *gur*, Betel nut and vermillion, *agarbatti* and *dhup* are used to worship these deities. Kali and Devi are worshipped by sacrificing goats.

All deities are worshipped either at the appointed time, or on special occasions. They are also worshipped due to any *manoti* or vows made by them. The *manotis* are made either at the time of disease or any natural calamity, or to fulfil any desire. When a sick person is cured or some desire is fulfilled such worship is performed. The promised amount of sweets or sacrifice is offered to that particular deity. Most of them also require the help of their priest but have their own sacred centres. Their sacred specialist is known as the *Bhagat.* The Bhagat generally belongs to the same caste.

The details of their deities, rituals and sacred articles used in worshipping a particular deity are given below:

Goraya Baba: This deity is normally enshrined at the side

of the village. Some stones are kept as the symbol of it at the sacred place. The belief is that Goraya Baba is the watchman of the village. They believe that the ignoring of the deity may cause an epidemic or any other calamity to the villagers. This particular deity is worshipped in the month of *Asarh* (June-July). Mostly it is worshipped with the *Devi*. This worship is called *Gramta*. The sacrifice of the goats, hens, pigeons, sweets and other puja articles are being offered in the worship. The people belonging to Schedued Castes as well as the other castes also worship this deity.

Barchi Vir or *Barchi Baba*: Southern part of the village has been chosen for this deity to be enshrined and is represented through a stone. He is also worshipped in the month of *Asarh* (June-July). It is worshipped on a community level by raising subscriptions from their own castemen. The goat and pig sacrifices are made. The *Bhagat* performs the ritual. The members of the Scheduled Castes under study believe that the oldest ancestor of the village is their deity.

Birbhayarata: This deity is commonly worshipped by the Musahars. But the Scheduled Castes also do the same. The sacred place of this deity is situated in the *Musahar tola*. No *Bhagat* is needed to perform the worship of this deity. This deity is supposed to be helpful in solving their difficulties.

Baskunit Baba: He is mainly be worshipped by the Dusadh caste, but other Scheduled Castes may also worship him. The sacred offerings in his case are the same but pig is an exception.

Rupa Baba: This deity is worshipped at the time of a wedding with sweets and puja articles. They worship this deity without help of *Bhagat*.

Masan Baba: According to name, this deity remains in the *Asmasan Ghat* (cremation ground). This Baba is worshipped at the time of marriage and only sacrifice of pigs or goats are performed without the help of a *Bhagat*.

Sevak Kunwar: The deity is a Gawala by caste but the other Scheduled Castes also worship him. The Gawala also believe Gomin Dak and the Sevak Kunwar as pirs. Both are worshipped at the same time. The difference is in the articles of worship. The Sevak Kunwar is worshipped with milk, *pera* (a sweet cake), jeeper etc. to protect the villagers from calamities. A *Bhagat* is not needed for this worship.

Madhu Dak: It is a small elevated pinda of cement situated in the north and southern corner of the villages. A Bhagat offers puja to this deity. They worship him by offering and sacrificing pigs, pigeons, hens. This worship is not done at family level.

Lohak Dak: No place is fixed for this deity. He can be worshipped at any place. The selection of the place is at the discretion of the worshipper. The Bhagat is not required to worship him. They believe that the deity removes all sorts of physical pains and sufferings.

Gomun Dak: It is believed that the deity is a Rajput by caste. A he-goat is offered to the deity and is believed that one may be cured of the evil effects of ghosts by the worshipping. The services of a Bhagat are again not required for such worship.

Bandhu Dak: Bandhu Dak is generally worshipped by the Musahars but others too worship him. His puja is offered in the month of *Asarh* (June-July) by sacrificing he-goats and pigs. This deity is placed at a sacred place as an earthen mound. It can also be worshipped at the house itself. The assistance of a Bhagat is not required. The Scheduled Castes worship with a strong belief that this deity removes all anxieties and diseases as well.

Lalgiran Dak: This deity is worshipped individually by the head of the family, in his house with mar (boiled rice water) *gur*, *batasa*, *mishri*, etc. He is also worshipped by sacrificing a pig, pigeon, hen, he-goats etc. He is in the form of an earthen mound. It is believed that this deity may bring back the dead to life.

Ban Deo: This deity is mostly worshipped by the Dusadhs but the other also worship him. They worship him on the fulfilment of any solemn promise made to the deity.

Magic, witchcraft, ghost and other superstitions are an essential part of the beliefs of most of the Scheduled Castes. Their belief is so strong that they ascribe the causes of all the diseases, accidents or natural calamities to these things and other superstitions. They consult the *Ojha* or *Guni* (watch-doctor) at first in case of any disease or physical abnormal behaviour. Only when the patient's conditions takes a serious turn, they run to Aurvedic, Homeopathic or Allopathic doctors. Due to improper treatment and care the condition of the patient begins to deteriorate and very soon results in death.

Regarding hosts they believe that those persons, who die before their scheduled time become ghosts. The persons who are not good-natured also become ghosts. About their form, they have an idea, that a ghost generally manifests itself or haunts in the form in which it was at the time of death. A female becomes a female ghost but it may change its form or body according to its will. A ghost hardly cares to age and sex in casting its evil eyes while haunting. A ghost roams about in the place of its death. For example, if a man commits suicide in his bedroom, his ghost is supposed to remain their itself. The other places where the ghosts dwell are *Asmashan Ghat* (cremation place), *Kabaristan* (grave yard) old disused wells, deserted houses, forests and desolate places etc. There are some trees which are favourite places of ghosts to dwell are *pipal, babul, jamun, pakar,* etc. and that is why a stem of *pipal* or *jamun* is kept on the bed of a pregnant woman because her family members are always afraid of evil spirits. It is believed that evil spirits or witches are particularly bond of casting their eyes on pregnant women but no one knows the reason.

Jinns can be of either sex and they have a special predilection for good-looking people of the opposite sex. A *Jin* can supply everything that one desires. But the victim begins to languish day by day if he discloses the matter.

The Scheduled Castes believe that witchcraft is not inborn but always acquired by training. The interested woman gets training from a witch. She goes to the *Amsahan* and there she is taught the *mantras*. This is generally done at night on the occasion of Dashara. She gets training during the 9 days. After repeating the process for several days, the pupil becomes an expert in her esoteric trade. After her training is over she is asked by her Guru to practise her skill on any one of her nearest relatives. As the result of which one of her dear relatives falls ill and ultimately dies. The witch takes out the liver of the dead man and then the pupil and other *Dains* (witches) eat a bit of it. When the witchcraft has proved to be successful, she becomes a witch, *Dain* or real witch. She has been only a probationer witch before doing so.

Thus the *Ojha* (witch doctor) is a person who has the power of *mantras* to undo the evil influences applied to man or woman by *Dains* or *Nayams*. He is a specialist in the skill of undoing the ill effects. They believe that any influence of ghost or witchcraft can be undone by the *Ojha*. He is very important in the life of the villagers. If any physical abnormality, he is asked by the family concerned. It is he who looks after the cases. The villagers go to the shelter of doctors only after his failure. In several cases, it has been observed that the hopeless cases which were not cured by the physicians or surgeons were seemingly cured by *Ojhas*. These incidents have established *Ojhas*. An Ojha is supposed to ply his craft with the help of some spirits and his mission is like that of the priest of some religion. He works for the sake of the people and so his place very useful and respectable amongst the people of his society.

Festivals: Like others, the Scheduled Castes also celebrate a number of festivals. Festival is celebrated at some religious occasion. But it provides recreation too. People forget their differences on festive occasions.

Holi is a great festival of the Hindus and is celebrated on the 1st day of *Chaitra*. It is not only a festival but also the first day of the Hindu calendar. The *Khaliyans* (threshing-ground) of the peasants as well as those of agricultural labourers remain full of Rabi crops during the occassion. Peasants sing *Fagua* songs throughout the month of *Phalgun*. Young men and children of the Scheduled Castes collect wood and cowdung cakes at a fixed place. The night before the Holi, a Brahmin set fire on the collected material. On the next day the Holi is celebrated with colours. The people of all castes without any feeling of caste, creed and economic categories, throw colours and water on one another. On the day, they rub *gulal* (a dry coloured powder) on the faces of fellow villagers. But they show respect and put *gulal* on the feet of the elders and take *Ashirbad* (blessings). Age and sex are not represented in the joking relationships and obscene songs are sung. It is undoubtedly a veritable saturnalia. Some of them who are economically handicapped don't make special preparations but in general, the people of the Scheduled Castes visit the houses of their peasant-employers and relatives and receive food and money. They eat, drink and sing and dance from door to door. *Chayata* as well as *Fagua* songs are sung on this day. This is because the month of *Chayat* begins from this very day.

Ram Nawami festival is celebrated in *Chayata* (March-April) on the ninth day of the *Sukla Paksha*. The worship of *Devi* also takes place on this day. Some people of the Scheduled Castes offer *gur, batasa, laddu* and other puja articles. Some also sacrifice he-goats.

Asharhi Puja festival is celebrated in the month of *Asarh* (June-July) on a community level. A fund is raised from the members of the community in order to purchase pigs, he-goats or other sacrificial items. They worship the spirits and ghosts. The blood of the sacrificed animal is poured on the earth for each of them. It is performed by the Bhagat.

Karma falls on the 11th day of *Bhado*. It is celebrated only by the sisters who keep fasting for the sake of their brothers' welfare and long life. They make a *pinda* of earth gathering in one place. The puja is offered with *arwa chawal* (a type of rice), *chana* (gram), *ganna* (sugar cane), *Makai* (maize), sindhoor (vermillion). On the next day, immerse this *pinda* in a tank, wrapping it in a new cloth.

Jitiya festival is celebrated by all the married women on the 9th day of the first fortnight in *Ashwin* (Sept-October) for the welfare of children or to get them. *Til, jau, madhu, gur,* and boiled rice are used for Puja. It is also celebrated for the ancestors. They pour *mar* (rice water) in the names of the ancestors. They celebrate this festival very enthusiastically. They wear masks resembling Rama, Hanuman etc. and move from door to door. The festival continues for seven days. The people donate money or crops.

Dasahara is celebrated by sacrificing he-goats collectively. They visit the house of their peasant-employers who offer them food and some money as *Salami*. They spend the night of Dasahara in merry-making. Some young men also go to Rajgir to see the image of Durga.

Diwali festival falls on *Amavasaya* (full dark night) of *Kartik* (October-November). In fact, Diwali is a mis-spoken form of Deepavali which means the row of lamps. As preparation for Deepavali, the people start cleaning their houses from a month before. This is actually done by the womenfolk. The houses are repaired after the rainy season. They are whitewashed and decorated with different materials. On the day of celebration the earthen lamps are lit in the evening. They try to keep them lit for the whole night. Some people gamble with a belief that one who wins this night will win throughout the year.

Chhat is also one of the most important all caste festival. It is celebrated on the 6th day of *Kạrtik* month after Deepawali. It is Surya Puja. It starts from the 3rd day of the month of *Kartik* and continues till the 6th day of the month. The festival starts with taking meal after bathing which is called *Naha-Khai*. The worshipper, either male or female, after taking bath takes the pious meal. Neither non-vegetarian meal nor the meal with garlic and onion etc. is allowed for the devotee. On the fourth day the devotee keeps fast for the whole day and night offering milk and *khir* to the moon and then they break it. But after that they take nothing including water till the final puja is over. On the next day too they keep complete fast and then in the last afternoon they offer puja to the setting sun. It is done on the banks of a pond or river. All the members of the family go to the tank with *soops* filled with sugarcane, fruits, home-made sweets, *dhup* and other puja materials two days continuously. The chief worshipper breaks the fast when they return after worshipping rising sun on the 6th day. This festival has a great social significance. As has been stated earlier it is a very pious and traditional puja being no question of untouchability during performance of puja. Everybody is expected to accept the *Prasad* of anybody. It is believed that if one does not accept the *Prasad* of an untouchable, he will be punished. White spots will erupt on whole of the body or any part of the body. So people have a great fear regarding this puja and they take proper care so that things take place strictly according to ritual.

Makar Sankranti festival falls on the 14th day of *Magh* (January). The Sun starts to move towards the Tropic of Cancer. It is celebrated in the form of a fair which is held near the *Kunds* of Rajgir. The people from the surrounding villages gather here. Villagers take bath in the *Kunda* and then donate eatables to the Brahmins. They donate chura, *gur* (molans), *til*. Then they eat chura and sweets made of *Til* and sugar or *gur* (molans).

The myth behind *Nag Panchami* is not known to the illiterate Harijans. The term itself reveals its meanings. Nag and Panchami, the day of the snake worship. It is celebrated on the 5th day of the *Shukla Paksha* of *Shrawan* (July-August). They draw pictures of snakes on the walls of their houses and worship with *lawa* and milk. They have the belief that snakes will not bite them if being they worshipped.

The following are the rituals related to the life cycle:

Birth: The Scheduled Castes, being every superstitious, are always afraid of witchcraft and evil spirits. They try to protect pregnant women from evil influence. A pregnant woman wears black coloured threads given by a *Bhagat* or

Faqir or *Guni Ojha*. They wear lockets with things made of iron as a safeguard. She also wears a *tabiz* (talisman) given by a *Faqir* or *Ojha*. If a pregnant woman has fallen a victim of evil spirits, a *Bhagat* or a *Faqir* is called to save the mother and the child in womb. They consider pregnancy as the most crucial period for every woman. If she gives birth to a child without any difficulty, it is a matter of grace. A woman has to face so many restrictions during this period, because her negligence not only affects herself but also the child which is in her womb. If an eclipse occurs during her pregnancy period she has to be careful. For instance, she is not allowed to do any work during the period of eclipse. Neither can she sleep nor sit. She is not allowed to cut anything, she either stands erect or moves failing which her child will be either deformed or mad. A pregnant woman is not allowed to cross a river or big *nalas*. She is not allowed to pass by a *Samsan ghat* (cremation place) or a place where there is possibilities of ghosts or witchcraft. She is not allowed even to go to latrine, alone. She cannot get out alone in the nights and does not lift heavy loads. It is noticed that a heavy work is not allowed for pregnant woman. Regarding these taboos, they are of the opinion that if a pregnant woman works hard and does not take rest, the child in the womb may be affected badly and sometimes an abortion may take place. But the nuclear family of a Scheduled Caste things oppositely and compels a pregnant woman to do all types of work, either light or heavy. A Scheduled Caste woman can be observed bringing water in a pitcher on her head, doing the work of harvesting etc. A pregnant woman is not allowed to eat meat, fish, curd and sugar etc. in order to keep digestive system good but in fact their economy does not permit them to eat such expensive food.

Pollution: After birth the first six days are counted as *Chutka* days during which the male members of the concerned family do not shave, they do not take non-vegetarian food or liquor. These things are strictly prohibited during the period of pollution. The sixth or sometimes the 12th day is known a

Chati. On this day a celebration is performed, which is called *Chatti Puja*. The house is cleaned alongwith the *Souri Ghar* (the childs birth place) by the womenfolk. The house is washed with water and cowdung. The head of the male members of the family and relations and invitees gets shaved. The barber gets Rs. 1.50 to 2 or 5 seers of foodgrains on the occasion of the birth of a child. The members are given a little mustard oil and Haldi to apply on their body and head before they take a bath. The wife of the barber, who is locally called *Naiyan*, is called to cut the nails of the women of family concerned, she pares the nails and paints the feet and palm with a red liquid which is called *alta*. She gets 50 to 75 paise and 2 seers of grains on the occasion. On this day, the family deity *Kuldevta* and other deities are worshipped. On the 20th day of the birth of child a ceremony is held, which is called *Bisori*. On this day, the mother and the child get a bath after whole house is cleaned. It is said that without completion of Besori a woman who has given birth to a child, should not cook the food. But in practice, amendments may be done keeping an eye on the time and facilities. A mother of a newly born child has to face so many restrictions to take only a restricted diet, not to take much spice especially red chillies and to take restricted diet at least for one month. It is believed that if she does not take restricted diet, many diseases may cause in the child who is completely dependent on her milk. As a result, both the child and the mother are surrounded by so many *tabiz*, *ganda* and other *totma mantra*. A child's eyes are marked by Kajol. The child and the mother wear articles made of iron, i.e. a ring, knife etc. in order to avert the evil eyes.

Death: They believe that death is natural and one goes to either heaven or hell according to one's deeds. They neither take meal on the day of the occurrence nor light a fire for cooking etc. and from the next day they take something simply boiled without oil and turmeric, upto 9 days from the day of death. Non-vegetarian food and liquor is avoided upto *Daswan* or *barshi* (10th day or 12th day). None of the members of the family are allowed to apply oil, soap and comb and the male members do not shave. The main prohibitions and customs are performed by the chief mourner (*Agdeva*) upto the *Daswan*. He wears a white *dhoti*. He eats only boiled things. His meal is prepared by a lady who does not come in contact with any other food. He sleeps in the same house, in which the deceased man was at the time of death. No *chauki* or *khatiya* can be used by him. He has to sleep on the ground. The mourner is not allowed to visit other people's houses during the period of mourning. On the *Daswan*, the barber shaves the head and beard and moustache of the relatives and the members of the family of the deceased. He also pares their nails. They touch turmeric and oil after taking bath. The womenfolk in the family perform the same rituals on the same day. After giving a Jati Panch Bhoj this ceremony ends. This Bhoj consists of rice, pulse and boiled vegetables. The *Barahawan* (12th day ceremony) is the final ceremony which is performed after cleaning the house well. A Brahmin is called to perform this work. It includes *Pinda-Dan* to ancestors and *Pakki Bhoj*. After that all ceremonies are put to an end. In this way, the period of pollution also comes to an end. Now the family is *pak*, (clean or pure) and is allowed to take part in all social functions. They are allowed to visit other's houses, to take food outside and to celebrate any auspicious functions like marriage etc.

Soul, Salvation and Rebirth: We mightt simply say: "Their beliefs regarding Soul, Salvation and Rebirth follow the common traditions of the Hindu masses". A man can get salvation by good behaviour and by leading a pious life. According to them following are the ways of salvation: 1. Honesty. 2. Love for others. 3. Good conduct. 4. Worship of God. A man can get salvation even without worshipped God if he has the three qualities. Honesty, love for others and good conduct are the fundamentals of a pious life. This may be due to Buddhist influences in the past. This agnostic attitude of a belief in certain virtues on the righteous way of life without postulating a Supreme Being may well have been due to the influence of Buddhism in the area, after the eradiction of Buddhism many Buddhists were re-converted to Hinduism and some once were within the Hindu fold but in a socially debased state. They became the followers of 'untouchability'. They said that although they were leading very nasty lives, worse than beasts, yet they also had the idea of salvation and rebirth. Their economic condition and the attachment to physical labour stand in the way of their departing from all these things. The wretched economic conditions do not allow these people to visit Hindu Tirthas like Varanasi, Gaya, Prayag, etc. which is supposed to be another way of getting rid of all their sins.

NINE

Role of Various Castes

Till some time ago, the Scheduled Castes were subjected to several forms of social disabilities. In all the areas of social interactions with the caste Hindus, social distance was extensively observed. The caste Hindus who were influenced by the narrow interpretation of the Hindu religion had no option but to treat the Scheduled Castes as low in status. Mary Douglas has also advanced a similar argument. "Defilement is never an isolated event. It cannot occur except in view of a systematic ordering of ideas". The Scheduled Castes were prohibited from the entry into temples and schools. Drawing water from common public wells and tanks, participation in religious procession, entry into caste Hindu streets and mixing with caste Hindus in public places, etc. were all denied to them on the grounds that they were not pure resulting from their unclean habits and occupations. In other words, untouchability was observed, in every field of social interactions by the caste Hindus. Untouchability continued unabated so long as the idea of purity and impurity continued to work in the minds of the caste Hindus. Dumont's report agrees with this. "It is clear that the impurity of the untouchables can not be separately from the purity of the Brahmin".

This attitude continued to be so till the middle of the twentieth century. In urban areas, the position improved to a great extent. But in the rural areas where the traditional outlook was very strong was no marked improvement. Besides the traditional areas of social distance, the practice of untouchability was extended to many new areas which were of public importance such as public parks, hostels, panchayats etc.

As soon as independence was declared, the popular Government, inspired by the Gandhian Philosophy and Principles, decided to put an end to this evil, particularly, in the rural society. So, the Government undertook several steps. The Constitution of India has several provisions to tear up the stigma of untouchability, exploitation and social injustice by roots. Untouchability has been abolished. The Scheduled Castes have been made equal to the rest of the population in the eye of law.

From time to time several committees such as the Elaya Perumal Committee have been appointed to study the prevalence of untouchability and suggest steps for its complete abolition. The Untouchability (Offences) Act, 1955 was enacted for this purpose. This law has several punitory measures to punish the guilty persons. Several administrative orders and circulars to District Officers, Village Panchayats and others have been issued by State Government.

Several other measures like punitive tax for the whole village, Dalit Weeks, inter-caste marriages, etc. has been suggested by the Government to bring the caste Hindus nearer to the Scheduled Castes. For the purpose cash awards are also earmarked.

There are several reports available which reveals that these measures have not worked well and untouchability still continues. That is why an attempt was made to study the various areas of the practice of untouchability and find out the extent and areas of change. It is also the aim of the study to assess the adequacy of Governmental measures to abolish untouchability.

Before proceeding to analyse the inter-caste relations in detail, it is compulsory to map the regions of traditional social discrimination which prevails in the rural areas still.

It is obvious that there are two extreme situations of the accessibility of the Scheduled Castes to several areas of social interactions. In areas of economic activities they have greater degree of approachableness while in areas of social and religious activities, both public and private, their accessibility is restricted beyond the proper limit.

With all the restrictions, it is quite important to note that changes have taken place during the last few decades. At one stage none of these was a possibility. However, it was noted that all the Scheduled Castes were not given the right to enjoy equal freedom and approachableness to public places. This poses the question as to who are all these privileged Scheduled Castes. What special benefits do they get over the others? It is reaccount of their own efforts that some of them are relatively better placed? It has been discussed in brief in following paras. Wood Cock's reference to the attempts of the Ezahavas to get over the stigma of untouchability is relevant to our current discussion.

REGIONS OF SOCIAL DISCRIMINATION

Regions of Social discrimination	*Respondents allowed*		*Respondents unallowed*		*Total*	
	N	%	*N*	%	*N*	%
Hotel	258	51.60	242	48.40	500	100.00
Saloon	236	47.20	264	52.80	500	100.00
Lundry	159	31.80	341	68.20	500	100.00
Shopping	480	96.00	20	4.00	500	100.00
Temple	63	12.60	437	87.40	500	100.00
Religious procession	63	12.60	437	87.40	500	100.00
Public wells	68	13.60	432	86.40	500	100.00
House entry	66	13.20	434	86.80	500	100.00
Dining	67	13.80	431	86.20	500	100.00

Note: 1. Row-wise percentages are furnished.
2. Social interaction is between the Scheduled Castes and Caste Hindus.

In the ancient period untouchability and illiteracy were closely associated. But with the extent of literacy among the Scheduled Castes, it was expected that the bonds of untouchability would become loose and ineffective. This is tested in the present study.

It was observed that so far as access to social, religious and private activities are concerned, literacy has no relevance, because there is a very high percentage of discrimination in respect of the literates also. There is a higher percentage of discrimination against the illiterates in regions of economic activity except shopping. But even in the case of the literates also, discrimination is seen. But it is very limited. In this connection, Smith has held the view that Legislation and education combined, however, can claim but limited success.

Therefore, the practice of untouchability has no relevance to literacy as much.

Untouchability is ordinarily expected to prevail extensively in rural areas due to the traditional outlook, the people have developed. However, untouchability is also expected to loose its rigidity because of the influence of urban life. The study shows that the category of villages has no impact on the observance of untouchability in matters which relates to temple, procession, wells, house entry and inter-caste dining. A major portion of the defendants in all the villages is subjected to the stigma of untouchability.

So far as the economic activities are concerned, untouchability is in practise in roadside villages nearer to towns and interior villages to a large extent. But in roadside villages near to the city its observance is less.

However, it is observed that only the category of villages does not help in identifying the persons those are subjected to untouchability because in the same village there are untouchable Scheduled Castes and touchable Scheduled Castes. It is explained in relation to sub-castes.

It has just been discussed that the practice of untouchability has not disappeared totally even among the literates and in roadside villages. Again it is also seen that in South India the practice of untouchability has disappeared in the interior villages to some extent. This is because there are certain sub-castes among the Scheduled Castes who are not considered as untouchables. It is observed that Bhovis, Adi-

Andhras, Korachas and Koramas are totally excluded from the operation of untouchability. Among the Adi-Karnatakas and Adi-Dravidas, untouchability is practised in varying degrees. The level of observance is almost 100 per cent in matters relating to religion, wells, inter-caste dining and house entry.

It was noted that majority of the Scheduled Castes is not inclined to create difficulties and disturbances in their relationships with the caste Hindus in the villages. The educated youths likely in the villages are generally wedded to a quiet and subdued life. They do not favour conflicts and clashes with the caste Hindus in their attempts to challenge the validity of the age-old social restrictions. The aged and elderly persons are also not in favour of differences and confrontations with the local caste Hindus. Then the only group of persons challenging the authority of the caste Hindus are the Scheduled Castes adult males in the age group of 30-40. These are the people who are turbulent and militant. Cohn reports that, "The change in mood among the Dalits is possibly to a definite amount of conflict, or even violence". Srinivas also reports such violent conflicts whenever the low castes attempt Sanskritization.

The consequential issue deserving a little consideration is the result of such conflicts, because their is nothing like success. Their winning in one place over one issue would open the eyes of others and they would follow suit. In the same way if they lose the battle, they may not venture to take up the same issue again and suffer humiliation and economic deprivation. The disadvantages which resulted due to the failure of the attempts made by the low castes to rise against social injustice have been narrated by Bailey and Epstein. The role of the leaders in the prevention of conflicts is another important issue that needs examination. The role of the Police Officers and the Panchayat leaders is also the same as before.

Mentioned below are some important issues around which centres the consideration of inter-caste relationship between the Scheduled Castes and the caste Hindus: 1. Four major rural social institutions, namely, village panchayats, cooperatives, schools and temples; 2. Saloons, laundry, shopping units and public places like hostels; 3. Dining; private places like house entry; 4. Relationship between master and servant.

A brief introduction to the conflicts that have taken place should be discussed before actual description of the various areas of social interaction. As a result of many attempts on the part of the Scheduled Castes to assert their Constitutional rights on one hand and the equally powerful counteraction on the part of the caste Hindus to prevent the Scheduled Castes from enjoying their Constitutional privileges at the cost of the local customs, on the other hand, conflicts arise. According to the reports of Beals, Srinivas and Shepperdson attempt to enforce legislations result in conflicts. "Now that anthropologists are fairly certain that conflict arises everywhere as a result of Constitutional and social forces and that it affects the functioning of human groups, it is time to move on to a consideration of the conditions which lead to the emergence of conflict at particular times and places" reports Beals. In the same way, Srinivas has reported with reference to the efforts made by the Scheduled Castes to enforce Constitutional rights that "... Naturally their attempts have led to an increase in the tensions existing between caste Hindus and Dalits." Shepperdson observes that conflicts arises between the Dalits and the caste Hindus when external power and norms influence the internal power structure and norms of the village.

Village Panchayats: By virtue of the seat reservation, some of the Scheduled Castes become members of the Panchayat. No caste barriers are reported in all their dealings as members, chairs and benches are kept in the Panchayat halls. But in the seating arrangements no discrimination of any sort is made. First comers take the chairs and those who comes late take the benches. Even the Brahmin members do not object to the Scheduled Castes taking chairs if they have come early. Brahmins sit by the Scheduled Castes members. The Scheduled Castes members come better dressed on the days of the meetings. When the Scheduled Castes members offer their suggestions and raise their problems, they are not opposed by the caste Hindus. When they address each other they show due respect. In other words, they are not addressed in the derogatory way such as in privacy by the caste Hindus. However, there is noticed some discrimination while admitting the general public to Panchayat halls. The Scheduled Castes population other than the members is not allowed to enter the Panchayat hall, whereas any person belonging to the high castes can enter the Panchayat hall and be an observer.

Cooperative Society: Unlike the village panchayats where the Scheduled Castes have a legal right to be members, membership of the Cooperative Societies is purely voluntary. Any person can become a member of the Society. Caste restrictions are not imposed on any person. A person who becomes a member, has every right to use the society to his own advantage so long as he is within the framework of the rules of the society. The Scheduled Castes do not have any restriction placed on their becoming members. Undoubtedly, the societies are dominated by the powerful and dominant caste Hindus. Nevertheless, membership is not denied on caste consideration.

Schools: Opening separate schools for Scheduled Castes children was the policy of the Government. With the passing of time Scheduled Castes children were allowed to study in the Government schools meant for all children irrespective of caste and religion. About two decades ago, when the Government schools were thrown open to the Scheduled Castes children, segregation was practised in the schools. The children were made to sit outside the classroom, near the entrance. Two type of social distance in the past is also confirmed by Mayer and Raja Bhoj. According to the reports the children had to sit on the floor. The caste Hindu students would sit inside the classroom and benches were provided for them. When the Brahmin teacher came to the class, the Scheduled Caste children had to stand at a distance till the teacher entered the class. When the Scheduled Caste children had to give slates to the teacher, they had to handover the slates to their classmates who in turn would give them to the teachers. In those days classes were held in the open areas. No Scheduled Castes child was allowed even though Muslims and other low castes were allowed. The Scheduled Castes children could not participate in any function along with the caste Hindu students. They were not allowed to participate in sports and games together. They were not allowed to enter the areas of the caste Hindu students. There was absolutely no social interaction between the Scheduled Caste students and the caste Hindu students either in the classroom or outside the classroom or in the village. The Scheduled Caste students had to suffer the cruelty of some teachers. They were beaten mercilessly for their very small and neglectable mistakes. The position is altogether different in the schools today. There is no discrimination between the students belonging to Scheduled Castes and the students belonging to caste Hindus. Arrangement of seats are made very commonly. The caste Hindu students including the Brahmin children sit side by side. They are treated alike by teachers. In some villages, caste Hindu teachers are very kind and helpful to the Scheduled Caste students. Some teachers have given them even fee concessions. Lady teachers are specially sympathetic. Scheduled Caste students and caste Hindu students may be seen playing outside the schools. In Primary Schools, all participate in the Ganapathi Puja and other functions. Teachers distribute *Prasadam* to all the children. But in High Schools discrimination is made. Scheduled Caste children are not allowed to distribute *Prasadam*. The Brahmin and Lingayat students play the role. This is the first experience of discrimination, on the basis of untouchability that the Scheduled Caste students have had in the high schools. Good friends among the caste Hindu students are had by the SC students. In the schools and outside the schools, they freely mix, exchange their thoughts and so on. Caste rigidity gets suspended for the time being. But the Scheduled Castes students would not visit the houses of the Vokkaligas and Brahmins. In some places, they go to the Vokkaliga areas but not to the Brahmin areas. According to the caste Hindu students, they have no hesitation to take the Scheduled Caste students to their houses. But our parents do not permit us. Parents know that they sit together in the schools, play together and all that. But they deny their entry in their houses.

Temple Entry Movement: In the past Scheduled Caste students were completely prohibited to enter the Hindu temples. This traditional religious sanction was implicitly obeyed by these Scheduled Caste. No attempt was made either to enter the temple or to allow them inside the temple barring in a few cases as reported by Hardgrave and Galanter. However, since 1930 there have been several attempts made by the Government as well as the enlightened Hindus to allow the Scheduled Caste to enter the temple. In Mysore the temple authorities being influenced by religious leaders allowed the entrance of Scheduled Castes in the temple at Melkote. However, this did not spread to other places. It was only in 1948 that the Government of Mysore made a law permitting all the Scheduled Castes to enter the temples in the State.

Present Position

Though nearly 54 years have lapsed since the State officially permitted the Scheduled Castes to enter the temples, there are various reports that in practice there is hardly any instance of such temple entry. The position of the Scheduled Caste in some South Indian villages is described in brief in the following paras:

The problem of temple entry is confined only to two sections of the Scheduled Castes, namely the Adi-Dravidas and the Adi-Karnatakas together called the untouchables, since the other Scheduled Castes are allowed to enter the temples.

The untouchables whether they are living in interior or roadside village are not allowed to enter the temples. Even in Konena Agrahara, Nagavara and Kadgudi which are the urban complex of Bangalore City, caste Hindu do not allow them to enter the temples.

In the same way there is no effect of their being educated or uneducated. Whether clean or unclean it has no relevance. Graduates and double graduates both are not allowed temple entry in their own villages. The only and a rare exception has been seen in Harohally. During the last 5 years, the Pujari of Chamundeshwari temple allows the educated Scheduled Caste boys and girls.

However, in the same village the Scheduled Castes cannot dare to enter the some other temples. The same educated boys and girls who visit the Chamundeshwari temple as said earlier are not allowed to enter the temples inside the villages although the local people know that these boys and girls visit the Chamundeshwari temple.

The Scheduled Castes which are untouchable carry coconut and other things for worship. These are handed over to the *pujari*. He offers puja, takes the conconut and money given to him and then gives the *Prasadam*. While giving the puja things, the untouchables do not touch the *pujari*. The things of worship in the plate are put on the earth. The *pujari* takes the things inside leaving the plate outside. In Solur, the *pujari* sprinkles water on the things and takes them inside. By sprinkling water on the puja things, he is removing pollution.

The Scheduled Castes are totally prohibited to enter the temples in Sondekoppa. The powerful Gowdas say "Just salute God from outside and keep quiet". Even temples managed by the Muzurai Department of the State Government are not allowed. Even in places such as Solur, Hullahalli and others where the Scheduled Castes are in numerical majority or numerically strong they are not allowed to enter the temples.

Among the Scheduled Castes there is divided opinion about asserting their right to enter the temples. The aged and the educated youngsters do not want to assert their right, whereas the middle aged group is assertive. The former category of Scheduled Castes advance two reasons, as to why they do not want to assert their right. First, they do not like to break tradition and create disturbance in the village. Secondly, they are afraid that the economic sanctions that the caste Hindus might impose on them would make them starve because mostly they are economically dependent on the caste Hindus. They do not want to risk their earning for the sake of temple entry.

When the educated boys of Harohally who visit Chamundeshwari temple were asked why they do not visit the village temples, they answered that most of their people are economically dependent on the caste Hindus. If the Scheduled Caste employees oppose their employers, they lose their jobs. They may not get loans and other economic assistance from them. Some sections feel that they might lose what little property they have in terms of small lands and houses too, if burnt by the caste Hindus. They are also have a fear of being beaten up by the caste Hindus.

The Scheduled Castes do not like to oppose the caste Hindu and face their enemity only for the sake of temple entry. One Scheduled Caste double-graduate said "I do not go to temples as I expect trouble. Even the Government does not come to our rescue".

It was also observed that it is only in respect of the temple entry that the caste Hindus are very rigid in comparison of hostels, schools etc. after initial resistance, they have allowed partially and in some cases fully. There are a few examples where the untouchables challenged the superiority of the caste Hindus in religious matters and had to fight but finally nothing tangible came out.

The village temple which is also common to all the castes in the village is not open to the untouchable Scheduled Castes. Mayer also reports that "Most public places are to some extent barred to the Harijans. The main village temple is the most strictly closed".

So far as the temples are concerned, no effort has been made by the Scheduled Castes to force open the gate of the temple even in villages practically dominated by them. The Scheduled Castes are not at all particular about forcible entry into temples in these villages unlike what it has been reported by Bailey about the efforts which are made by the Broad outcastes in Bisipara village in Orissa to forcibly enter the caste Hindus temples. But the position assumes a little different colour in matters which relates to the taking out of religious procession and also offering prayers at the village tank. There are some reported clashes between the caste Hindus and the Scheduled Castes in these areas. A very short description is being given here about these clashes.

In the early part of 1970 in Solur the Scheduled Castes and the caste Hindus had a fight during the Dussehra festival. The Scheduled Castes also took out a procession of their god. It so happened for the first time that both the processions reached a particular place. The Scheduled Castes requested the caste Hindus to have both the processions together, side by side, or one after the other. The caste Hindus used foul language and insulted the God of the Scheduled Castes. As a result the Scheduled Castes had a fight with the caste Hindus and thus the procession was abandoned.

The same night the caste Hindus complained against the Scheduled Castes alleging that they had stolen the costly jewels from the person of their God. The Scheduled Castes objected this blame. They said that it was completely a false case. However, with the intervention of a common leader, there was a settlement. In this case Police sided the caste Hindu so it was suggested to act carefully in the matters of such type.

In Baglur also there was a clash between Scheduled Castes and the caste Hindus in 1968 during the yearly village tank celebration. As usual the Scheduled Caste were not expected to participate. But during that year a few middle aged Scheduled Castes challenged the traditional social practice while illumination was going on. Just then an open fight started.

Some of the Scheduled Castes were severely beaten and taken to the Police Station and there were further harassed for disturbing the peace in the village.

Thus ended the futile efforts made by the Scheduled Castes to assert their Constitutional rights for participating in religious functions. The local caste Hindu leadership, the Hindu religious practices and also the local police took their efforts as a challenge.

Public Activities

Hotels: In the ancient times there was no problem of hotel entry because hotels were not found in the rural areas. But the question of admission of the untouchables arose when hotels were started in some of the rural areas. This was also not a problem then because the untouchables did not go to the hotels because of the want of money which was necessary for eating in the hotels and above all the traditional outlook also implied that hotels were not meant for them.

When awareness grew among them that hotels are commonly public places and they have a right to enter there they made efforts to enter the hotels. Thus once again the same problem arose.

The untouchable had no permission to have anything from the hotel on the ground that they were unclean and their presence inside or outside the hotels might pollute the environment and the caste Hindus could not tolerate it. So long as the Scheduled Castes were not keen on visiting the hotels or taking anything from there, everything was alright. But once the Scheduled Castes were determined to visit hotels, then clashes with the caste Hindus became inevitable.

In Northern India, in rural areas usually, the hotels are maintained by high caste Hindus, OBCs, Sikhs and Muslims. In some hotels, the Scheduled Castes are not allowed at all. In some hotels partial entry is allowed. The details are discussed here.

However, in semi urban and urban areas, there are

absolutely no restrictions placed on the Scheduled Castes. About ten years ago in some small towns they were not allowed to enter the hotels. But gradually one after the other started entering the hotels. Their entry in hotels were not protested against by the proprietors and the caste Hindus and hence without any more difficulty their entry in hotels became very easy.

A different position is observed in the villages located both on the roadside nearer to towns and also the interior villages. Comparatively, roadside villages appear to be slightly better. The position is still extremely bad in interior villages. Even now, there are some places, where the Scheduled Castes are not allowed inside but have to stand outside the door. A few cups are kept there and a bucket full of water is also available. The Scheduled Castes customer has to wash the cup and then the server pours tea or coffee in to the cup. After drinking it, he has to wash it again. The server then collects money from him. In such villages, no Scheduled Caste man has ever thought of making an attempt to enter the hotel. Two reasons are advanced for this. First the Scheduled Castes are extremely ineffective there. They are completely dependent on the caste Hindus. The second reason is that all the hotels belong to the upper castes, who are the landed class and are very powerful. The Scheduled Castes dare not confront them. However, at strange places, the untouchables have no problem as they are not identified as untouchables. But they are beaten up if any caste Hindu can recognise them. Once, X, an untouchable from a neighbouring village entered the hotel in another village. He was taking tea. Seeing him one upper caste person became very angry. He caught hold of him and beat him in public abusing him and his caste. He is reported to have told the untouchable "Look here, if you or any of your people dare enter the hotel again, your hands will be cut off and exhibited in the village". All the people near the hotel witnessed this but none of them made effort to rescue the untouchable. The untouchable reported the matter to his people who appeased him saying that they were helpless because they were economically dependent on the high caste people.

However, the other side of the picture is not so dark. there was one hotel owned by an enlightened Brahmin who allowed the Scheduled Castes to enter the hotel and they were behaved equally along with the caste Hindus. This was resented by the caste Hindus who did not enter the hotel for some time. But the proprietor was not disturbed. He had a strong will and faith in the Gandhian philosophy. Later on, all the caste Hindus also started visiting the hotel. It was noticed that while sitting in the hotel, the untouchables were glued by themselves in one corner. They did not have any intention of claiming equal rights.

But there are other hotels where Scheduled Castes either do not go or when they visit them they are not equally served. There is a hotel which is owned by a caste Hindu, who is very conservative. However, the untouchables say, that he may not deny them if they visit. But they have not visited because they are afraid of other caste Hindus. A Muslim tea shop is also there. It is not visited by the Scheduled Caste since they are not used to drinking tea. Those who do take tea have visited this tea shop and there is no problem.

In other hotels where the Scheduled Castes are allowed, discriminatory behaviour is given. Separate cups and saucers are kept for them and tiffin is served on leaves. They are made to sit on the floor. They are offered inferior quality tumblers, mostly aluminium are provided to them and these are all kept outside. They are forcibly made to wash them before leaving the hotel. In any case, no tension prevailed in this village any time as far as hotel entry was concerned.

Then come some other villages where hotel entry resulted in tension and conflicts. Some years ago in a particular village, the untouchables were not allowed to enter the hotels. But they can go in all of them now, except one. For them two benches are kept outside. Cups and other pots are kept separate. They are served food on leaves. It was reported that once two untouchables attempted to enter the hotel. A Jat and a Brahmin beat them up. When the Scheduled Castes told them that they would take this case to the Court, the proprietor made haste in lodging a complain against them on the ground that they had beaten him. For want of witnesses the case was dismissed because there was no proof. The Scheduled Castes feel that left to himself, the Brahmin proprietor would not have gone to the Court. But others instigated him.

The remaining two hotels in the same village were not approachable for them. But they lodged complaints in the Police Station and the duty conscious Sub-Inspector favoured the untouchables and advised the proprietor to allow them inside, failing which he would be prosecuted. The proprietor accepted to allow them inside the hotel. But equal treatment was not offered to them. They sit separately. Muslims sit with them but not the caste Hindus. Even educated Scheduled Castes get the same treatment. No separate cups and saucers are kept for them. But the proprietors are reported to have their own way of dealing with the Scheduled Castes. More money is paid by them. More salt is added to their curry and less sugar is used in the coffee and tea served to them. If they object, they are abused and threatened that urine would be mixed and given to them. This has created fear in the minds of the Scheduled Castes and that is why they do not like to go to these hotels.

In another village, the Scheduled Castes were not allowed to enter the hotels until 1969. The Scheduled Castes were made to stand outside and served, in the usual discriminating manner. In 1969, the middle aged Scheduled Castes who were aware of the legal rights are reported to have forced their entry into a hotel run by a Rajput. The proprietor not only refused to allow them but also mustered a reasonable number of the other Hindus to disperse the Scheduled Castes people. A free-for-all battle began. Heavy damage was caused to the hotel property and the hotel was closed down temporarily.

In the meanwhile the Scheduled caste Hindus drew a plan to finance a local Muslim to start a tea shop and take revenge of the humiliation they had experienced earlier. The Scheduled Castes people who had maintained good relations with the Muslims thought there would be no problem for them. But they were surprised when they were refused entry into the tea shop. After initial differences, they resorted to forcible entry. The Muslims who had the support of the caste Hindus attacked the Scheduled Caste people. A very dreadful and fierce battle was pitched among Muslims and Scheduled Castes.

After the end of the fight Scheduled Castes were complained against to the local police for trespass and assault. The Scheduled Castes people also wanted to lodge a counter complaint. But the Sub-Inspector effected a compromise and pacified the Muslims and the Rajputs, Yadavs and others.

The older hotel also began functioning as before and the Scheduled Castes were allowed inside. But they were not allowed to sit among caste Hindus. Their seats were arranged separately. They were happy that their efforts in asserting their rights bore fruit at least to some extent.

Common Wells and Tank: The common wells are another area where the Scheduled Castes and the caste Hindus confront each other. In some villages the Scheduled Castes have their own wells. But in summer their wells get dry, so they have to fetch water from some other areas. In some villages the Scheduled Castes have no wells, but they have to fetch water from some other areas.

There are two possibilities – either they have to draw water from the common wells in the village or go to distant gardens and bring water. Caste Hindus do not allow them to draw water from any well located in their areas. In some villages, the caste Hindu women draw water from the wells and pour it in the pots of the Scheduled Castes. In some other villages, the Scheduled Castes are allowed to use tap water but only after 10 p.m. The argument advanced is that there is water scarcity and yet the Scheduled Castes have to wait till 10 p.m. when all the other caste people have had their share of water.

In a certain village, a Scheduled Caste asserted his right to draw water from the well. The caste Hindus resisted and threatened the Scheduled Castes with dire consequences. A suit was filed in the court by Ramaiah and it was compounded. Even now the Scheduled Castes are not permitted to draw water from the well. However, this incident opened the eyes of some of the educated Scheduled Castes who realised that they were not even aware that they had a right to sue the caste Hindus. Srinivas has also referred to such an awakening among the low castes.

In the past in a particular village, the Scheduled Castes were not even allowed to approach the Government owned tank. However, now they can only take water from the lower part of the tank but not from the upper part. This is only to retain the inferiority of the Scheduled Castes. Such instances are also reported by the Commissioner for Scheduled Castes and Scheduled Tribes.

Shaving Saloon: Four sources of hair cutting facilities are available to the Scheduled Castes. They are: self, the casteman, the service casteman in the village and the service casteman outside the village. Self means a person taking a shave without any one's help or two persons also may help each other in shaving and hair dressing. The profession of a barber is taken up by castemen in some villages. In a limited number of cases, the service casteman (a professional barber) entertains the Scheduled Castes.

The caste Hindus are not in favour of the Scheduled Castes entering the saloons. They feel that the razor used for the Scheduled Castes would be dangerous for health of the others. In a case study a barber, was of the view that personally he was not against the Scheduled Castes. He had confessed the fact that his status was as low as that of the Scheduled Castes. He was also an outcaste in every sense.

The Scheduled Castes were entertained by a barber named 'Y' in a village. The reward he got from the caste Hindus was that he was driven out of the village. In the same village, Z, another barber denied to do hair dressing when one Scheduled Caste school teacher went to him. A suit was filed by the teacher in the court. The barber came to know the consequences. He agreed to serve the Scheduled Castes. The case was compounded. The barber kept up his promise for one year at the end of which the local castemen drove him out.

Another barber refused to serve an outcaste. He lodged a complaint with the Police. The matter was taken to the Magistrate. A very influential local leader interfered and the case was compounded in 1959. Since then the Scheduled Castes are allowed to enter the saloon to shave and dress their hair.

There were two saloons on the roadside in a village. The untouchables tried their best to gain access to these saloons. But they were refused by the barbers. During the fight between the Scheduled Castes and the caste Hindus, the barbers closed the shops and started serving the caste Hindus only in their houses. When the Scheduled Castes questioned them, they are reported to have said that "This is a private place and I live here with my family. None was allowed to enter the house". Even later, the Scheduled Castes did try their best, but they did not succeed.

Laundry: Laundry is generally considered to be a feature of urban society. In rural areas only a limited number of people give their clothes to the washermen. Caste has nothing to do. However, as far as the Scheduled Castes are concerned, clothes from them were refused by the washerman. Srinivas reports that "The washerman similarly washes the clothes of every family in the village, except families belonging to very low castes". The services of barbers and dhobis are denied almost at every place. Washermen are more rigid than the barbers.

Shopping: Generally, whenever, the Scheduled Castes go for shopping there is no discrimination shown in the villages, Haimendorf's observation supports this trend. There is no restriction on occupational cooperation in agriculture and commerce. They can buy whatever goods they want. If there are caste Hindus, specially the Brahmins, the Scheduled Castes themselves will hesitate to go till the caste Hindus leave the shop.

Inter-caste Dining and House Entry: The third major region of social interaction relates to dining and house entry. In several occasions a large number of people are invited for dinner, from both the Scheduled Castes and caste Hindus. Generally Scheduled Castes are not invited by the caste Hindus excepting in some cases where only some non-untouchable Scheduled Castes are invited. Nor do all the Scheduled Castes also invite them. Some of them invite the caste Hindus and some of them attend the function. It is depending upon the status of the inviter. Even Brahmins attend the marriages and other functions. But this is also not very frequent. Other outcastes, if they come, are fed at the end, outside the house of the caste Hindus. A few SCs are allowed to enter the house. Caste Hindus barring the Brahmins come to the house of some non-untouchable Scheduled Castes. Entry into the untouchable Scheduled Caste region by a caste Hindu was almost a taboo in the past. So also the untouchables were not allowed to enter the streets of the caste Hindus, particularly so in the case of the Brahmin areas in the past. But the observation made recently shows that the position now has changed a little but not completely.

Jeeta System: Jeeta is a famous word for servitude. Servitude has been originated from slavery. Any form of slavery is not valid or legal in the eyes of Indian Constitution. Even servitude which is an off-shoot of slavery is prohibited type of relationship between the master and the servant. In the ancient time whenever a Scheduled Caste was in need of financial assistance in the form of a loan, or whenever he felt that it was difficult for him to withstand the burden of his family expenditure, he would just then go to the caste Hindu and pledge his son or himself for monetary consideration and this could be redeemed only on clearance of the loan together with the interest. In past Jeeta system was extensively practised but nowadays it is not seen in the same form as before. Every

Scheduled Castes family contributed atleast one person to the Institution of servitude then. Today it has been decreased. No example of survitude is found in the roadside villages nearer to the city. However, out of the eight remaining villages, roadside villages nearer to towns and interior villages, in five villages servitude is still practised. In some of these villages, it is to the extent of about 50 per cent of the families. The relationship between Master and Servant was too much cordial. In many cases the entire family of the servant was at the disposal of the master. Srinivas has also reported that "Formerly it was not unknown for a man to spend all his working life between ten and seventy years of age in the service of one master".

Servants Outside

Servitude: Orders and instructions of the masters were generally carried out by the servants. When, on a few occasions, the Master beat the servant out of sudden provocation, the servant would not retaliate. The master too was humanitarian in equal form. He would soon realize his mistake in beating the servant and would give a little quantity of ragi and commodities to make suitable amends. The servants would feel secure under all circumstances of stresses and strain. "When our masters are there why should we worry about our living?" Is the consensus among the servants as reported by Rao. But the position has changed now to a great extent. The servants have a longer sense of independence now. They are no longer prepared to withstand the onslaught of their masters. As against that community type of relationship, it is now found to be contractual of associational relationship. Though economically they are not completely free from their masters, on whom they depend for their livelihood, they feel that they are no longer the traditional slaves in the hands of their masters. The servants of present time demand higher wages as a result of the increase in the cost of living. But the masters resist to the extent possible. This leads to minor frictions between the two.

Social distance which was the main feature of the inter-caste relationship between the Scheduled Castes and the caste Hindus in the past, is found to be strong even in the present day. The distance between Scheduled Castes and caste Hindu seems to be strong in present times also as it was in the ancient time. Scheduled Castes cannot enter the temples even now. Marginal changes are noticed in matters relating to religious processions which are in a few cases taken to the Scheduled Castes regions. The only change that is worth noting in religious matters, is that the untouchables may offer puja things and receive *prasadam*, but they can perform it from a distance.

They can not take water from public wells. Even in the case of tanks owned by the Government they are discriminated by caste Hindus. Further, barring a few marginal exceptions, saloons and laundry are not accessible to them.

In the region of schools maximum changes have taken place. Now Scheduled Castes may go to schools and they are offered similar position to the other castes in school. Discriminations in this area have almost disappeared.

A significant change has developed in the relationship between the caste Hindu masters and the Scheduled Castes employees. They are governed by contractual relationship. There is a lot of awareness among the Scheduled Caste employees. However, servitude is widely in practise even now due to economic reasons.

PART THREE

Problems and Issues

TEN

The Modern Era

All social reforms and Dalit awakening in India are due to the impact of western education and culture, science and technology as well as industrial revolution of Europe. There was all chaos and no strong central authority in the country when the British Crown took direct control of India. There was also no sympathy for the untouchables and deep-rooted caste system as well as superstitions ruled over the society.

The 19th century social awakening came in the elite class of Bengal when Raja Ram Mohan Roy (1772-1833) appeared on the horizon as a powerful force. He founded the Brahmo Samaj and acknowledged the virtues of western education, liberal outlook and legal institutions. He made all efforts for the removal and banning of the Sati system. He was all against social injustice and impropriety of the British land policy. He was against caste system and untouchability, superstitions, ignorance and narrow religious outlook. He gave equal status to women in society.

In fact, Lord William Bentick supported his reformative outlook, as well as free and frank views on social ills. Here critics of Ambedkar should note that Roy may not have succeeded without the backing of the British administration. Like Roy, Ambedkar was also appreciated by the government of his time for his social priorities. He was first a rebel and reformer and politician afterwards. Whatever Roy and Ambedkar, did it was for the welfare of the entire society.

For Roy caste was undemocratic, inhuman and anti-national. Throughout his life Roy fought the orthodox elements in Hindu society.

Iswar Chandra Vidyasagar (1820-1891), Kesub Chandra Sen (1838-1884), Devendra Nath Tagore (1807-1905) concentrated on social reforms, ill treatment of women, individual liberty and eradication of caste system. While they stood for moral values, they pleaded for freedom from the bondage of scriptural authority, abolition of caste distinctions and useless customs.

In Bombay Presidency Mahadev Govind Ranade (1842-1900) founded Prarthana Samaj in 1867, just after a decade of 1857 mutiny. Ranade was keenly interested in social change, abolition of priesthood and idolatry. His Prarthana Samaj took great interest in the abandonment of the caste system; introduction of widow remarriage, encouragement of female education, abolition of child marriage and social prejudices.

There was also a wave of social reforms in Punjab during the end of the 19th century. In 1887 Deva Samaj was founded in Lahore which attacked social evils, caste system and injustice done to the untouchables in the form of social humiliations and denial of opportunities for education and better professions. Sikhism had already advocated the cause of the Shudras and the oppressed people and restored equality, religious tolerance and individual freedom.

The continuity of social and religious reforms was also maintained through the Arya Samaj, a popular socio-religious movement which was founded by Dayanand Saraswati (1824-1883) in 1875 at Rajkot in Gujarat. He believed in the authority of the Vedas, but had progressive views and stood for social reforms and abolition of social evils. His advocacy for justifying the social order based on Varna system made it a militant and aggressive Hindu organisation against the reformative and enlightened, liberal but progressive Brahmo Samaj, Prarthana Samaj and Deva Samaj. Dayanand was against the current classification and basis of caste which divided the humanity and created injustice and human wastage it produced. He, pleaded that a low caste man may rise to superiority by leading a virtuous life and emphasised on the work of Shuddi and condemned conversions.

The Radhaswami Samaj was founded at Agra in 1861 which worked for social reforms, removal of caste distinctions and untouchability but in a big way stood for spiritual awakening. The Samaj believed in national regeneration through organizing educational institutions. But all the followers were not free from the caste hierarchy or Varna system. Therefore, Samaj ceased to be a social force in existing sócio-economic setting and political developments.

Ramakrishna Mission was duly founded in 1879 in Bengal for social action and spiritual awakening. Ramakrishna Paramhansa (1834-1886) was the driving force behind this movement. Ramakrishna, though a mystic had a compassion for suffering humanity. Social customs, social evils and monster of caste have cause, much anxiety in his mind. In fact in the chain of 19th century social reforms the Mission was inspired by the traditional mysticism and devotion, as well as Western Philanthropy and social welfare work. The Mission took care of the suffering people and allowed non-Brahmins and Shudras to be initiated in the Mission's work through the devotion of God.

Individuals as Reformers

Besides these organisations and personalities who stood and worked for spiritual and moral progress, social reforms and enlightenment, there came some individuals as reformers like Swami Sahjanand (1781-1839), Swami Ramalingam (182 31874), Mahatma Jyotiba Phule and Savitri Bai Phule, Karsondas Mulji (1832-1871), G.G. Agarkar (1857-1895) in 19th century, who strongly opposed the oppressive character of caste system and the stigma of untouchability which hampered the growth of society. They all protested against the existing social inequalities and stood for social reforms and female education. They influenced the events of their times in bringing social transformation.

Swami Sahajanand of Gujarat was a puritan theist. He encouraged holy sessions (Satsangs) led by a group of disciplined saints and formed Sivonti Nurcrvon Sect. Like other Bhall sects, this sect also welcomed the Shudras and untouchables. The Swami stood for various social reforms His a humanist.

Swami Ramalingam of the Tamil region developed a compassion for all human beings. In his religious devotional songs he sang the miseries of the people and preached against caste system. Untouchability and unequal treatment of women. He asked people to shun caste prejudices, injustice and malpractices. His Sanmarga Sabha, though a small organisation did a lot in Tamil Nadu for tile upliftment of the downtrodden.

The History of Dalit awakening in Maharashtra and elsewhere is basically the History of Dalit Movement in India. Paranjpe (Caste, Prejudice and Individual: 1970) has taken much pains in sketching a short survey of the history of the early non-Brahmin movement and socio-political awakening in Maharashtra.

Dr. Ambedkar's speeches and writings are the most authentic references on the Dalit awakening and Dalit revolt. Some historians and social scientists have made efforts to trace the historical background of the Dalit awakening during the 19th and 20th century. Jyotiba Phule and Dr. Ambedkar's entire movement itself is the modern history of Dalit awakening.

Indian National Congress in the pre-independence days (1885-1947) has no doubt done remarkable work in eradicating the caste system and untouchability under the leadership of Mahatma Gandhi. He did a lot for their uplift. Nationalist Dalit leaders like Babu Jagjivan Ram also deserve mention in bringing social awakening and revolution among the Dalits of northern India. Among Dalit leaders Jagjivan Ram was a true democrat.

Social Awakening and Democracy

We can quote Will Durant, who after a lifelong study of civilizations summed up the lesson of history which has great significance for India. He said, that Democracy is the most difficult of all forms of government since it requires the widest spread of intelligence and we forgot to make ourselves intelligent when we made ourselves sovereign.1

In democratic system Dalits can make progress, but cannot do so in toto, as they are poor and exploited class whereas the concentration of political and economic power in few hands is alarming. There is no committed judiciary. Then how can they get social justice? It is a matter of debate that for social justice and equality, distribution of power and sharing in governance is properly defined and implemented, that was the dream of Dr. Ambedkar in his writings and speeches, his deeds and actions till his death.

Elimination of poverty, illiteracy and restoration of social justice, all require urgent attention for the success of the democracy. It is argued very often in academic as well as bureaucratic circles whether India has fully succeeded in achieving the fruits of democracy, even after more than 5 decades or so, when millions of depressed classes and other ignored sections of society live below poverty line under terror and oppressive situations. Who can dare to deny that millions of them are still illiterate and even their sons and daughters have not been provided means of elementary education. The landless labour, artisans and unskilled workforce is running out and migrating from villages to cities in search of gainful employment. The Dalit and exploited people are crying for social justice and employment opportunities, for better education and a honourable position and status in the society after searching their identity. At present there seems to be no agenda on national level for their uplift and betterment except high hopes and big promises. The mechanism for restoring social justice is not so efficient and quick in decision making.

Winston Churchill doubted India's ability whether we will run our democracy successfully or not as early as in 1948. He also expressed hope that things should be judged after 50 years. Though India has already celebrated 50 years of Republic as merely a ritual, the country is facing grim challenges and there are much more hard days ahead, more acute problems.

Lincoln said that you cannot fool all the people all the time, but you can fool enough of them to rule a large country. It is all that is happening here in case of Dalits.

The centuries old problem of casteless society is still a dream. The untouchability has been abolished on paper, or rather legally, but it is still practised in villages and remote areas. It has changed shades. Even in the civilized cities, there are hell like clusters, the ghettos for the members of the exploited and neglected class of ex-untouchables and Dalits. Where is total meaningful education for them, and education linked with gainful employment and elimination of poverty? Dalits are the basic pillars of Democracy. The survival of democracy is in their hands. But where is social justice and employment for them'? As Prof. VKRV Rao says: "It will not be wrong to suggest that the Depressed Classes need total education for the success of the democracy. For elimination of poverty and injustice in all forms, more and more channels of employment should be made available to them."

According to Dr. Ambedkar the new social order demands the establishment of just, liberal and equal relationship between man and man, irrespective of caste, colour, race and religion.

In India, the voice of a small educated minority in power belonging to the dominating castes is today mistaken to be the voice of the majority of people. The rich are becoming richer while the poor, becoming more poor. The Dalits are not only poorer and uneducated, but also the ruling small minority, well organised and highly educated, is not serious about this class. The social justice, equality and individual freedom which are enshrined in our constitution cannot be achieved in toto unless mass education is provided to each and every citizen of the country.

Tell a man that he is exploited and illiterate, he will surely revolt next day. India has already discarded authoritarianism, exploitation and adopted socialism, a democratic form of government.

In the Dalit elite class there is social awakening, they

have become economically and socially better compared to those brethren who are still landless, illiterate and living below poverty line.

Fiery speeches and radical writings alone cannot change the fate of the Dalits. Their problems cannot be solved unless a proper 'Dalit National Agenda' (DNA) is formulated. More employment is created, land reforms implemented and social justice restored. If it is not done, thins will he otherwise.

Non-Brahmin Movement in Maharashtra

Here we will trace and analyse the history of the non-Brahmin movement which emerged prior to Dalit movement in modern India. Paranjpe writes: "The history of Brahmin-Kshatriya rivalries in India can be traced back to millennia. According to pre-Ramayana myth, Parshurama, a Brahmin warrior, tried to immolate the Kshatriya race from the face of earth fourteen times in succession. One need not trace the history so far back. It would be both relevant and convenient to start the historical account from Shivaji, an important landmark ill the history of Maharashtra during the 17th century." Shiva wars believed to have been born in a non-Kshatriya caste and hence was denied the right of initiation by the contemporary Brahmins. At the beginning of the 20th century, Shahu Chhatrapati, the prince of Kolhapur and a descendant of Shivaji, was similarly denied the right to perform Vedic rituals by the contemporary Brahamins (Latthe, 1925). The history of Maratha empire is replete with examples of Brahmin-Maratha rivalries. By the end of the Peshwa period, which was the period of decline of the Maratha hegemony, the Brahmins acquired supreme political power. The last Peshwa Bajirao II became notorious for wasting, colossal amounts of money to appease Brahmin priests. He is reported to have entertained over thirty thousand Brahmins every day with feasts in the Shravana Month of 1797A.D. (Sardesai. 1932, p. 548). Brahmins arrogated themselves when religious economic, and political power was concentrated in their hands. There are several references about the miserable plight of the untouchables in the history of the decline of Peshwa rule."2

The early British period (the second half of the 19th century) was marked by a bitter reaction of the non-Brahmins against Brahmin supremacy. The educated Brahmins added to their power by entering the British bureaucracy. The village clerks (Kulkarni), money-lenders and lawyers - most of whom were Brahmins accumulated wealth. The ignorant and illiterate village-folks were exploited. We can see the reaction against this exploitation reflected in the contemporary literature. Lokahitawadi (1823-1892) and Phule exposed the hypocrisies of Brahmins through their writings. They bitterly criticized the ascribed status of the Brahmins, the futility of their learning, their greedy nature, and so on.3

Jyotiba Phule Movement

Both Mahatma Jyotiba Phule (1827-1890) and his wife Savitri Bai Phule were great social reformers and educationists of their age. Phule was the pioneer of the non-Brahmin movement, which became a powerful force in Maharashtra. He opened several schools for female education at Pune. Perhaps he is the foremost reformer who started social awakening and love for education amongst the depressed classes and the Shudra communities, specially the womenfolk during the 19th century. He not only championed the cause of social reforms in a practical form by opening such institutions, but also opposed the rigidities of the caste system and practice of untouchability by organizing the downtrodden, first in Pure and at other places afterwards.

The aim of the Satya Shodhak Samaj, founded in 1873 was to save the non-Brahmins and the untouchables from the hypocrite Brahmins and their irrational opportunistic scriptures. He tried to establish a society where caste distinctions based on birth hit, no place. His Satya Shodhak Samaj became very popular amongst the lower classes throughout Maharashtra not only in fighting social evils and spread of education but also in social awakening, spirit of unity and brotherhood. Phule tried to gain social and political recognition for the non-Brahmin castes, specially the Shudras and the Other Backward Classes.

His devoted wife always assisted and inspired hull in all his social, educational and political activities. She managed and helped in running the educational institutions meant for Dalit and unfortunate women.

Phule and his wife in fact were active and creative as early pioneers of educational enterprises with the co-operation of both non-Brahmin and Brahmin colleagues. He and his friends, not only worked for social unity and awakening in the poor masses but also used every channel and influence to urge the Government for helping and spreading mass education and equal treatment to the non-Brahmins. The Malis, Kolis, Mahars, Mangs, Chambhars and other non-Brahmin and untouchable communities joined his Satya Shodhak Samaj, which was actually Bahujan Samaj Reformative Movement.

His Satya Shodhak Samaj awakened the masses against Brahmin supremacy and propagated an egalitarian philosophy. The folk arts, folk music, ballads and songs (Tamasha) were utilized as a medium of propaganda to communicate their principles to the masses. The Samaj rejected the priesthood who were regarded as agents between the God and worshipper, and as such the role of the priest in religion was despised. The Samaj also tried to convince the illiterate masses of the importance of education and also undertook a drive against untouchability.

The writings of Vishnushastri Chiplunkar indicate the intellectual awakening and also revival of nationalist spirit and anti-British national feeling.

Most of the political leaders like Gokhale, Ranade and Tilak were Brahmins. Tilak was the most powerful leader in Maharashtra till his death in 1920. Though he was regarded as a leader of the masses, he was conservative. He joined the orthodox Brahmins in saying that Shahu Chhatrapati of Kolhapur was not eligible to adopt Vedic rituals. The controversy over the eligibility for Vedic rituals (Vedokta Prakaran) continued for a long time and widened the rift between Brahmins and non-Brahmins.

Shahu Chhatrapati

Prince of Kolhapur Shahu Chhatrapati5 furthered the cause of education in Maharashtra amongst the non-Brahmins and Dalits. He created awakening in the poor untouchables. As a reaction against the orthodoxy of Brahmin priests, Shahu Chhatrapati tried to create it rival class of Kshatriya priests. The drive against Brahmin priesthood was in keeping with the principles of the Satya Shodhak Samaj which he had embraced. However, instead of driving out the concept of priesthood which was regarded its all unwanted agency between the worshipper and the God, he created a new class of priests. He tried to build enthusiasm about education among people. He built residences not only for Maratha students but also for Lingavats and Jains, untouchables and Muslims. The non-Brahmin movement during this period was non-political and concentrated its efforts on social welfare and education. To a certain extent it was against the nationalist movement which was at that time led by the Brahmins.

It is claimed in Maharashtra that Shahu played it leading a role in organising the non-Brahmin movement. In the first quarter of the 20th century the Maharaja assisted Ambedkar and helped the Mahars, Mangs and Kolis to rise to the equal level of the forward Marathas.

Interestingly, the Maharaja was so loyal to the British Raj that while Delhi Durbar was held in January 1903 a local celebration was organised by the state Residency attended by all those sardars and state officials who had not gone with Maharaja to Delhi; the state battery fired a royal salute and money was distributed among the poor. The grand-royal celebrations were held at Delhi from December 1902 to January 1903 in honour of the coronation of Edward VIII, King and Emperor. Lord Curzon was Viceroy at that time.

The Maharaja of Kolhapur, recipient of title of Sir descended from Shivaji, the founder of Maratha Empire was also present at the coronation of the King in London in 1902. In 1903 Delhi Durbar, the Maharaja himself attended the Royal function accompanied by his brother Piraji Rao and 500 persons and was awarded Grand Cross of the Royal Victorian Order, in the presence of Princes and chiefs of India for his loyalty to the British Crown. Actually in the history of India at no previous occasion have so many British supporters mainly chiefs, nobles, Zamindars and wealthy persons had an opportunity of meeting together for weeks to exchange their ideas how best they can be the friends of the Empire and rule over the masses.(Stephen Wheeler: A History of Delhi Coronation Durbar, 1903)

In the wake of the growing nationalism during the third decade of the 20th century the feudal mentality of the ruling chiefs changed entirely. In view of this Kolhapur chief also changed his outlook and took keen interest in non-Brahmin movement and reformative activities. In Ambedkar he found a western educated promising young man who might sincerely go ahead to work for the untouchable masses of India. Ambedkar first started his socio-political and humble career as Mahar leader but he had soon since 1930 appeared on the national scene as a champion of the Dalit cause.

After 1920 the non-Brahmin movement took a political colour. The political reforms announced by the Montague Commission of the British Government in 1918 and the subsequent grant of adult suffrage brought the non-Brahmin movement into the political arena. Inspired by the activities of the non-Brahmin party in Madras Province. The non-Brahmin leaders of Maharashtra sent Bhaskarrao Jadhav to Britain in order to negotiate for reservation of separate constituencies for the non-Brahmins. The demand was partly granted. In the following elections non-Brahmin leaders like Bhaskarrao Jadhav, Shripatrao Shinde, Keshavrao Jedhe organized effective propaganda and brought about a political awakening among the non-Brahmins. During the elections held in 1920, 1923 and 1926, several non-Brahmins were elected to the Provincial Council and a separate non-Brahmin political party was constituted. This party fought for educational facilities for the non-Brahmins for special concessions in qualifications for entrants into Government Service, and also passed a bill for abolition of the rights of village priests (abolition of Joshi Watan). Though the non-Brahmin party was politically conscious and guarded the interests of the masses it avoided participation in the nationalist movement. In fact, it was alleged to have been pro-British.6

In the year 1930 a marked change in this position came about Keshavrao Jedhe, the most prominent leader of the non-Brahmin party during the twenties was aware of the pro-British nature of his party (Jedhe, 1955). Inspired by the nationalist movement under the leadership of Mahatma Gandhi, Jedhe entered the Congress Party along with his followers. After 1930, the Congress gained a stronghold in the rural areas among the majority of non-Brahmins and the separate existence of non-Brahmin party disappeared from the political scene. The Congress was led by Brahmin leaders like Gadgil and Shankarrao Deo, as well as by non-Brahmin leaders like Keshavrao Jedhe and Shankarrao More till the struggle for independence succeeded in 1947.

The rift between the Brahmins and non-Brahmins appears to have continued in more latent and subtle forms. Many a Brahmin youths were attracted by revolutionary movement led by Savarkar and also by the more conservative political party, the Hindu Sabha. These movements got little support from the non-Brahmins. To a certain extent, there was also a split in the non-Brahmin castes. The traditionally ascribed higher status of the Marathas, a greater spread of education among many well placed Maratha families and a more decisive majority of the Maratha votes allowed the Maratha caste to grow stronger than the other castes. There was a feeling of resentment about the Maratha domination among the non-Maratha castes. A reflection of these feelings can be seen in the writings of K.S. Thakare.

After independence the Brahmin-non-Brahmin split became manifest in different ways. The leaders of the former non-Brahmin party who had joined the Congress in 1930 left the Congress again. Jedhe and More started a new party called the Peasants and Workers Party (Shetkari Kamgar Paksh). It proclaimed the acceptance of Marxist Ideology. There were only a few Brahmins in this party. The leaders gave a Marxist interpretation of the non-Brahmin movement as a class-struggle of the masses against the privileged Brahmin class. However, only a few years later Jedhe and More, the powerful founder leaders of the Peasants and Workers Party, joined the Congress again. This reduced the strength of the Peasants and Workers Party considerably.

The anti-Brahmin feelings took a very violent turn in 1948 when Mahatma Gandhi was murdered by a Maharastrian Brahmin. Many Brahmins were alleged to have rejoiced over Gandhi's murder. Mob fury was let loose and the property of the Brahmins, especially in the rural arms, fell a prey to it. A large number of Brahmin families from the rural areas migrated to the cities. The diverse reactions of the Brahmins to this violence were expressed in a series of articles published in the Sahyadri Magazine in 1948 (Bhide; Divekar: Gadgil; Khadye; Karandikar Pendse).

In the words of Paranjpe: "The other line of cleavage which has disrupted the Hindu society in this region is the struggle between the touchables and untouchables. Untouchability is the worst form of discrimination resulting from the caste system. The concept and practice of untouchability may or may not be as old as that of the caste system itself but its origin certainly dates as early as Mann who codified and sanctioned it. 'The plight of the untouchables seems to have been at its worst in the latter Peshwa period in Maharashtra when even tile shadow of an untouchable falling on a Brahmin would bring the former a severe punishment.

The end of the Peshwa rule must have eased the situation at least to the extent that a legal sanction behind such punishment was withdrawn.

In the early British period some individuals like Lokahitawadi and Vishnubuwa Brahmachari in Maharashtra started expressing sympathies for the untouchables. It was Mahatma Phule who first went beyond verbal sympathies. He not only exploded myth of Brahmin superiority but also started attempts at elevating the position of untouchables by opening a school for them. He flung his private water-tank open for their use in 1868.

The pioneering efforts of Phule were followed by the social reform movement led by Shivram Janba Kamble. He started magazine to propagate his views and made petitions to the British Government to improve their lot. Vithal Raniji Shind started the Depressed Classes Mission Society in 1906 which undertook educational activities.

Shahu Chhatrapati of Kolhapur passed a Mahar Vatan Abolition Act in his state in 1918. The Mahars thereby became out-right owners of their land and were freed from the slavery of doing a hundred odd jobs for the village in return for a small piece of land they were allowed to cultivate. He recruited untouchables as clerks in the state service and admitted a few educated untouchables to the bar. In 1919 he legally prohibited the segregation of untouchable children in schools.

After Phule and Shahu Chhatrapati the leaders of the Satya Shodhak like Jedhe, Bhaurao Patil, et. al. also undertook a campaign against untouchability. Like Shahu Chhatrapati, Sayaji Maharaj Gaikwad the ruler of Baroda also supported the movement for the uplift of untouchables. He employed Ambedkar, the leader of untouchables in his state and also financed his education abroad.

There is one more important figure in Maharashtra whose name is associated with the movement which attempted to uplift untouchables. S.M. Mate from Poona started a society in 1917 for eradication of untouchability and also started several schools for untouchables. He taught untouchables cleanliness. He associated and mixed with the untouchables so freely that the orthodox Brahmins passed remarks against him. Many of the leaders for the advancement of untouchables in its early stages were mainly from the upper castes. It would seem that attempts were born out of compassion. Traditionally the untouchables would accept the low position as ordained to them by destiny as a result of their own sin in past incarnations. The untouchables' own attempt towards improvement of their lot started only after some of them learned the new egalitarian ideas. The new opportunities for education paved the way for the spread of new ideas. The educated untouchables became aware of their rights and the most enlightened and mighty soul among them B.R. Ambedkar became the harbinger of a revolution.

Ambedkar returned to India with a Ph.D. from Columbia University in 1917. Soon after, he started awakening and organizing the untouchables. In 1927 he organised a Satyagraha at the Chawdar water tank at Mahad, a small town on the Western coast, to establish the right of the untouchables to draw water from a public reservoir. In 1929 and 1930 he organized a Satyagraha for entering the Parvati temple in Poona and Kala Ram Temple in Nasik. Thus he started an agitation against social and religious discrimination.

The Revolt of Untouchables

Dr. Ambedkar himself has very clearly stated: The movement of the untouchables against the injustice of the Hindu Social Order has a long history behind it, especially in Maharashtra. The early period of his socio-political life is full of hardships and struggle for the cause of the Dalits. This history falls into two stages. The first stage was marked by petition and protests. The second stage is marked by open revolt in the form of direct action against the Hindu Established Order. This change of attitude was due to two circumstances. In the first place it was due to the realization that the petitions and protests had failed to move the Hindus. In the second place Government had declared that all public utilities and public institutions are open to all citizens including the untouchables. The right to wear any kind of clothes or ornaments are some of the rights which the British Indian Law gives to the untouchables along with the rest. To these were added the rights to the use of public utilities and institutions, such as wells, schools, buses, trams, Railways, Public offices, etc., were now put beyond the pale of doubt. But owing to the opposition of the Hindus the untouchables cannot make any use of them. It is to meet the situation, the untouchables decided to change the methods and to direct action to redress their wrongs. The change took place in about 1920.

Of such attempts at direct action only few can be mentioned so as to give an idea of the revolt of the untouchables against the Hindu Social Order. Of the attempts made to vindicate the right to use the public roads, it is enough to mention one most noteworthy attempt in this behalf was that made by the untouchables of Travancore State in 1924 to obtain the use of the roads which skirted the temple at Vaikom. These roads were public roads maintained by the State for the use of everybody, but on account of their proximity to the temple building, the untouchables were not allowed to use certain sections which skirted the temple too closely. Ultimately as a result of Satyagraha, the temple compound was enlarged and the road was realigned so that the untouchables even if they used it were no longer within the polluting distance of the temple.10 Of the attempts made to vindicate the right to take water from the public watering places, it is enough to mention the case of the Chawdar tank.

This Chawdar tank is situated in the town of Mahad in the Kolaba district of Bombay Presidency. The tank is a vast expanse of water mainly fed by the rains and a few natural springs. The sides of the tank are embanked. Around the tank there are small strips of land on all sides belonging to private individuals. Beyond this strip of land on all sides belonging to private individuals, lies the Municipal road which surrounds the tank and beyond the road are houses owned by the touchables. The tank lies in the heart of the Hindu quarters and is surrounded by Hindu residence.

This tank is an old one and no one knows who built it or when it was built. But in 1869 when a Municipality was established by the Government for the town of Mahad, it was handed over to the Municipality by the Government and has since then been treated as a Municipal i.e., public tank.

Mahad is a business centre. It is also the headquarter of a Taluka. The untouchables either for purposes of doing their shopping and also for the purpose of their duty as village servants had to come to Mahad to deliver to the Taluka officer either the correspondence sent by village officials or to pay Government revenue collected by village officials. The Chawdar tank was the only public tank from which an outsider could get water. But the untouchables were not allowed to take water from this tank. The only source of water for the untouchables was the well in the untouchables quarters in the town of Mahad. This well was at some distance from the centre of the town. It was quite choked on account of its neglect by the Municipality.

The untouchables therefore were suffering a great hardship in the matter of water. This continued till matters got going. In 1923 the Legislative Council of Bombay passed a resolution to the effect that the untouchable classes be allowed to use all public watering places, wells, Dharnrashalas which are built and maintained out of public funds, or are administered by bodies appointed by Government or created by Statutes as well as public schools, courts, offices and dispensaries. Government accepted the resolution and issued the following orders:

"In pursuance of the foregoing Council Resolution the Government of Bombay are pleased to direct that all heads of official should give effect to the resolution so far as it related to the public places, institutions belonging maintained by

Government. The Collectors should be requested to advise the local bodies in their jurisdiction to consider the desirability of accepting the recommendations made in the Resolution."

In accordance with this order of the Government, the Collector of Kolaba forwarded a copy thereof to the Mahad Municipality for consideration. The Mahad Municipality passed a resolution on 5th January 1924 to the effect that the Municipality had no objection to allow the untouchables to use the tank. Soon after this resolution was passed there was held at Mahad, a Conference of untouchables of the Kolaba district over which Dr. Ambedkar presided. The Conference met for two days, the 18th and 20th March 1927. This was the first Conference of the untouchables held in the Kolaba district. Over 2,500 untouchables attended the Conference and there was great enthusiasm. On the first day of the Conference, Ambedkar delivered his presidential address in which he exhorted them to fight for their rights, give up their dirty and vicious habits and rise to full manhood. Thereafter high caste Hindus who were present and who held out that they were the friends of the untouchables, addressed the gathering and told the untouchables to be bold and exercise the right that is given to them by law. With this, the proceedings of the first day were closed. The subject committee met at night to consider the resolution to be moved in open Conference the next day. In the subject committee, attention was drawn by some people to the fact that there was great difficulty at Mahad for the untouchables in the matter of obtaining water for drinking purposes, and that this difficulty was felt particularly by the members of the Reception Committee of the Conference which had to spend Rs. 15 an enormous amount to employ caste Hindus to dole out water in sufficient quantity to satisfy the needs of those who had attended the Conference.

Next day on the 20th, the Conference met about 9 in the morning. The resolutions agreed upon in the Subject Committee were moved and passed by the Conference. It took about three hours in all. In the end one of Ambedkar's co-workers moved a vote of thanks to the President and others who had helped to make the Conference a success referred to the question of the difficulty in the matter of getting water and exhorted the untouchables present to go to the tank and exercise their right to take water from Chawdar tank, especially as the Municipality had by resolution declared it open to the untouchables and that their- Hindu friends were ready to help them. The Hindus who had exhorted them to be bold and begin fearlessly to exercise their- rights, instantly realised that this was a bombshell and immediately ran away. But the effect upon the untouchables was very different. They were electrified by this call to arms. Nearly, 2,500 untouchables led by Ambedkar and his co-workers marched in a procession through the main streets. The news spread like wild fire while crowds thronged the streets to witness it.

The Hindu inhabitants of the town saw the scene. They were taken by storm. They stood away witnessing this scene which they had never seen before. For the moment they seemed to be stunned and paralized. The procession in form of fours marched past and went to the Chawdar tank, and the untouchables for the first time drank the water. Soon the Hindus, realizing what had happened, went into frenzy and committed all sorts of atrocities upon the untouchables who had dared to pollute the water.

The assault committed by the Hindus on the untouchables at Mahad when they entered the Chawdar tank was undoubtedly a challenge to the untouchables. The untouchables on the other hand were determined not to be satisfied with merely exercising their right but to see it established. They naturally felt that they must take up the challenge thrown at them by the Hindus. Accordingly a second Conference of the untouchables was called. The untouchables were told that they must come fully prepared for all eventualities for Satyagraha (i.e., for civil disobedience and even for going to the goal).

The Hindus, when they came to know of this, appealed to

the District Magistrate of Kolaba for issuing an order under Section 144 of the Criminal Procedure Code against the untouchables, prohibiting them from entering the Chawdar tank and polluting its water. The District Magistrate refused and said that the tank was a public tank open to all citizens and he could not by law prevent the untouchables from taking water therefrom. He advised them to go to a Court of law and get their right of exclusive user established. The dates fixed for the Conference were 25th, 26th, 27th of December 1927. As these dates drew near, and as they heard that the untouchables were quite in earnest, and knowing that the District Magistrate had refused to come to their rescue, they did the only thing that was open to them, namely, to get their right to exclude the untouchables from a public tank established by law. Accordingly, nine Hindus drawn from different castes joined as Plaintiffs in filing on 12th December 1927 a suit No. 405 of 1927 as representatives of the Hindus, in the Court of Sub-Judge of Mahad. Ambedkar and four others were made defendants as representing the untouchables. The suit was for obtaining a declaration that the said Chawdar tank is of the nature of private property of the touchable classes only and that the untouchable classes have no right to go to that tank nor take water therefrom and also for obtaining a perpetual injunction restraining the defendants from doing any of those acts. On the same day on which the suit was filed, the plaintiffs appealed to the court for a temporary injunction against the defendants restraining them from going to the tank and taking water therefrom pending the decision of the suit. The judge holding that it was a fit case, granted a temporary injunction against Ambedkar and the other defendants on the 14th December 1927.

The temporary injunction issued by the Judge was sent to Bombay and was served upon Ambedkar two or three days before the Conferences actually met. There was no time to have consultation and no time to postpone the Conference either. He decided to leave the matter to the Conference to decide.

The Conference was called with the specific object of establishing the right to take water from the tank which was challenged by the Hindus last time. The District Magistrate had left the way open. But here was a Judge who had issued an order banning such action. Naturally, when the Conference met, the first question it was called on to consider was whether to disobey the order of injunction issued by the Court and enter the tank. The District Magistrate who had been favourable to the untouchables now took a different view. He explained his view very clearly to the Conference which he came and addressed personally. He said that if the Civil Court had not issued an injunction, he would have helped the untouchables in their attempt to enter the tank as against the caste Hindus, but that as the Sub-Judge had issued his order, his position had become different. He could not allow the untouchables to go to the tank because such an act would amount indirectly to help them to break the order of His Majesty's Court with impunity. He, therefore, felt bound to issue an order prohibiting the untouchables, should they insist on going to the tank notwithstanding the injunction not because he wanted to favour the Hindus but because he was bound to maintain the dignity of the Civil Court by seeing to it that its order was respected.

The Conference took what the Collector had said into its consideration and also the reaction of the Hindus to the attempt of the untouchables going to the tank in defiance of the order of the Court which they had obtained. In the end, the Conference came to the conclusion that it was better and safer for them to follow law and see how far it helped them to secure their rights. It was therefore decided to suspend civil disobedience of the order of the Judge till the final decision of the suit.

The occasion for civil disobedience never came because the untouchables won the suit and the Hindus lost it. One of the principal reasons which led the untouchables to follow law and suspend civil disobedience was that they wanted to have a judicial pronouncement on the issue whether the custom of untouchability can be recognized by the Court of law as valid. The rule of law is that a custom to be valid must be immemorial, must be certain and must not be opposed to morality or public policy. The untouchables' view is that it is a custom which is opposed to morality and public policy. But it is no use unless it is declared to be so by a judicial tribunal. Such a decision declaring the invalidity of the custom of untouchability would be of great value to the untouchables in their fight for civil rights because it would seem illegal to import untouchability in civic matters. The victory of the untouchables in the Chawdar tank dispute was very great. But it was disappointing in one way that the Bombay High Court did not decide the issue whether the custom of untouchability was valid or not. They decided the case against the Hindus on the ground that they failed to prove that the custom alleged by them in respect of the tank was not immemorial. They held that the custom itself was not proved. The tank became open to the untouchables. But the untouchables cannot be said to have gained their point. The main issue was whether the custom of untouchability was a legal custom. Unfortunately the High Court avoided to give judgment on that issue. The untouchables had to continue their struggle.

Kala Ram Temple and Burning of Manusmriti

The next item in this history of direct action which is worthy of mention relates to the entry in the famous Hindu Temple at Nasik known as the Kala Ram Temple. These are instances of direct action aimed to achieve specific objects. The movement includes two cases of direct action aimed at the demolition of the Hindu Social Order by applying dynamite to its very foundations. One is the burning of the Manusmriti and the second is the mass refusal by the untouchables to lift the dead cattle belonging to the Hindus and to skin them.

The burning of Manusmriti took place at Mahad on the 20th December 1927. The function was a part of the campaign for establishing the right to take water from the Chawdar tank. The burning of the Manusmiriti invited publicity as it took place openly in a Conference of Untouchables. Before burning the Manusmriti, the Conference passed certain resolutions. According to Dr. Ambedkar these resolutions form a landmark in the history of the movement of the untouchables, as given below:

Resolution No. 1. Declaration of the right of a Hindu: This Conference is firmly of opinion that the present deplorable condition of the Hindu Community is only an illustration of how a community becomes fallen by reason of its tolerating social injustice, following erroneous religious beliefs and supporting economic wrongs. The fall of the Hindu community is due entirely to the fact that the masses have not cared to know what are the birth-rights of a human being and much less have they cared to see that they are recognised and not set at naught the base acts and deeds of selfish people. To know what are these birth-rights of man and to endeavour to see that they are not trampled upon in the struggle between man and man and class and class, are the sacred duties of every person. In order that every Hindu may not know what are in the opinion of the Conference the inalienable birth-rights of man, this Conference resolves to issue the following proclamation containing a list thereof :

(i) All Hindus have the same social status from birth. This equality of social status is an attribute which they retain till death. There may be distinctions and differences between them in point of their functions in society. But that must not cause differences in their social status. This Conference is therefore opposed to any action-whether in the political, economic or social field of life-which would result in producing a difference in social status.

(ii) The ultimate aim of all political, economic or social changes should be to maintain intact the equal status of all Hindus. That being the view of the Conference, the Conference strongly disapproves of all literature of the Hindus, whether ancient or modern, which supports in any way the pernicious doctrine of inequality underlying the Hindus social system.

(iii) All power is derived from the people. The privileges claimed by any class or individual have no validity if they are not granted by the people. This Conference therefore repudiates the social and religious privileges enjoyed by some classes of Hindus in as much as they are founded upon the Vedas, Smritis and Puranas and not upon the free consent of the people.

(iv) Every person is entitled as his birth-right to liberty of action and speech. This liberty could be limited only for the purpose of saving the right of another person to his liberty and for no other purposes. Further this limitation can be imposed only with the sanction of the people and not by any injunction of the Hindu Shastras. This Conference therefore repudiates at restraints on religious, social and economic freedom imposed upon the thought and action of the Hindus in as much as they are imposed by the Shastras and not by the people.

(v) Hindus can be deprived of their rights other than their birth-rights only by law. What is not prohibited by law, a Hindu must be free to do and what is not obligatory by law, a Hindu must not be forced to do. For this reason there must be no obstruction to persons using public roads; public wells and tanks, public temples and all other public utilities. Persons, causing obstruction in matters where law has laid down no prohibition are in the opinion of this Conference enemies of the public.

(vi) Law is not a command of an individual or a body of individuals. Law is the peoples prescription for change. That being so, law to be respected, must be made with the consent of all and must have equal application to all without any distinction. Social divisions if they are necessary for the ends of society can only be made on the basis of worth and not of birth. The Conference repudiates the Hindu caste-system firstly as being detrimental to society, secondly as being based on birth and thirdly as being without any sanction from the people."

The Second Resolution passed by the Conference was worked as follows:

Resolution No. 2. Taking into consideration the fact that the laws which are proclaimed in the name of Manu, the Hindu law giver, and which are contained in the Manusmriti and which are recognised as the code for the Hindus are insulting to persons of low caste, are calculated to deprive them of the rights of a human being and crush their personality. Comparing them in the light of the rights of men recognised all over the civilized world, this conference is of opinion that this Manusmriti is not entitled to any respect and is undeserving of being called a sacred book to show its deep and profound contempt for it, the Conference resolves to burn a copy thereof, at the end of proceedings, as a protest against the system of social inequality it embodies in the guise of religion. A cursory reading of these resolutions will show the line which the Conference adopted. Although the Conference met to redress a particular wrong, it showed that it was not going to be satisfied with the redress of petty wrongs. The Conference felt that the time had arrived for laying down the goal of the untouchables. The goal laid down by it was far-reaching. The Conference proclaimed that the Untouchables wanted a complete overhauling of the Hind social system. It proclaimed that this reconstruction must rot be on the old foundation of Shastras. It proclaimed that whatever character of the new foundations, they must be consonant with justice and equity between Hindu and Hindu and to leave no doubt that in the matter of this reconstruction, they would not consent to Hindu Shastras being drawn upon. The Conference not only repudiated them but actually went to the length of burning them to ashes.

It was an echo of Voltare's denunciation of the Catholic Church of his time. For the first time a cry was raised against the Hindu Social Order 'Ecraze la Infame.' It is also clear that these resolutions were absolutely revolutionary in character. Manusmriti and other scriptures are sacred to all Hindus. Every Hindu believes in their sanctity and obeys their injunctions. Manu not only upholds caste and untouchability but gives them a legal sanction. The burning of the Manusmriti was a deed of great daring. It was an attack on the very citadel of Hinduism. The Manusmriti embodied the spirit of inequality which is at the base of Hindu life and thought just as the Bastille was the embodiment of the spirit of the Ancient regime in France. The burning of the Manusmriti by the Untouchables at Mahad in 1927 is an event which has the same significance and importance in the history of the emancipation of the untouchables which the Fall of Bastille had in the liberation of the masses in France and Europe.

The second instance of direct action against the frame of the Hindu social order itself is the refusal to skin the dead animals belonging to the Hindus and carrying them.

One often hears the untouchables being condemned for having brought upon themselves the curse of untouchability. The main ground on which this accusation rests is the adoption by the untouchables as their occupation, the carrying of the dead animals of the Hindus and skinning them and eating the carrion.

Even so great a friend of the downtrodden as the Abbe Dubois writing about the Pariahs of the Madras Presidency said: "What chiefly disgusts other natives is the revolting nature of the food which the Pariahs eat. Attracted by the smell, they will collect in crowds round any carrion and contend for the spoil with the dogs, jackals, crows and other carnivorous animals. They then divide the semi-putrid flesh and carry it away to their huts, where they devour it, often without rice or anything else to disguise the flavour. That the animal should have died of disease of no consequence to them, and they sometimes secretly poison cows or buffaloes so that they may subsequently feast on the foul, purifying remains. The carcasses of animals that die in a village belong by right to the Thoti or scavenger, who sells the flesh at a very low price to the other Pariahs in the neighbourhood. When it is impossible to consume in one day the stock of meat thus obtained, they dry the remainder in the Sun and keep it in their huts until they run short of their food. There are few Pariah houses where one does not see festoons of these horrible fragments hanging up; and though the Pariahs themselves do not seem to be affected by the smell, travellers passing near their village quickly perceive it and can tell at once the caste of the people living there .....

"It is to be wondered at after what has been just stated that other castes should hold this in abhorrence? Can they be blamed for refusing to hold any communication with such savages, or for obliging them to keep themselves aloof and to live in the separate hamlets?..."

It is true that this occupation has created a feeling of repugnance against the untouchables in the mind of the Hindus. But the Abbe or those who adopt this reasoning forget to raise two very important questions. First is why do the untouchables eat carrion? Will the Hindus allow the untouchables the freedom to give up skinning and carrying their dead animals?

No one would prefer carrion to flesh meat if it is available. If the untouchables have been living on carrion it is not because they like it. They eat carrion, because there is nothing else on which they can live. This will be clear to anyone who realizes that on account of untouchability they have no way left to earn a living. All professions have been closed to them. There is no land on the produce of which they can live. There is no trade which they can engage in. Their main stay is therefore the food they collect from the villagers and the carrion which is left to them. Without carrion they would literally die of starvation. It is therefore clear that the fault does not lie with the untouchables. If the untouchables eat carrion it is because the Hindus have left no honourable way of earning a living open to them.

To the second question the answer is equally clear. If the untouchables skin and carry the dead animals of the Hindus, it is because the untouchables have no choice. They are forced to do it. They would be penalized if they refused to do it. The penalty is legal. In some provinces the refusal to do this dirty work is a breach of contract. In other provinces it is a criminal offence involving fines. In Provinces like Bombay the untouchables are village servants. In their capacity as village servants they have to serve the Government as well as the Hindu public. In return for this service they are given land which they cultivate and on the produce of which they maintain themselves. One of the duties of the untouchables is to skin and carry the dead animals of the Hindus in the villages. If the untouchables refuse to perform these duties to the caste Hindus, the land which they live on is liable to be confiscated. They have to choose between doing the dirty work or facing starvation.

In Provinces like the United Provinces refusal to do scavenging by sweeper is made an offence. The United Provinces Municipalities Act II of 1918 contains the following provisions:

Section 210 (1) "Should a sweeper who has a customary right to do the house-scavenging of a house or building (hereinafter called the customary sweeper) fail to perform such scavenging in a proper way, the occupier of the house or building or the board may complain to a Magistrate."

(2) "The Magistrate receiving such complaint shall hold an inquiry and should it appear to him that the customary sweeper has failed to perform the house-scavenging of the house or building in a proper way or at a reasonable intervals, he may impose upon such a sweeper a fine which may extend to ten rupees, and upon a second or any later conviction in

regard to the same house or building may also direct the right of the customary sweeper to do the house scavenging the house of building to the forfeited and thereupon such right shall be forfeited."

Exactly similar provision is to be found in Section 165 of The Punjab Municipalities Act of 1911. The Punjab Act is an advance over the U.P. Act, in as much as it provides for punishment of a sweeper who is not customary sweeper but a contract-sweeper. (3) The Punjab Act adds: "Should any sweeper `other than a customary sweeper), who is under a contract to do house-scavenging of a house or a building, discontinue to do such house-scavering without fourteen days' notice to his employer or without reasonable cause, he shall on conviction be punishable with a fine which may extend to Rs. 10."

"227, Every order of forfeiture under Section 165 shall be subject to an appeal to the next superior court, but shall not be otherwise open to appeal."

People may be shocked to read that there exists legal provision which sanctions forced labour. Beyond doubt, this is slavery. The difference between slavery and free labour lies in this. Under slavery a breach of contract of service is an offence which is punishable with fine or imprisonment. Under free labour a breach of contract of service is only a civil wrong for which the labourer is liable only for damages. Judged in the light of this criterion, scavenging is a legal obligation imposed upon the Untouchables which they cannot escape.

Given these conditions, how can the untouchables be accused of doing these dirty works voluntarily?

The question whether the untouchables can be accused of having invited the curse of untouchability upon themselves for doing the dirty work of the Hindus is really beside the point. What is important to note is that the, Conference of the untouchables which met in Mahad resolved that no untouchable shall skin the dead animals of the Hindus, shall carry it or eat the carrion. The goal of these resolutions was two-fold. The one object was to foster among the untouchables self-respect and self-esteem. This was a minor goal. The major goal was to strike a blow at the Hindu Social Order. The Hindu Social Order is based upon a division of labour which reserves for the Hindus clean and respectable jobs and assigns to the untouchables dirty and mean jobs and thereby clothes the Hindus with dignity and heaps ignominy upon the untouchables. The resolution was a revolt against this part of the Hindu Social Order. It aimed at making the Hindus do their dirty jobs themselves.

This is a brief summary of the history of the revolt of the untouchables against the established order of the Hindus. It originated in Bombay. But it has spread to all parts of India.18

The story of the revolt of the untouchables tells how the old is ringing out and the new is ringing in. What is the reaction of the Hindus to this revolt? It is clear that his attitude is one of opposition. It might be difficult to understand why the Hindus should oppose. But there can be no manner of doubt that he is opposed.

The reasons why the Hindus are opposed to this fight for rights of the untouchables for their rights will not be difficult to understand if certain important features of the relationship that is now subsisting between the caste Hindus and the untouchables are borne in mind.

The first and foremost consideration that must never be forgotten is the sharp division between the touchables and the untouchables. Every village has two parts, the quarters of the touchables and quarters of the untouchables. Geographically the two are separate. There is always an appreciable distance between the two. At any rate there is no contiguity or proximity between them. The untouchables have a distinct name for their quarters such as Maharwada, Mangwada, Chamrotti, Khayakana, etc., de jure for the purposes of revenue administration or postal communication the quarters of the Untouchable are included in the village. But de facto it is separate from the village. When the Hindu resident of a village speaks of the village he means to include in it only the caste Hindu residents and the locality occupied by them. Similarly when the untouchable speaks of the village he means to exclude from it the untouchables and the quarters they occupy. Thus, in every village the touchables and untouchables form two separate groups. There is nothing common between them. They do not constitute a folk.

The second thing to note with regard to this division of the village into two groups is that these groups are real corporations which, no one included within them, can escape. As has been well said the American or European belongs to groups of various kinds, but he 'joins' most of them. He of course is born into a family, but he does not stay in it all his life unless he pleases. He may choose his own occupation, residence, wife, political party, and is responsible, generally speaking, for one's acts but his own. He is an 'individual' in a much fuller sense because all his relationship are settled by himself for himself. The touchables or untouchables are in no sense individuals because all or nearly all of their relationships are fixed when they are born in a certain group. 'Their occupation, their dwelling, their gods and their politics are all determined for them by the group to which they belong. When the touchables and untouchables meet, they meet not as man to man, individual to individual, but as members of groups or as nationals of two different states.

This fact has an important effect upon the mutual relationship between the touchables and untouchables in a village. The relationship resembles the relationship between different clans in primitive society. In primitive society the member of the clan has a claim, but the stranger has no standing. He may be treated kindly, as a guest, but he cannot demand 'justice' at the hands of any clan but his own. The dealing of clan with clan is a matter of war or negotiations, not of law; and the clanless man is an outlaw, in fact as well as in name, and lawlessness against the stranger is therefore lawful. The untouchable, not being a member of the group of touchables, is a stranger. He is not a kindred. He is an outlaw. He cannot claim justice nor any rights which the touchable is bound to respect.

The third thing to note is that the relationship between the two, the touchables and the untouchables, has been fixed. It has become a matter of status. This status has unmistakably given the untouchables a position of inferiority. This inferiority is embodied in a code of social conduct to which the untouchables must conform. What kind of code it is, has already been stated. The untouchable is not willing to conform to that code. He is not prepared to render unto Caesar what is claimed by Caesar. The untouchable wants to have his relationship with the touchables by contract. The touchables wants the untouchables to live in accordance with the rules of status and not rise above it."

The Bombay Chronicle on the occasion of the entry of the untouchables in Chawdar tank at Mahad wrote:

"The procession was most peaceful one and everything passed off quietly. But after two hours some evil minded leaders of the town raised a false rumour that the depressed classes were planning to enter the temple of Vireshwar, whereupon a large crowd of riffraff had collected all armed with bamboo sticks .... but the depressed classes were held back by their leaders and thus a far more serious riot was averted. The rowdies finding no occasion for provocation began patrolling the main street and assaulting the members of the depressed classes, who were passing along on their way to their villages." This was the courage shown by the leadership of Dr. Ambedkar.

Ambedkar's first public political plea in 1919 resulted in failure. The Southborough Committee, ignoring Ambedkar, Gawai and a number of caste Hindus from Bombay, including Vithal Ramji Shinde, V.J. Patel, R.P. Paranjpe and M.M. Joshi, who urged direct representation of the Depressed Classes, gave them one nominated representative in the Bombay Legislative Assembly. The first man selected for representation was D.D. Gholap, a Mahar from Satara who had been in charge of Ambedkar's paper, Muknayak. Following the Muddiman Committee Report on the working of the Montague-Chelmsford Reforms in 1925, which among many other matters contained an admonition of the need to correct the Depressed Class status, another nominated untouchable representative was added to the Bombay Legislative Council and Ambedkar was named to this seat in 1926."

It was during 1923 that two untouchable leaders urged the Bombay Legislative Council that public places and institutions maintained by public funds be opened to Untouchables.

As mentioned in earlier pages during the end of the 19th century Phule, a Shudra social activist, had started his education movement in Pune which spread throughout Maharashtra and gave a lead in educating and awakening the people of lower classes.

"In the decade between the sessions of the Southborough Committee and those of the Simon Commission in 1928, which provided the next opportunity for untouchables to plead for direct representation, a great deal of organizational and educational work went on in the Mahar community. In the pre-Ambedkar era, Shivram Janba Kamble had organized Conferences as early as 1903; the Depressed Indian Association was formed in Nagpur (and continued to function in the 1920s, but without Ambedkar's co-operation); and four Conferences were held in Bombay in 1917-18, some under caste Hindu leadership, all concerned with the untouchables and their increased political importance in the coming reforms. Ambedkar's first full-scale Conference seems to have been in March 1920, at Mangaon in Kolhapur, a princely state whose ruler, Shahu Maharaj had been active in the non-Brahmin movement of the Marathas and in education for backward classes, including untouchables. Ambedkar also spoke at the first All India Conference convened by untouchables at Nagpur later in 1920, before his return to England. At Nagpur, he persuaded all Mahar sub-castes, at that time endogamous groups, to eat together, although not all untouchables castes were prepared to interdine. Ambedkar also propounded a theory at Nagpur, which has held for the subsequent Mahar political movement, that the caste Hindu could not know the mind of the Untouchables, and hence could not lead him. He criticized Vithal Ramji Shinde, the most active of the caste Hindu workers among Untouchables, for suggesting that untouchables representative should be selected by members of the Legislative Council rather than by the Government or institutions of the Untouchables themselves. Direct representation was their goal if that was not possible, then a neutral British government or their own organized groups should select members, not a largely caste Hindu today."

On the basis of documentary proofs Zelliot has derived a conclusion that participation of Dr. Ambedkar in Mahad Satyagraha of 1927 created awakening in Dalits of Maharashtra. All these efforts had established Dalit identity in social life.

As the Mahar political movement gathered momentum, the non-Brahmin movement, with which it was partially identified, died away, or rather took a new form as its leaders were slowly absorbed into the Congress. The two movements had some things in common: both groups had grievances against the Brahmins; both looked back on the 19th century figure of Phule as a prophet, such non-Brahmin leaders as Shahu Maharaj and Keshavrao Jedhe knew Ambedkar and attended Untouchables Conferences. But the caste difference between the two groups and their social situations the Marathas were a land owning dominant caste, the Mahars a nearly landless minority--worked against any real co-operative effort between them. Although the Mahar grievances were voiced chiefly against the Brahmin, the Mahar village protests in the form of quiting Balutedar duties or claiming some form of social equality increased, and the village boycott directed by the non-Brahmin castes proved an effective weapon against the untouchables. The inability of a leader like Ambedkar to accept a subordinate role in a caste Hindu organization also mitigated against co-operation. Just as the Justice Party in Madras failed to include significant number of Untouchables, the non-Brahmin movement in Maharashtra could not make common cause with the untouchables.

If non-Brahmin movement and Dr. Ambedkar's untouchables movement have worked on a common platform things would have been different in Maharashtra and elsewhere in pre-independence politics and even after that.

Simon Commission

In 1927, when the British Government appointed Simon Commission, situation in the Country had undergone a tremendous change. The freedom movement had become strong and widespread. Muslim leadership has emerged. The Congress had inspired social welfare work specially the removal of untouchability through change of heart.

Congress strongly boycotted the Simon Commission and organised protest rallies and agitations throughout the Country. At this juncture Dr. Ambedkar welcomed Simon Commission and addressed Conferences in support. According to Zelliot:

"The reaction of the Depressed Classes to the Simon Commission's tour of India was far different from that of the Congress or the moderates. Eighteen Depressed Classes associations testified willingly to the Commission, sixteen of them asking for separate electorates for untouchables. While his students walked out of his class at Government Law College in protest, Ambedkar told the Commission that the untouchables were relieved of anxiety because the Simon Commission did not include an Indian, since such a nominee could not be truly representative of all groups. However, he did not renew his 1919 request for separate electorates. Adult franchise and reserved seats, up to 22 in all in a Bombay Assembly of 140 (15 according to their numbers and seven as weightage to insure their rights), would satisfy him and the organization he spoke for, the Bahishkrit Hitakarini Sabha

(Depressed Class Association). He also requested guarantees from the Depressed Classes as did an appeal from the Central Provinces Depressed Class Association, signed by five Mahars (including Kisan Fagoji Bansode), two Chamars, one Mang and one Bhangi, which expressed a similar view of rights and privileges in even stronger and more distrustful language. This group requested: (1) an increase in the government power of veto for protection of the minority, (2) separate representation not only in legislatures, but all public bodies including universities in proportion to their numerical strength (3) posts in government service for Depressed Class members, with minimum qualifications required (4) representation in the cabinet dependent only upon Depressed Class votes, (5) special grants for education (6) no application of a bill affecting the Depressed Classes if three-fourths of the community opposed it. Both the Vidarbha and the Bombay demands reflect the feeling of the need for education (2.9 per cent of the Mahars were literate, according to the 1931 census), the need for government jobs (Ambedkar pointed out that there was not one Depressed Class clerk in government service), and a desire for the Depressed Classes not only to participate in all public bodies but to be able to control any legislation affecting them.' Motilal Nehru ignored the Depressed Classes in 1928.

As D.K. Baisantry in Ambedkar: The Total Revolutionary (p. 90) observes: " But when the Constitution prepared by the Nehru Committee published in 1930 saw the light of the day, Ambedkar was shocked. He was forced to criticise the Nehru Report as one intending to `preserve the upper class hegemony and Brahminical rule in the society. The Committee it is worth mentioning had invited all sorts of organisations for consultations, but not the Depressed Class Organisation, led by Dr. Ambedkar. Nay nor any other Scheduled Castes leaders."

The young, emerging leader Dr. Ambedkar had become the voice of the Depressed Classes through his speeches, writings and agitations all aimed at awakening the Dalits as well as for expressing free and frank views on social and national issues facing the country. But when he was invited by the British Prime Minister to participate in the RTC held at London during 1930-32 he emerged as a champion of the Depressed Classes.

Non-Brahmin Movement in South

In Tamil Nadu the non-Brahmin movement took place only after the 1910s. But long before it took an ideological shape 32 Panchalar from Salem in 1840 protested against offering Brahmins all the responsible public offices and requested for employing all classes without caste distinction. In 1896, more than one dozen men from Anantpur deplored the control of public offices by a family of a Brahmin coach as disastrous.

The Visvakulotharana Association of Madras in 1897 voiced its grievances against the Brahmin supremacy. In Nellore 50 Brahmins of a family controlled revenue establishment and European officers were shocked to detect this fact when the matter was brought to their notice in 1853-1854. The Madras Revenue Board in its standing order thus warned the collectors in 1853 to see that appointments should be made from all castes. WK. Cornish, Census Superintendent of Madras issued warning in 1871 but till 1880 the order were neutralized. But non-Brahmins became alert and conscious to keep the Brahmins in check. Due to educational reforms and expansion of education since 1890s, the percentage of educated Brahmin boys was very high while of non-Brahmin Hindus very low during nearly two decades, naturally Brahmins had a larger share in British service. The opposition of Brahminical supremacy crystallized into the South Indian Liberal Federation (Justice Party) and the release of the non-Brahmin manifesto in 1917. Thus a radical, creative and reformative movement took birth in Madras Presidency for safeguarding the interests of the non-Brahmins. It was a movement against the domination of Brahmins and other dominating caste Hindus in the fields of education, employment, economic and political life.

In fact the non-Brahmin movement was led by the rich and powerful backward agriculturist classes like Reddys, Kammas, Vellalas, Velamas and Nairs and their supporters. The non-Brahmins declared themselves as Dravidians and branded the Brahmins as Aryans. Under the Government of India Act of 1919 the non-Brahmins were allotted 28 reserved seats out of the 98 elected seats in the Madras Legislative Assembly. This was a big achievement for the Justice Party. In November 1927 in a Communal Quote GO Communal ratios were introduced in public services, allocating in unit of 12 appointments, five (41.7%) to non-Brahmin Hindus, two (16.7%) each to Brahmins, Anglo Indians and Christians and Muslims and one (8.3%) to others. It is to be mentioned that Brahmins were only 3 per cent of the total population in Madras Presidency, whereas before non-Brahmin movement their representation in British public services was cent percent in high offices and a good number in lower places. It is argued that the beneficiaries of the non-Brahmin movement were from the forward non-Brahmins and the very purpose of equal opportunities for all and injustice to none was defeated. The dominating non-Brahmins achieved socio-political ascendancy during a period of three decades (1920-1950). However, the Depressed Classes, who were the untouchables and Shudras as well as Backward Class Hindus could not get much during this period.

Prominent Dalit leader in Madras M. C. Rajah in 1923 led a deputation to the Governor accusing Justice Party of ignoring the claims of the Dalits to the legislature and local bodies, appointment in services and education preferences. He asked for adequate number of scholarships to Depressed Classes students and liberal admission policy. On behalf of the Adi-Dravida Mahajan Sabha, Rajah in 1924 demanded the Governor to include one member in the Cabinet and Executive council and creation of a Department of Depressed Classes Welfare. When the Simon Commission visited India, during 1928, the

Congress opposed its country wide tour. The Adi-Dravida Mahajan Sabha welcomed the Simon Commission and insisted on separate electorates for the Dalits. A Provincial Conference of the Madras Depressed Classes Federation and a series of other conferences expressed solidarity with its demands and appealed to British Raj against transferring power fearing Hindu dominated Congress Raj would crush them. Rajah worked with Ambedkar and under the Government of India Act 1935, Madras Depressed Classes were allotted 30 out of the 215 seats in legislature.

In 1923 there was a no-confidence motion against Justice Party ministry in Madras, which however was defeated. Some artisan caste combines (Viswa Brahmins) though socially backward with the support of P.C. Ramamurti and 27 other members of the Madras Legislative Council in 1932 demanded inclusion of Viswa Brahmins in D C list. Viswakarma Young Men's Association, Literary Association. Rajahmundry supported this move but the government rejected this demand which was thought to be unfair to DC's and other non-Brahmin castes. Again in 1934, Ramamurti and others asked for preferential treatment to Viswa Brahmins, Setti Balijas, Chaklis, Devangis, Nadars, Nambudri Brahmins and other backward communities without inclusion in DC list. The demands were repeated again in the following years.

The Vanniyars in 1935 pleaded for separate representation and Nanjappa claimed that they were 6.3 percent of total population and quite an ignored class. In 1938, the Vanniyakula Kshatriya Maha Sangam founded in 1888 in Madras, demanded fair representation in education and employment. From 1938 to 1940 the Vanniyars brought pressure stating that British Raj did justice to the poor backward communities while the Justice Party and Brahmins have totally ignored their just demands. Only the forward non-Brahmins were getting preferential treatment.

The Madras Provincial Backward Classes League founded in 1932 and registered in 1935 as a social non-political organisation worked for the socio-economic development of the Backward Hindu communities. M.A.M. Nayakar, S.A. Nanjappa, P.K. Ramachandra Padayachi and H. A. Gowder were the driving force behind this movement.

In November 1933, C. Basudev claimed that few forward non-Brahmin Hindus were getting the benefits and poor unrepresented Backwards were being marginalised. The Revenue member of the Governor's Executive Council met the deputation led by Basudev. In 1937 the matter was brought to the notice of C. Rajagopalachari who was Chief Minister of Madras. But he hardly cared for such demands being tough Brahmin.

The Backward Classes League started its paper, held conferences, led delegations, put demands repeatedly and in 1947 the GO was revised and Backward Hindus also got their share in jobs, education etc.

After independence, in the wake of the Madras High Court ruling in 1950 declaring Madras Government order as ultra vises of the Constitution, EX Ramaswamy Naicker the pioneer of the non-Brahmin and Dalit Movement organised a vigorous campaign, Communal GO Safeguard Processions protest meetings etc., throughout the state. Fearing social unrest and rendering justice to the less advanced communities in 1951, the Madras Legislature carried a resolution authorizing the government to adopt such measures as are necessary to for admission in schools and colleges and appointments in Government jobs for the welfare of all classes of citizens. The government reintroduced reservation quota of 15 per cent for SCs/ STs, 25 per cent for socially-educationally Backwards and the rest for open competitions for the entire population.

Following the recommendations of the BC Commission of 1969 the Dravida Munnetra Kazgam (DMK) ministry led by M. Karunanidhi enhanced the reservation quota from 25 to 31 percent and for the SC/STs to 18 percent. In 1979 All India Anna Dravida Munnetra Kazgam (AIDMK) ministry led by M.G. Ramachandran, for ensuring that the benefits of reservation should really reach the backwards among the BCs and were not cornered by the affluent upper crust announced the increase in the reservation for BCs from 31 to 50 per cent. However, following unit petitions challenging the validity of the GO the Supreme Court in 1982 directed the Tamil Nadu Government to appointment a new commission to review the existing list of BCs for a factual and scientific investigation.

There was much politicalization of the reservation policy and leg pullings and pressures, the Government therefore did not table the BC Commission Report, submitted in 1985 instead issued a series of GOs and made selective use of the report to avoid social unrest and communal chaos. The Vanniyars have agitated and struggled during 1980-1988 in a big way for meeting their long pending demands by the government. The Vanniyars movement turned very violent in 1987 and claimed at least 20 lives in clashes with police and Scheduled Castes followed by participation and arrest of over 20,000 persons. Though their agitation was against government policy, the agitators clashed with SCs also though both have much in common in matters of backwardness and poverty.

Narayan Guru: Izhavas and Vaikam Satyagraha

The lzhavas or Ilavans (Ilavas) of Malabar, Cochin and Travancore appears to be the powerful-dominating community amongst the untouchables of Kerala. By the end of the 19th century and beginning of 20th century they arose as socially and politically strong because of their rich economic background as an agriculturist and toddy-drawing caste. Sri Narayan Guru (1857-1925) himself an Izhava was a great philosopher, saint and reformer among them. He was progressive in his outlook and spiritual leader of the Depressed Classes. In 1902-03 his followers founded Sri Narayan Dharma Paripalan Yogam (SNDPY) as a reformative educational organisation, which took active initiative in bringing social reforms, removal of untouchability and caste system as well as temple entry.

Izhavas or Ilavas socially-economically united themselves and in 1918 appealed to the Travancore government for opening state temples to all Hindus including Depressed Classes. Narayan Guru's principal followers Dr. Palpu and T.K. Madhavan were successful in bringing the Izhavas under the Gandhian influence. Many Adi-Andhara Dalits of South were influenced by the philosophy and teaching of Narayan Guru. 1921 Izhavas threatened that if they were not treated at par with the caste Hindus, they will embrace Christianity. In 1924-25 the Travancore Vaikam Satyagraha even drew the attention of Gandhi who got an opportunity to act publicly on behalf of untouchables and non-Brahmins on Kerala for the removal of prohibition against untouchable's use of the road way passing the temple at Vaikam. Although the Nambudri Brahmin priests known for the rigidities and the then government finally agreed to open the road passing by the temple but it was not perhaps clear whether the untouchables were actually allowed to enter the temple, until 1936. It may be looked into carefully that the unity amongst the Depressed Classes, growing awakening due to Ambedkar movement and rise in feelings of nationalism, the Izhavas constant threat to convert to Christianity and finally in the light of Gandhi's pressure and intervention forced the government to enact a law opening its state temples to the untouchables. Thus Travancore was the first state in India to frame such legislation. In his speech in 1924 Ambedkar referred to the vaikam Satyagraha which was of social and political importance to India's millions of untouchables. In the following year, again Ambedkar stated that vaikam Satyagraha was the most important event in the country today. Strangely enough except. Gandhi very few public figures expressed their sincere concern to this sort of discrimination and denial of right to worship.

Other Non-Brahmin Movements in South

In Madras, Praja Mitra Mandali was established by C.R. Reddi to work for social uplift and political rights as well as non-Brahmins Opposition Forum. Reddys in Tamil Nadu have been an agriculturist class, socially and politically neglected and educationally backward. Earlier to this organisation, Lingayata Education Fund and vokkalinga Sangh have been forward in Karnataka as a non-Brahmin Movement. They demanded social-political rights and preferential treatment in Government jobs.

The Lingayats have a great history as a sect. In Tamil Nadu and Karnataka the Lingayats are a religious community who were recognised as powerful sect in the 12th century. Farquhar says: "the mass of the people had been either Jains, Digambaras or Sivas, and the new sect seems to be essentially a formation meant to give the Sivas a more definite theology".

In 1914 Mannath Padmanabha Pillai founded the Nayar Seva Samaj in Travancore. He organised the people and brought social reforms in the Nayar society. The Nambudri Brahmins of Kerala had become prosperous and influential in the society. They even did not pay land revenue though they controlled big farms and exploited the landless farmers who were Shudras. They did not allow untouchables in the temples where they worked as priests. Under the able leadership of K. Ramkrishna Pillai and Mannath Padamanabha the Nayars struggled hard and raised their voice against Brahmin domination. They demanded the Travancore Durbar for social and political rights as well as equal treatment. Nayar Samaj took keen interest in social reforms and spread of education, profess a non-caste religion and the four-fold divisions of caste scheme are not applicable to them. It is believed conversions to the Lingayat faith were made from various castes from time to time. Because of their unity Lingayats became a powerful force in South.

Role of Naicker

Known truly as Ambedkar of South India, EX Rama Swamy Naicker was a great fighter against caste oppression and social disabilities arising from the caste system. As true social reformer he worked genuinely for the establishment of casteless and classless society. His father Venkatappa Naicker was a trader.

As a protest against ill-treatment to the Dalit students he left his studies at the age of 10 years. Again in 1885 he was admitted in a primary school, but left the school as the Dalit boys were not allowed to mix up with upper caste Hindu boys. From his childhood he opposed caste system, social evils and Hindu ritualism; and even the worship of various gods and goddesses. He was married at the age of 19 years in 1898 with Nagammai.

He worked as a Congress leader during 1919-1925 and was secretary Tamil Nadu Congress Committee in 1920. He visited Russia, Germany, England, France and Spain in 1931. He was elected Chairman of the Justice Party in 1938 when he was in prison.

He was a great critic of Rajagopalachari, but both were fast friends in personal life. Annadurai was his adviser and disciple.

In 1930 he left the Congress because of Brahmin domination. He established Dravida Kazgam. He burnt the Constitution and the National Flag. He fearlessly spoke against north dominance and Brahminic supremacy, Aryan invasion and struggle with non-Aryan Dravidians and highlighted the atrocities committed on Dalits by the caste Hindus. His speeches and writings were more radical and he has been a better practical visionary than Ambedkar. The Brahmins blamed him as a supporter of the British Raj and the Englishmen in the same manner as Ambedkar was criticised and blamed. But like Ambedkar he also never bothered for his critics. No doubt Naicker was a great visionary, social revolutionary and radical thinker.

Non-Brahmin and Dalit Movement in North India

There are historical records and evidences that Shudras, Dalits and untouchables in Northern India have actively participated in the freedom movement, beginning from the first Sepoy Mutiny of 1857 till 1942's Quit India Movement.

The Backwards and the untouchables have been landless labour and very few own agricultural land. They were mainly engaged in village crafts and cottage industries, which after independence have been crushed by the highly mechanised industrial revolution which began in the second half of the 19th century.

In Bihar, Jagjivan Ram organised the Depressed Classes under the banner of Bhartiya Dalit Varga Sangh; which became a political organisation in the 40s. In 1937 he was appointed as Parliamentary Secretary in Bihar Government and joined the Nehru cabinet in 1946, when the Interim Government was formed. It is most unfortunate that very few Western and Indian scholars have attempted to study and analyse the Depressed Classes Movement started and led by Jagjivan Ram which was of national character.

Bhagat Amin Chand established All India Harijan league at Lahore in 1932. Till 1947 its reformative and social activities were limited in the pre-partisan Punjab, Kashmir and Himachal Pradesh but after independence it shifted its headquarters in Delhi. Bhagat entered in the Delhi Legislature as a member in 1952 and was Whip of the Congress Assembly Party, when Chaudhary Brahma Prakash was Chief Minister of Delhi. The All India Harijan League worked for the removal of untouchability and caste system, socio-economic uplift of the Depressed Classes and was active in Northern India till 1980. It was patronized by the national leaders as a representative organisation which in fact has emerged after the Poona Pact to voice the grievances of the oppressed people. Harijan League was very popular in Punjab, J & K and Delhi.

In Punjab, as a religion Ad-Dharma existed in each and every village. It was a social and religious movement amongst the untouchables. In urban elite class it was a symbol of status, which accorded pride and a honourable place in society and community leadership. It was quite different from Sikhism, Arya Samaj, Deva Samaj and Sanatan Dharma led by the wealthy Punjabi reformers.

In the post independence phase apart from Gandhi's Harijan movement Tilak Chand Kureel (Kanpur), Dr. Manik Chand

JatavVir (Agra), Ch. Biharilal (Bijnor), Swami Achchutanand (Mainpuri), B.R. Jayant (Etah), T.P. Sahyogi, Bhagwan Dass and Pandit Kanhaiyalal (Hathras), Dr. Dharam Prakash (Bareilly) and K.L. Balmiki (Bulandshahar) did appreciable work for the removal of untouchability and spread of education in Northern India. They not only worked for the untouchables but also took interest in the welfare of the Backward Classes.

Similarly, Baldeo Singh Arya, a well known social activist, advocated the cause of the hill untouchables. In Uttranchal Depressed Classes were not allowed to take out marriage processions and use of Doli-Palaki was banned. Arya started agitation against this high-handedness and ban as a stigma of untouchability and aroused public opinion. Gandhi intervened and lauded the efforts of Arya. Today Arya is known as Gandhi of Uttranchal.

During the first quarter of 20th century Jats, Yadavas,Chaurasias and Kurmis in U.P. and Bihar, Kolis in Gujarat, Kaivartas in Bengal, Sainis and Jats in Rajasthan, Punjab and Western UP, Tantis and Tells (Sahus) in Bihar organised themselves and emphasised on social reforms and education as well as tried to gain power and social status. They were interested in OBC status. Some of their leaders in pre-independence days participated in the national movement. Lohars who migrated from Bihar to Bengal got a DC status to achieve preferential treatment.

Kaivartas called themselves as Mahishas. Nai (barbers) and Badhai (carpenters) became Thakurs and Brahmins. Tells of U.P. tried to become Sahus and Lohars as Panchals.

There is much awakening in Chattisgarh Chamars and they have assumed new status as Satnamis. There is renaissance in Jatavas and its sub-castes in Uttar Pradesh.

In princely states of Rajasthan and Madhya Pradesh Raigars, Meenas and Kolis refused to work as slaves or forced labour. Rajput landlords have a history of oppressing the Depressed Classes since long. Meenas are STs and a very powerful community, while Raigars and Kolis enjoy SC status.

In 1910-20 the poor Alloors (Yadavas) and Kttrmis of Bihar refused to work in the fields of big Zamindars, maintained by richYadavas, Kayasthas and Bhootnihars. In due course of tune, struggle of forward and backward castes took political shape. Now Yadavas have emerged as a powerful community in Bihar and Eastern UP While Pasis, Dusadhas, Chamars and Koris are landless labour, Kurmis own land. Untouchables of this belt have produced leaders and social activists of state and national level. Namshudras of Bengal struggled for their rights and raising socio-economic status in pre-independence days.25 Besides caste conflicts and intercaste rivalaries between the forward-backwards and the Dalits, a new trend of Sanskritization has emerged amongst the non-Brahmin and Dalit elites.

ELEVEN

The Emancipation

Talking of the progress of Dalits, any evaluation of the measures by the State for the progress of the Scheduled Castes and Scheduled Tribes should appropriately begin with a review of progress in the conventional frame. Progress of the members of a community has two facets—Progress in absolute terms and Progress in relative terms *vis-a-vis* people of other castes in the nation. So far progress in absolute terms is concerned, it is comparatively a much more easy task particularly when the concerned people like members of the Scheduled Castes to begin with may have been at the rock bottom. They had not only been living in scarcity in terms of resources but were also facing the worst form of exploitation even as labourer, artisans and professionals. The position of members of the Scheduled Tribes is, however, different. They have been in good position, enjoying until very recently full and effective command over the resources in their respective areas. It is only in the wake of opening up of their territories that serious inroads have been made in regard to the access to and command over resources by other people. These consists of a variety of institutions both in the private sector and the public sector and even the State. Accordingly while the graphs in some items like area under irrigation may show an upward trend. There may be regression in actuals with regard to the vital question of land ownership. The community may not be better off even in absolute terms not withstanding the visible progress for some.

The measurement of the progress of a community in a developing economy to be realistic should be in terms of its relative position in the national economy. This will depend on two important factors. Firstly, the overall rate of growth of the economy and secondly the share of the concerned community therein. No systematic studies or estimation has been done which can be used to assess the relative position of the Scheduled Castes and Scheduled Tribes in a time sequence. However, the overall position in some respects is well-known which could give us a reasonable base for first order estimates of the long-term process and relative changes affecting these communities.

Our national economy comprises of both the organised and the unorganised sectors. The former includes the modern industrial sector and the associated infrastructure, commercial organisations and economic institutions, modern social and professional services and the variegated apparatus of the State. The unorganised sector comprises of agriculture and allied activities, village and household industries, traditional professional services and such like. The modern industrial sector is the leading sector of our economy which is growing at a faster rate compared to the rest. Major benefits of modern science and technology and also organisations as such are becoming an integral part of the organised sector. On the other hand, many activities in the unorganised sector are facing backlash. Therefore, the gap between the two sectors is growing at a fast rate, especially where economy is concerned.

A significant feature of the structural transformation of our economy is that the maximum extraction from new opportunities in the organised sector have gone to those who had the benefit of being nearer to the emerging centres of power or to those who had the benefit of early start because of their heritage or better access to education. Due to the marked difference in the quality of education and the near absence of good educational institutions in rural areas, only the elite class particularly those who owned land, could send out their children for higher education. It is only in a comparatively smaller segment of the organised sector that are able to avail the services under Government and public sector in which the policy of positive discrimination has enabled members of the Scheduled Castes and Scheduled Tribes to get a foot-hold. The big differential in the access to education and in the opportunity to get timely initial start has thus created an environment of unequal competition for the new opportunities in the organised sector bulk of which have gone to members of the upper castes. Thus the intersectoral and intrasectoral polarisation has acquired a social base.

While the gains in the organised sector for the members of Scheduled Castes and Scheduled Tribes have been rather limited and the position within the traditional sector is also very similar. It has been noted earlier that the social and economic drawbacks of the traditional system, particularly the latter, have not relented. Moreover, there is growing polarisation within the unorganised sector in general and rural economy in particular. Not only members of higher castes have command over bulk of the resources in the beginning but even now they are in a better position so they could consolidate their command and expand it with the new weapon of the power of technology, money and influence. These are the people which have entered the organised sector in general and Government establishment in particular. They now have fully consolidated their position.

If we look from other angle, we find the process of deprivation of the rural economy in general and agricultural sector in particular are affecting most adversely to the members of weaker sections, particularly members of the Scheduled Castes, as earlier noted from the condition of landless labourers. Therefore, while members of higher castes are taking advantage of their links with the organised sector and are migrating from concern rural areas due to the pull factor caused by intersectoral polarisation, members of weaker sections, particularly the Scheduled Castes, are being compelled from rural areas due to intrasectoral polarisation within the rural economy. They are largely joining the amorphous mass of the unorganised sector in urban areas. Thus it appears that except the gains that the members of the Scheduled Castes and Scheduled Tribes have made through reservations in services in addition they got nothing their relative position in the national economy has deteriorated. In fact, the inability of the members of middle castes who comprise the second wave of educated people to enter the organised sector, where major share of the opportunities in the national economy rest, is at the root cause of the sporadic struggles for reservations in services which is the only way to make an entry, mere token and of no consequences to the masses, in the privileged sector that is modern and organised.

The position of members of the Scheduled Tribes is still worse except in the hill areas of the North-East. They are far behind and not as yet ready for participation in the organised sector of the national economy and their representation even in the limited area of public services is small. They are facing severe backlash of development in all directions as their areas are being opened up and the tentacles of the organised sector are gradually spreading out to the remotest areas now. The tribal people are losing their lands along the new arteries of communication and are being incessantly pushed back from wherever new opportunities are arising. They are compelled to squeeze or forced to flee on their own, firstly as their lands are acquired by new establishments and then in the face of successive waves of migrants who begin to pour into these areas and spread out. The new openings are emerging as islands of affluence and centres of tremendous power and authority in which the tribal has no place or at best can creep in only to occupy the substratum of the new economy as also the new social system. The tribal people are losers on all counts and ironically are victims of the depredation of the system which is conveniently accorded the aura of inevitability, sparing those responsible for policy making even the allusion of embarrassment and qualms of conscience.

We will revert to the implications of the relative deprivation which members of the Scheduled Castes, and

Scheduled Tribes are facing in general while a substantial section amongst them, particularly members of the Scheduled Tribes, are losing even in absolute terms. Nonetheless, there are some gains, even though the coverage is not as much large as it should be and the pace is also rather slow. Moreover before a clear perspective about their position is drawn with reference to the larger national frame it will be necessary to evaluate the gains and also the setbacks in the conventional frame referred as earlier. It will assist more if we begin with the brighter sports in a mixed scene of light and shade.

Education

The major achievement in absolute terms has been noticed in the field of education. The level of literacy amongst the Scheduled Castes and Scheduled Tribes has grown up considerably during the decades 1951-2000 while the gap in their literacy levels and that of the rest has also increased during the same period. The percentage of enrolment of children belonging to these communities has also been increasing at all levels. The proportion of Scheduled Caste children amongst those enrolled at the primary level more or less corresponds to their relative strength in the population. But there is a marginal decline at the middle school level, particularly amongst the Scheduled Castes, after which, however, their position stabilises. At present there are more than a million and half postmatric scholars belonging to the Scheduled Castes.

These gross figures of literacy levels, scholarship holders, etc., however, can be taken as reference indicator of increasing coverage of the Scheduled Castes. These do not represent the real state of achievement. Firstly, the figures in many cases might be overestimated. Secondly, the figures of enrolment at the elementary level are highly inflated due to bulging of enrolment in primary class. A substantial proportion of these children in primary class are unable to move to the next stage and are unable to cross even the illiteracy barrier. Thus the pace of advancement in this crucial area has remained slow, particularly when it is compared to what was envisaged in the Constitution. This is primarily because the significance of education for the welfare and advancement of the Scheduled Castes, specially the latter, has not been fully realised. The role of education as a cultural accomplishment has been recognised for ages. Its importance as a crucial investment for economic development was realised after the Second World War which distinguished it from other purely welfare measures. But so far as the vulnerable sections of the commmunity are concerned, the role of education has another dimension. Education is vital in their struggle against inequity and oppression in a system where scales are heavily loaded against them. Ignorance is their biggest enemy.

Education is particularly critical for small tribal communities in the new context. Their traditional institutions are being gradually superseded by a powerful formal structure of the modern States about whose ways they are unaware. In the absence of education which could provide to them the key to the new system, they are defenceless. Their traditional command over resources which have provided them sustenance through ages is at stake. Moreover, they are also not duly prepared for taking advantage of the new opportunities which are being created in these areas around the use of resources which they have traditionally commanded. The present state of the tribal people in the North-East and in the middle India, which was almost the same in the beginning of this century, presents a striking contrast which is largely relatable to the place of education in the scheme of development in the two regions. In the North-East education preceded development of their economy which continues even to this day at the pre-agricultural stage. But in middle India economic development took precedence over education which has remained neglected. Whereas the tribal people in the North-East are now ready for a leap forward in development based on the resources which have remained under their command, those in middle India have fallen prey to the adverse processes of development and are facing disorganisation, many of them having been rendered resourceless.

The only reliable indicator of educational progress at present is the level of literacy. But on an average literacy level for the Scheduled Castes and Scheduled Tribes referred to above do not give a real picture in the field. A large number of community are far behind in the scale, some of them does not have a single matriculate even today. The evaluation of community-wise figures which are available is revealing these tacts that Chandigarh which has to its credit the high literacy level for non-Scheduled Caste population amongst the States/ UTs has a poor rating for the Scheduled Castes people and in fact, it has the dubious distinction of reporting the lowest literacy level for any community. The Union Territory of Delhi also shows good for non-Scheduled Castes. But SCs in this state are still struggling. The Union Territory of Pondicherry also shows a similar pattern.

In fact, the real position in the field is still worse. Most of the educated youth specially in the rural areas migrate from the communities for seeking opportunities elsewhere. Consequently, it becomes very difficult to find the overall level of education achieved by a community as indicated by the statistics. It does not give the real picture of the low literacy and education amongst those who are still struggling for their survival against heavy odds in their traditional setting.

Another facet of educational developmental programme is that only those who have succeeded to get education at the primary and secondary levels are in a position to claim liberal support of the State in various forms such as Scholarships at the post-matric level. This process has a cumulative effect resulting in polarisation among between different communities as also within each of them. It is a matter of rethinking that why a substantial section of these people, specially the Scheduled Tribes, cannot avail of the educational facilities even at the primary level. But the weakest link in the educational structure for a variety of reasons is the secondary level. The network of primary schools has been spread extensively, except in remote areas, as a result of the State's special effort for universalisation. Similarly the elite's demand for higher education has led to tremendous growth of higher secondary schools and colleges. But the geographical spread of secondary schools, which is the middle stage, is rather limited and highly uneven. This has serious outcome for education in the tribal areas. Firstly, by this stage the children, become real help to their parents. Therefore, if the child wishes to continue further studies, he has no option except to move out of home and stay away from the family. Secondly, because there is hardly any assistance offered from the State in the form of scholarships and stipends at this stage, they are unable to support their child to send him away from home for education which is impossible dream for ordinary people. The girls' education is the worst hit on account of this phenomenon.

The scheme of scholarships are stipends, which in absolute terms seems to be quite large, leaves much to be desired. For example, the need for continuous revision of pay packet of people in the organised sector, who are not only well above the poverty line but quite easier living has been well recognised and there is an automatic linkage with the cost of living. The economical outlays for meeting that commitment are treated just like a charge on the State exchequer, having precedence over everything else. But the quantum of assistance to the students concerning the weakest sections of our community, where parents can ill afford even a square meal, remains unchanged for years on end even as the prices skyrocket and everyone may agree in principle about the need for a substantial rise.

Inadequate provision for education is not only incongruous in any plane of things but goes against the grain of basic social values. No family can ever consider of putting the needs of its children at a lower priority compared to items of comforts, let alone indulgence in luxuries, unless of course there is a streak of irresponsibility. Tightening of belt is the natural response. The same logic applies with equal force, if not greater, in the management of national economy. But any lapse on this count by managers of the economy with regard to the education of the weaker sections of the community is reprehensible. In their case the advantages of education cannot be refused even for a single day without compromising the basic rights and forcing those already deprived to lifelong drudgery and indignity for no fault of theirs.

Education occupies a central place amongst the safeguards provided for the weaker sections in the Constitution and inadequate provisions in this region deprive them of the due protection as envisaged for them by the founding fathers. Let education be the first charge on the outlays which may be earmarked for the development of Scheduled Castes. In this I am echoing the feeling of the common man who shows it the moment the subject is touched. He cannot find an answer to a very simple question as to why such a vital need of theirs on which depends the future of their children is refused to them when the State can squander huge sums on innumerable schemes of doubtful value. Their representatives in the State Assemblies and Parliament also shows the same feeling but are unable to see through and pierce the web of the formal system in which they are enmeshed.

It may, however, be said here that condition is over where general formulations about education may do. What needs to be attended to are (i) effective coverage of the more difficult regions, (ii) bringing the poorer groups under the educational fold, (iii) making education relevant to the economy of the people and (iv) raising its quality to a level comparable to the new convenience assumed to be the right of exclusive institutions. A strategy has to be worked out with reference to the specific situation of each community or a group therein and for difficult region. Micro planning for the educational development of the Scheduled Castes and Scheduled Tribes has been admitted as an important element in the new education policy. It has to be ensured that it does not become a ritual. The priorities should not be allowed to get mixed up as has happened with a spartan scheme like Operation Blackboard. It is already facing constraints of means even before ordinary blackboards have been provided to bulk of the ordinary schools specially at the tail end. The irony is that it is in the names of the simple schools and under the guise of providing blackboards that many an elite institution have received windfall gains unsolicited. Even though means do appear as a constraint which, however, should not be the case with any State following right priorities, it cannot be witness of those States whose performance in comparison is unsatisfactory ordinarily with regard to the education of the Scheduled Castes and dismal for the weakest amongst them, which cannot be explained in any way but want of concern for this vital sector.

Education is a precious acquisition for enabling members of disadvantaged communities to take advantage to the policy of positive discrimination. The scheme of reservations under the general policy of positive discrimination initially began with employment under Government. Its area has been expanding gradually. The banking industry and the public sector undertakings have by now been fully covered under that policy frame. The policy frame has also been admitted by educational institutions though, in some cases, it is only partial-limited largely to non-academic positions only. The highly professional and scientific condition, however, continue to remain outside its purview.

The review of the progress of representation of the Scheduled Castes in public employment shows that the position has ordinarily improved. However, its pace has been rather uneven. The shortfalls in many regions still remain quite substantial. The representation of the Scheduled Castes in Group D of Central Government services was already above the stipulated level in 2000 and that level has also been attained for ranks in Group C. But the representation for Group A and

B is not satisfactory. The position of employment of Scheduled Castes in the public sector undertaking during this period has also amended and their proportion has moved up at all levels. While the position in Groups C and D is now good, as their representation was reached the stipulated level, the position in Groups A and B continues to be far from satisfaction.

While the principle of positive discrimination has been by and large internalised by the system, it is obvious that there are still some areas of weaknesses which need to be particularly attended to. The representation of the Scheduled Castes at the higher ones in the services continues to be low for which special attempts have to be made. The vertical mobility through promotions is especially tardy due to built-in resistance and a variety of impediments which come in their way and are sometimes even contrived. One of the regretable aspects of implementation of the policy of positive discrimination is that it is generally accepted in a formal way without much regard for the sprit behind it. The result is that even innocuous technical points can be used to deny the rightful due to members of the Scheduled Castes. Sometimes such apparently innocuous measures like introduction of time-bound promotion, appointment to particular pay posts and 'objective' criteria accepted for postings after transfer prove to be inequitous. What is worse, instead of removing the anomalies the authorities tend to stick to their position quoting the rules. Thus, the irritants which needed to be automatically deleted persist and Herculean attempt is required to move the system to make even minor changes.

A number of very simple issues are not attended even at the policy level in Government even though they may have far-reaching implications for employment of members of the Scheduled Castes. For instance, the proportion of the Scheduled Castes in the population is highly variable from one region to another even within the same State. Yet most of the States have not taken the trouble of considering this elementary aspect of the situation and prescribe area-specific reservation quotas for the Scheduled Castes. This is a case of transparent inequity in the name of equity and principles. Another persistent difficulty is the fate of Scheduled Caste candidates at interviews. No action has been taken to ensure that if candidates with the prescribed educational and/or technial qualifications are available they shall not be rejected at an interview. Consequently, qualified candidates remain unemployed while posts reserved for them go abegging. The administration conveniently permits such vacancies to lapse without showing any concern for them. The basic question here is about the validity of reliance on the judgement of an interview board, which meets a candidate just for a few minutes, vis-a-vis his educational credentials which are based on a series of assessments of the same person by the academic system spread over many years.

The most glaring example of bias in interviews came to my notice from none else than the prestigious Jawaharlal Nehru University which is known for its leaning towards the under-privileged. One of their own Scheduled Caste students was awarded dismally low marks in the interview for admission to a higher course even though he had got a first class in the master's examination from the same university and had also scored high marks in the written part of the admission test. The University has since reviewed its procedure to avoid similar inconsistencies. If this can occur in a citadel of learning whose hallmark is rationality and scientific spirit, the stranglehold of vicious tradition and prejudice elsewhere can be easily imagined. Non-action by the States is not a matter of surprise. Nor has one to discover the reason why they have not still formalised the position about fixing the responsibility for fulfilling this social obligation.

Recounting the vicious play of prejudice, the most pernicious example is the blatant bias against those engaged in the 'lowly job' of maintaining cleanliness in certain public sector enterprise. These employees are refused the benefits of organised sector enjoyed by all workers through the devious device of assigning those jobs to contractors. No one seems to be concerned about the fact that those engaged in this crucial service do not have the status of a worker of the enterprise and can be paid exploitative wages taking advantage of their low bargaining capacity and the traditional low rating for their job prevalent in the society.

This shows how even the so-called modern organisations can be insensitive and inhuman dealing with the weakest sections of the community and the system can look on unconcerned. The ostensible plea of the management is their concern about the quality of work in as vital an activity as maintaining minimal standards of cleanliness which, they feel, can be assured only through contract system. This is not acceptable: A management which claims to be rational and modern must follow the practices which it preaches and also follow for other employees like introduction of suitable incentives or organising the work on cooperative lines with a sense of involvement rather than reverting to the tyrannical practices of slave-driving.

Reference has already been made to the differential growth amongst different communities concerning to the Scheduled Castes. This procedure is possibly to get further accentuated as the chances in the larger economy become available to members of the Scheduled Castes equitably. The implications of differential growth for the weaker communities and the late starters are becoming increasingly clear. The representation in the recruitment to the All India Services is highly skewed. A few communities are accounting for bulk of these positions year after year while the bulk of the Scheduled Castes, specially the latter, who are educationally backward cannot claim even a handful; some of them have yet to start the score. The competition for reserved vacancies at the all India level thus is becoming a competition amongst unequals. Same situation is also arising in other States and there is a feeling of discontent, albeit subdued, amongst members of those communities who are unable to compete with the comparatively advanced groups. This issue has been sought to be decided in the States of Meghalaya and Nagaland, which are tribal majority States and governed by tribal elite, by adopting a policy of reservation for comparatively less advanced tribal communities according to the relative strength of their numbers. As the advantages of education reach out to the weaker groups and the distant areas, the first generation educated youth will find it difficult to make a mark even in the limited competition for reserved positions.

It is time that this issue is considered in all its aspects and the less advanced amongst the Scheduled Castes are enabled to enter the public sector through a policy of special positive discrimination in their favour. As far as, scheduling is concerned, it is required to be critically and carefully examined. The Constitution envisages the scheduling of castes, races or tribes as Scheduled Castes, as the case may be, within each State. No provision has been made in the Constitution for a caste, race or tribe being scheduled in the whole country. The reason is that the use of the same nomenclature by caste, race or tribe cannot be taken to be a powerful enough ground for admitting that they include the same people throughout the country. The people using the same name to indicate their caste may occupy completely different positions in the local setting. Consequently, the scheduling of castes, races or tribes, as the case may be, has to be done firmly State by State after considering the qualities of the case for each of them separately. Even here the provision of the Constitution calls for a cautious approach. According to Articles 341 and 342 the President may specify 'the castes, races or tribes or parts of or groups within castes, races and tribes' (emphasis added) as Scheduled Castes in to a State or a Union Territory, as the case may be. Thus even before a caste, race or tribe is to be thought to be scheduled in a State, it has to be observed whether all people throughout the State covered by that name qualify for inclusion in the schedule. It could be a group within the caste or a part of that caste, e.g., those living in a special area who may be eligible for the special dispensation. Reference here may also be made to clause 5 of the Fifth Schedule to the Constitution according to which a law can stand improved through a notification in its application to the entire Scheduled Area in a State or any part thereof.

Thus the Constitution envisages a discriminating and cautious approach on the part of the executive. It is expected that the tribal situation will not be subject to routine and generalised treatment. The case of each community or parts of or groups within the community will be thought with reference to each area in the State so that the legal frame and the State's action for the welfare and advancement of the tribal people are in consonance with the tradition of each group which may vary significantly from one section to another. Any generalised approach with regard to tribal affairs, therefore, is indicative of the unwillingness or unpreparedness of the executive to discharge the responsibility cast on it by the Constitution. Therefore, such an approach is violative of the Constitutional safeguards which each tribal community is expected to enjoy according to the Constitutional scheme. The initial scheduling of the castes and tribes after coming into force of the Constitution followed generally the status assigned to those communities before Independence under the appropriate legal provisions of British India or the Indian States as the case may be. There were some anomalies no doubt. But the situation became quite complex after formation of linguistic States which resulted in bringing together of many areas with different administrative histories under the new States. Consequently, all communities which had been recognised as Scheduled Castes in the former States were mechanically pooled together and put in one list for every of the new province. In those States where the new list retained the association of some communities with the territories of the erstwhile States, there were apparent anomalies some of which were genuine. In this process, which involved substantial assortment of territorial administrative units, a crucial point about the tribal communities – their intimate linkage with a well-defined geographical area – receded in the background and got neglected. The real anomalies, which agitated the people in some areas, were no doubt removed but recognition of all communities in all parts of the new States created many problems alluded to earlier.

The growing incidence of fake claims by other people in the names of the Scheduled Castes, specially the latter, taking profit of similar caste names, surnames, titles, etc., has many adverse effects which should be urgently attended to. For instance, transfer of land in violation of the law can be effected through misrepresentation on either side, e.g., a tribal vendor may be shown as a non-tribal or a non-tribal vendor may claim to be a tribal. The manipulation and even flagrant misuse of the law becomes quite easy with the connivance of the official machinery. In the case of employment the procedure for verification of genuineness of the caste/tribe to which an individual belongs is comparatively more streamlined. It also has the deterrence of penal action in case of forgery. Even then issue of false Scheduled Castes certificates has reached menacing proportions. Therefore, suitable procedures should be evolved to check this growing misuse.

In case of transfer of land by a tribal to a person not residing in the same village, who claims to be a tribal, it may be made obligatory for the vendee to produce a community certificate before the land transfer can be formally effected. The procedure of issue of community certificates for the purposes of employment may be streamlined. For example, all members of the Scheduled Castes may be issued community certificates with computer numbers alongwith their High School Examination certificates. These certificates may be deemed to be the conclusive evidence of the caste/tribe of an individual unless otherwise proved on the similar lines as the date of birth entered in the High School Examination certificates is taken as the conclusive evidence of age for the purposes of entry into service and retirement.

Economy

Measures for the progress of the economic interests of members of the Scheduled Castes have been taken from the very beginning of national planned economic development. However, since the basic premise in the beginning has been that members of these communities would partake in the advantage of general developmental programmes like others in the normal course, special programmes for their progress were in the nature of supplementation. It was thus envisaged that in due course the initial gap could be made good and the handicaps which they were subjected to would be neutralised. This supplementation had to be quite substantial for the areas in view of the lack of infrastructure and their general conditions of underdevelopment. The effect of these programmes was inadequate for two reasons. Firstly, the benefits of general developmental programmes did not percolate to the weaker sections as envisaged. On the other hand the programmes for Scheduled Castes which were expected to supplement the general efforts in effect supplanted them. The position somewhat improved when special programmes were formulated for the weaker sections in general like the marginal farmers and agricultural labourers and disadvantaged areas like the drought prone regions. A substantial section of these target groups belongs to the Scheduled Castes. Accordingly, a proportion of benefits has been earmarked for these groups. Even though there are numerous hurdles in the way of due share really accruing to the Scheduled Castes, particularly the later, the position is significantly better here compared to that in other programmes. However, even these programmes are not considered as adequate for the task in view of the inherent handicaps of the situation, both social and economic for the Scheduled Castes which begins with the Sixth Plan represents a watershed in the strategy of development of the Scheduled Castes, notwithstanding within the conventional frame. Here was an attempt to consider the issues which associated with the welfare and progress of these communities in their totality and work out programmes cutting through the formal trappings of the system with a clear objective of bringing members of these communities to the level of the rest of the people within a settled time frame.

The special plans include a variety of poverty instigation programmes, minimum needs programme, employment generation schemes, integrated rural development, individual schemes of different Ministries/Departments and at least supplemental effort under the TSP and SCP. The indicators of achievements under all these schemes are in terms of the economical outlay and expenditure and the number of beneficiaries. The increasing economical allocations are indicative of the fact that poverty mitigations in general and economic progress of Scheduled Castes in particular have been high on the agenda at least in a formal sense. The strategy of the TSP and the SCP have brought into the light the issues of their development.

Today we are at least in a position to attempt a realistic review of the acquirements and also identify inadequacies in the attempt, thus bringing this vital national issue out of the realm of vague generalisations and good intentions. The outlays for tribal and Scheduled Castes development had a quantum jump after the introduction to these strategies. They have continued to rise steadily thereafter even though they still require substantial stepping up and putting the system to order. The cumulative effect of all the programmes which mentioned above taken together gets reflected in the number of persons who still continue to subsist below the poverty line. According to the figures the proportion of people below the poverty line had reduced considerably by the end of the Ninth Plan. This is enough notwithstanding the correct numbers specially in the context of the continuously rising prices and a rather stationary poverty line which can be reviewed only at long intervals. The reports of various schemes shows that the total number of beneficiaries is quite impressive. However, it represents the general total of beneficiaries under different developmental programmes. This sum does not shows the actual number of beneficiaries due to overlap. And then one cannot really know what happens after the beneficiaries get the assistance. Moreover, the processes of deprivation rooted in the national economic system are relentlessly pushing bulk of the people subsisting in the unorganised sector towards the margin. In this way one can never knows how many persons have crossed the poverty line in the reverse direction.

Poverty is not a matter of only figures and absolute numbers. It is a dynamic phenomenon relatable to the national socio-economic milieu which prevails at a given time. Therefore, even though the financial conditions may improve in absolute terms, the increasing disparities in the country would endanger the feeling of relative deprivation and it is made more and more acute and pervasive.

Even after discounting the above observation the achievements are enough specially where the targets are specific and quantifiable. It is satisfactory that most of the landless people are reported to have been allotted house-sites; they can now have a piece of land which they can call as their own—a great psychological boost. This is in striking contrast to the earlier situation where many of these disinherited people had to accept conditions of near serfdom simply because there is not a single place belonging to them to stand on. The human institution of bonded labour which had been pushed under the carpet and forgotten after a bevy of laws were passed by the States after Independence has been brought into the open. The worst forms of the practice now are exceptions which, however, cannot be condoned. Yet, it can be said that ordinarily bondage is now more in the form of adverse economic relationships rather than physical duress, even though some abominable cases do come to light occasionally. It is gratifying to note when people in some remote areas acknowledge that the moneylenders have disappeared for the simple cause that their investment is no longer safe. Even though these are exceptional instances, they are important because they are indicative of what can be achieved even within the existing frame. The laws which are enacted for the safety of the poor have provided open legitimacy to their demands and the detractors have been on the wrong side of the fence. The role of social activists who have taken advantage of this situation and mobilised the people on specific issues has made a important contribution in many of these cases.

It has already been made clear that Scheduled Castes have advanced in owning lands. The programme of irrigation wells has yielded important results even though the number falls too short of the big potential which can be developed. The general salary level in many areas has risen though not commensurate with the people's due entitlement. The provision of minimum wages has helped the poor in this regard by providing them a privilege for which they can fight even though the machinery for its implementation is almost non-existent.

Rural electrification has reached out to some of the most interior regions which covers all the villages in some regions. The States have taken special measures to take electricity lines to predominantly Scheduled Caste habitations even though, at times, the coverage may be notional, limited to a single pole-light which may not burn. Although there made no improvements in remote areas accessibility yet network is being extensive. A large number of habitations, hamlets and villages have been provided hand pumps even though some may not work occasionally. These include the positive side of the situation which gives one hope even though the gloomy side is also quite pervasive.

There being more in the nature of processes rather than were packages of developmental programmes is a distinguishing feature of TSP and SCP. As our review shows even though there has been a spectacular step up of economical outlays and there are important achievements in some activities, specially in comparison to poor performance of the earlier period, the inherent potential of the new strategy has not been realised. The achievements fall too short of expectations and are rather inadequate compared to the work ahead for securing members of these communities a place of similarity in the national economy particularly in the preference of the emerging situation in which the relative position of these communities in the national economy has not improved, may, rather have deteriorated. It seems that some visible gains to small groups are taken as evidence of general progress and highlighted as such which create a wrong impression and a sense of complacency. It is probably this psychological make-up that explains why even after formulation of workable strategy there are serious lapses in their follow-up over a period of time and even simple operational details are not attended for years but from one Plan to another. It is an exasperating experience to witness the monotonous routine year after year—review of situation, identification of problems and proposed action plans — without moving forward in any real sense.

Let us begin with the first basic premise of the new strategy, viz., the welfare and progress of the Scheduled Castes as a national task which has to be distributed by all citizens according to their respective positions in life. A beginning had clearly to be made by Government organisations each of which is charged with some responsibility or the other in the broader national life. The Union Government did take the welcome initiative and the States formulated the TSPs and SCPs. But it is distressing to observe that even single Ministry at the Centre has not even initiated this exercise in its true and real spirit even after more than two decades of the first minute recorded by the Prime Minister in this regard in 1974. None of them has prepared a perspective for the development of the Scheduled Castes in their respective sectors which should appropriately comprise, (i) the present status, (ii) a statement of special problems and the tasks ahead, (iii) the attempts made by the State Governments and (iv) the plans drawn by the Ministry to ensure accomplishment of the tasks. At best some mechanical exercises have been undertaken and token outlays are showed against programmes relatable to the development of the Scheduled Castes. When the mass which the Central Ministries have gathered are looked the only conclusion which can be drawn is that there is not only want of will power but disinclination to admit the responsibility for this national work.

The assistance of the Central Government has to be supplemental for the welfare and progress of the Scheduled Tribes in accordance with the provisions of the Constitution. The recurrent refused with this premise, which had been specifically noted by the Shilu AO Committee, was sought to be rectified in the Tribal Sub-Plans by giving guidelines and adoption of appropriate procedures. The same principle was later extended to the welfare and advancement of the Scheduled Castes in the Special Component Plans. The States were expected to prepare a comprehensive plan of action on the basis of what could be provided from the general State Plan. This basal investment was to be suitably supplemented by the concerned Central Ministries in their respective areas of responsibility. At last the nodal Ministry incharge of the Scheduled Castes was expected to fill in the gaps through the Special Central Assistance. The basic introduction of this scheme that the Special Central Assistance should become supplemental to the State's attempt has not been achieved.

While the general position is as stated above, the particular situation varies significantly from one State to another. Moreover, there is considerable difference between the position about the Special Component Plans and the Tribal Sub-Plans. The expenditures for the SCPs in the State Plan continue to be determined on an ad hoc basis depending on the initiative of individuals and Departments in each State. There is scarcely any linkage with the Special Central Assistance. Accordingly there is no mechanism to ensure that the Special Central Assistance for the Scheduled Castes is supplemental to the State's effort in real senses. In the case of the Tribal Sub-Plans the position is somewhat better. While separate budget subheads have been created for the Tribal Sub-Plans in all the States. Separate demands for TSPs has been established by some of the states. This is the first step towards ensuring that the SCA is additional. But there is no monitoring of this vital aspect even though it does not require any special effort except a clear perception about the objectives particularly because all items and relevant figures have got to be reflected regularly in the budgets of the concerned States.

The indiscriminate clubbing together of all types of programmes under one demand has an too much deleterious effect. The capital intensive projects are easy to execute and can devour all funds – whatever their size. But programmes of real significance to the tribal people contain small outlays which are difficult to plan and still more difficult to execute. The success of such programmes depends their widespread and large canvas. But the irony is that shortfalls in such programmes are welcome to any one – they ease the ways and means position of the State and also provide alibi to the administration when resource position is tight for non-action in difficult areas which saves them even the bother of making some attempt even for the good of form.

The preliminary analysis based upon the most favourable interpretation of the figures given in the Plan documents of the eight States referred to above and those given by the Ministry of Welfare shows that a substantial part of the Special Central Assistance, if not the entire assistance, released to the States during the Ninth Five Year Plan except for Himachal Pradesh has remained unused. A detailed analysis is bound to express a worse situation. It also may be added here that firm budgeted figures are available only in the cases of Andhra Pradesh, Gujarat, Madhya Pradesh, and Maharashtra. The figures for Orissa and Rajasthan are not based on authorised statements. So far as Bihar is concerned the figures given even in the same document are discordant and are not quite reliable. In other states where the budgeting mechanism is not proper the position is not likely to be very different.

It is noted that even the preliminary steps to operationalise the supplementation principle have not been taken in most cases in the concern of special Central Assistance for the Scheduled Castes. The allocations for the Special Component Plans are generally notional and sometimes may relate to programmes which may have no relevance for Scheduled Caste development. The Special Central Assistance has no linkages whatsoever with the State Sector programmes. In sum, bulk of the Special Central Assistance, both for the Scheduled Castes, during the Sixth Plan period has not been used to supplement the States attempts for the welfare and progress of these communities. It has been used in such a way as to reduce the State's own commitment for the development of the Scheduled Castes and Scheduled Tribes. It is thus a violation of a cardinal principle enshrined in the Constitution.

Now, the State Governments may be asked to make a supplemental outlay equivalent to the amount which remained unspent during the Ninth Plan which may be over and above their Tenth Plan outlay to be used exclusively for growing the level of elementary education in the tribal areas and should be over and above the outlays already provided for elementary education during the Tenth Plan.

At this stage I may invite attention to a vital issue belonging to reintroduction of the matching principle in a few schemes concerning tribal development. Even though the quantum of assistance involved is small at present, it is crucial matter since it is not in keeping with the basic premise of the supplementation principle. According to the first proviso to Article 275(1) of the Constitution the Union Government are obliged to provide whatever economical assistance is compulsory after the need of a programme for tribal welfare has been established irrespective of the fact whether the State Government are able to contribute something towards it or not. It is within the frame of this Constitutional scheme that the methodology for determining the outlays for the Tribal Sub-Plan has been worked out. The base investment is determined first from within the State's own resources. Once this outlay is fixed keeping in view the situation in each case, the Central Government are obliged to make the necessary means available through the Special Central Assistance to reach the agreed tasks in tribal welfare. The matching principle, irrespective of the share of the State, makes the Special Central Assistance contingent on the State's ability and willingness to contribute and not the merit of the proposal which is in infringement of the stipulation of the Constitution which is referred to above.

The matching principle is not only violative of the Constitution in purely technical terms but is also inequitous to those tribal communities which belong to the financially weaker States. The people belonging to tribal castes would get no benefit of the national scheme because these states may not be able to provide their share of investment in the scheme. On the other hand, the economically stronger States may be able to draw upon the same on the strength of their contribution even though that investment may not be required. As stated elsewhere, any generalised formulations as this about tribal welfare are also violative of the basic tenets of the Constitution about tribal welfare. The matching principle refuses the tribual people the benefit of the safeguard provided for them in the Constitution.

The tribal cause is hurted by this scheme in another important way. If the States know that they will be obliged to find means later for attracting Central funds for certain schemes for the welfare of the tribes it is quite natural for them to keep that in view in the course of the first exercise for determining the outlays for the welfare of tribes itself. Thus every State will have to keep something apart for that contingency. In other words, the outlay for tribal welfare will be kept at a lower level intentionally compared to what the State means can otherwise be expected to provide. It is not so much the fact that a somewhat smaller provision is made which is significant here. What is to be objected is that an exercise which is supposed to be objective gets vitiated. It is also possible that while keeping the outlays artifically low the States will be tempted to lower the same to the maximum having no relationship to what could be reasonable in the normal conditions. In this process objectivity in determining the States' attempts for tribal welfare gets a back seat and the outcome would depend on how different partners fare in what becomes a war of wits, an undesirable situation in the context of the value attached to the cause of the tribal people in the Constitution. As will be argued later, the nodal organisations belonging tribal welfare at present are rather weak who do not always get success in pressing even what is desirable and fully justified on plain computing. This rationalisation of under provision, even though implicit, makes for compromising their position in vital deliberations about determining the Plan attempt.

It is not also plausible to note that the Union Government were satisfied by the mere issue of an order extending the scope of the Special Central Assistance to the whole tribal population without any preliminary exercise or even follow-up action to make sure that this assistance was tied up with the States' own programmes and did not result in supplanting the States' own attempt outside the Sub-Plan areas. If the analysis presented earlier is any pointer, it should not be surprising if this would have happened on a significant scale.

The provision of outlays for the welfare and progress of the Scheduled Castes and Scheduled Tribes by the State Departments and the Union Ministries which have been discussed above was hardly the first compulsory step in the direction of preparation of a comprehensive plan for their welfare and progress. Therefore, the type of anomalies and even distortions noted earlier, especially in the case of the Tribal Sub-Plans, could perhaps be hoped in any first exercise. That they have not only persisted but have received formal approval, albeit implicit is distressing. Moreover, the exercise of quantification of outlays by different Departments has become mechanical with little concern about what meaning the sum total of all those little bits makes for the concerned people. The right course after the first assessment of what in concrete terms was being done by each Department through the disaggregation exercise should have been to reverse that process and determine the total attempt for the development of the Scheduled Castes and Scheduled Tribes keeping in view (i) the position of their economy, (ii) the difference between the levels of development of the Scheduled Castes and Scheduled Tribes and the rest of the community, (iii) the rate of growth for the national economy or the State economy as a whole, and (iv) the time period within which members of the Scheduled Castes and Scheduled Tribes could be expected to catch up with the rest of the people. Thus the rate of growth for the people who start with a handicap both in terms of the level of their economy and the socioeconomic constraints had to be higher than the rate of growth of the National/State economy as a whole.

This approach was not denied in principle given by the Planning Commission for the Tribal Sub-Plans beginning with the Sixth Five Year Plan and for the Special Component Plans beginning with the Seventh Plan. The States were asked to work out the overall outlays for the development of the Scheduled Castes and Scheduled Tribes separately. They were also asked to determine the sectoral composition of those outlays in accordance with the needs of the development of these communities. It is sorrowful that no action was taken in this regard nor do they seem to be ready at the moment for any such exercise. Since the Government of India are already convinced about the need for the change in the process of planning for the welfare and progress of the Scheduled Castes and Scheduled Tribes. I can only reiterate the same and state that it is high time that this crucial step is taken by the Government so that a real beginning can be made for preparing developmental plans for the Scheduled Castes and Scheduled Tribes in consonance with the spirit of the Constitution.

A significant character of the new strategy was the realisation that conventional developmental programmes could not provide the full answer to the complex difficulties which members of the Scheduled Castes faced. In the concern of the Scheduled Tribes the issues are more complicated even today because of the distinctive social and economic features of their situation. These people have a holistic view of life which cannot be neatly dissected into personal, social, religious and financial slices which may be separately handled. Accordingly it is not possible to make a distinction between the so-called developmental and non-developmental facets of administration. They are interwoven in an extreme distinguishable manner and one without the other may have no meaning, nay, may even become dysfunctional. For instance, unless effective measures are taken for safety of land, its development will make the tribal still more vulnerable as added value of developed lands inflames the greed of others while he himself is at odds to manage the same with his traditional abilities and restricted resources. Any attempt to increase production is without much meaning in a situation there where the tribal does not get even a fraction of reasonable market price of what he is already producing and standing crops may have to be sold in advance to discharge the debts incurred during the lean season. The offer of casual wage employment in forestry cannot interest a people whose traditional rights for meeting the daily requirements from the neighbouring forests and collection the MFP are being refused. How can a people be aware about the benign nature of the State when their first contact with the formal system is marked by the non-recognition of what they cherish as their tradition, nay, at times even branding them as unlawful or unethical? And how can an administration, which is wielding tremendous authority by quality of its inherent power and also the contradictions of the situation in which the tribal people are pushed on the wrong side, be hoped to function in the interest of the people especially when those who man it are sent to these areas without any consideration of their personal sensitivity and other qualities and, not infrequently, as a matter of punishment?

It is cleared by the review that the Sub-Plan strategy for tribal development was hoped to take care of the special situation in tribal areas. While the Tribal Sub-Plans were hoped to provide the major thrust by way of needed investment on the economic front, the provisions under the Fifth Schedule to the Constitution were to be used for the compulsory administrative thrust. However, all tribal majority areas were not covered by the Fifth Schedule which seemed to be compulsory in the new context. Accordingly the Fifth Schedule to the Constitution was reformed in 1976 to empower the President to grow the Schedule Areas.

In the 'Statement of Objects and Reasons' placed before Parliament at the time of the introduction of the Bill to reform the Fifth Schedule to the Constitution it was mentioned that with a view to intensifying development of tribes effort in the Five Year Plan all areas with more than 50 per cent tribal concentration, besides the existing Scheduled Areas, had been delineated in different States and Union Territories. Particular programmes had been prepared for these areas under the Tribal Sub-Plans. It was further added: The Fifth Schedule to the Constitution are accorded by the Sub-Plan. Highest priority to elimination of exploitation including tackling the problems of land alienation, bonded labour, indebtedness, etc. makes special provision for the administration of tribal areas and provides a broad and flexible frame for effective legal and administrative action. The powers under the Fifth Schedule can be used for effective implementation of developmental programmes and promptly tackling the difficulties of exploitation in different forms... While bulk of the Sub-Plan area is covered under the Fifth Schedule some areas are outside. This presents an anomalous situation because effective simultaneous action cannot be taken throughout the Sub-Plan area. That the area presently covered under the Fifth Schedule may be rationalised so that the Scheduled Area may cover the entire Sub-Plan area in these States is, therefore, considered desirable.

In pursuance of the above objectives the Scheduled Regions in seven of the eight States under the Fifth Schedule were rationalised by suitably extending them and further they were made coterminous with the tribal majority areas covered under the TSPs during the Fifth Plan. Till date, the exercise taken up in A.P. remains incomplete. The additional tribal majority areas in these States which were brought under the TSP later during the Sixth Plan, however, have so far remained outside the Fifth Schedule. Moreover, the question of scheduling the areas of tribal majority in other States which did not have any Scheduled Area, except Tripura, has not even been taken up.

While rationalisation of the Schedule Areas has to some extent remained incomplete. It is distressing that even the first step towards effective legal and administrative action as envisaged under the new strategy and especially mentioned in the 'Statement of Objects and Reasons' referred to above using the special provision of the Fifth Schedule has not been taken even after so many years of the amendment of the Constitution specifically for that aim. For about a decade a comprehensive Regulation for the Scheduled Areas of Madhya Pradesh has been under active consideration of the Central and the State Government now. As a result the administrative structure has grown phenomenally in a routine fashion as the level of economical investment had risen rapidly during and after the Fifth Plan itself. The *ad hoc* measures and scattered attempts to rationalise and integrate the existing institutions have resulted in a still bigger confusion. New organisations have been established with a wider charter but earlier institutions could not be disbanded. The single line of authority sought to be established with the creation of Integrated. The sectoral authorities continue to function independently tribal Development Projects (ITDPs) has been a non-starter. In different personnel were continued to be attracted by tribal areas with rare exceptions, and not infrequently are saddled with wrong persons as a matter of punishment postings with ominous consequences for the good of the tribal people. In sum, the administrative situation in the tribal areas has become worse after the TSPs were launched.

The position in relation to the priorities accepted in the programmes for the welfare and progress of the Scheduled Castes, specially the latter, is unhappy one. The new strategy for tribal development rightly accorded the highest priority to elimination of exploitation which has followed by programmes aimed at building up the inner strength of the community. Economic programmes were about to disappear in a natural manner. This scheme of priorities was not followed in actual practice. In reality even though some measures were initiated for elimination of exploitation these did not acquire the due primacy in the scheme of development. It is the subject of pity that elimination of exploitation as an item of the highest priority does not find a mention even as a principle in subsequent Plan documents and, what more, has been glossed over at the national level. The most crucial facet of the situation thus has remained largely neglected.

TWELVE

Identity in the New Millennium

Delhi Seminar

The first national seminar on Dalit Identity in the New-Millennium was organised in Delhi University on June 25, 2000. It was attended by union ministers, governors, secretaries to the Government of India and states, academicians, intellectuals, sociologists, historians, judges and social activists. Delegates from all over India participated in the seminar in the University campus. Earlier a keynote address was discussed at length and the participants expressed their views on the future of the Dalits in the New Millennium.

The speakers concentrated on the socio-economic problems of the Dalits and focussed their attention for establishing a casteless egalitarian society within the constitutional and democratic set up. It suggested ways and means for their proper education, social justice and economic betterment and reviewed the progress and achievements during the last 5 decades or so. As a developmental planning strategy this seminar emphasised the abolition of poverty and ignorance and appealed to the Planning Commission and the Centre to prepare a National Policy for socio-economic development of the Dalits.

The seminar took a serious note of the widespread terrorism which was a great threat to humanity and democracy. Though fight against global terrorism is going on, but the problem has posed grave danger to several countries like U.S.A. and India. For the last five decades or so India is facing and fighting terrorists.

India as an emerging nation is seriously engaged and

concerned with the eradication of poverty, fight against hunger, as well as centuries old social ills. The noblest ideals of the great visionaries and fighters for national freedom were to ensure for the country certain fundamental rights and to safeguard the interests of the weaker sections and to guarantee liberty for all citizens irrespective of race, caste and creed. Architects of our Constitution have talked and provided fundamental rights and human freedom as permanent and inalienable.

The world community, rich or poor more advanced or in the process of making developments is much concerned with global peace, prosperity and liberty. India being the largest democracy in the world has the gravest problem of population explosion. Growing population to alarming proportions has posed dangers to our planning mechanism. In clear words the very purpose of planning is being defeated. In the keynote past and present of Dalits was analysed and suggestions for future made.

Though this is an age of science and technology, computer skills and automation, but a vast majority of our Depressed Classes still live a miserable life, and have no access to education and even jobs. They face large number of problems, disabilities and disadvantages of all sorts-social, economic and educational, and have to struggle for existence. Our Constitution provides and empowers them for enjoying preferential treatment, besides, sharing in the Democratic Institutions and governance. But a large number of people still remain in dire need of employment, and social equality and social justice constantly denied to them because of their ignorance and disunity.

Dalit awakening actually emerged in India when Phule started his pioneer work of education and social reforms. Dr. Ambedkar remembered Phule (1 827-1890) as the "Greatest Shudra of Modern India, who made the lower classes of Hindus conscious of their slavery to the higher classes, and who preached the gospel that for India, social democracy was more vital than independence from foreign rule." A new era of social democracy had begun during the time of Phule, and the cycle was completed by Dr. Ambedkar.

We all are aware that with the growth of nationalism, in the beginning of the 20th century, a new chapter began in the Constitutional History of India. Patriotic feelings gave rise to humanism, liberalism and individual freedom. It was so because the nationalist forces worked for social reforms, for enlightenment, for education and modernization. They advocated the cause for industrial and economic development. This was the tune, when India's National Struggle was being led by the Moderates.

But very little was done in the earlier days by the nationalist forces, regarding the centuries old inhuman conditions and appalling poverty of the untouchables and the Dalits as a class.

A National Agenda for their economic betterment in the New Millennium must be prepared by the Planning Commission. Roughly the caste Hindus control 90% of the country's wealth which is concentrated in their hands. The economic concentration, including control of agricultural land has certainly been monopolized by the upper castes, due to caste system and practice of untouchability. Unfortunately, there is no socio-economic plan for their betterment and everything is on paper.

For centuries untouchability was not merely a religious observance, but it was an economic exploitation in the larger context. It created a master class and a servile class. Nearly one third of slave India's population, divided into castes and sub-castes, was kept and forced to do dirty jobs.

According to John Gunther: "Caste is as old as India. It is the inner citadel of Hinduism. It is the institution which makes India unique, the device breaking up Indians into fixed categories that has no approximation elsewhere in the world. Every Hindu is born into a caste and his caste determines his religious, social, economic, domestic life from the cradle to the grave. No man may leave his caste, except to be expelled. It is impossible to progress from caste to caste. This device of partition, and exploitation has been very much true and alive till today."

We have been witness to social boycott and social degradation, exploitation and discrimination of all kinds; disabilities, and injustice done to the humble people for nearly 5000 years. And it is very amazing that within a very short span of time of fifty years, this crushed and unprivileged section of the society has risen to meet all the challenges faced by the nation, though untouchability, inequality, hard and harsh social evils and practices still continue; and are not fully abolished, particularly in rural areas, the feudal village set up.

From the time immemorial the majority of India's millions of untouchables, the depressed and oppressed people, the landless labour, the traditional artisans, have been living in miserable conditions in villages, like slaves and serfs, animals and wretched creatures, constantly being ill-treated and suppressed in the hands of the dominating communities the Brahmins, the Kshatriyas and the Vaishyas. Age old slavery and poverty, socio-economic ills, superstitions and nomadic character still seem visible in society and there is not much change in their socio-economic status. There are claims and counter claims, regarding percentage of progress achieved, but except a small number of people of a few communities the condition of Dalits is still miserable.

Great personalities like R.C. Dutt and Dada Bhai Nauroji spoke about the poverty of the country in a very impressive manner, but the British Rule hardly strived for economic betterment, till we got freedom. Whatever village industries and crafts existed in the pre-independence India have been ruined because of new technology. This ruination of cottage industries is really alarming.

It is evident in the beginning of 20th century, no political heavy weight raised his voice against the tyranny, oppression and injustice done to the Dalits in the hands of the so called upper castes, till the entry of Mahatma Gandhi, who returned from South Africa in 1914 fighting against Racial

Discrimination, and struggling for restoring human rights to the people of Indian origin.

Dr. Ambedkar pointed out that the Hindus were the masters, and the untouchables were slaves. And slavery is kept alive on the cradles of caste hierarchy and practice of untouchability. We must draw the attention of our planners, economists and social scientists to these facts. There is no exclusive National Agenda, a National Policy or a Blueprint for the all-round development of the Depressed Classes till date. Everything is in piece meal.

During the last fifty years or so, nearly half of the rural Dalit population has left their ancestral homes, in search of jobs in industrial towns, as they don't have land for farming. It is a horrible situation that majority of landless labour and artisans belonging to Depressed Classes are running from rural areas in search of gainful employment, rather to die of poverty and hunger and remain oppressed forever in villages.

Many communities and high societies, have touched the sky in socio-economic, cultural and educational fields, whereas the landless labour, traditional artisans and self employed class of the village craftsmen all belonging to Depressed Castes have lost their ancestral occupations, because of high technology and rapid industrialization. Faulty planning and industrialisation, from a feudal agrarian system to an industrial society have resulted in creating a class of unemployed and jobless people belonging to Depressed Classes. In Europe also during 18th and 19th century, this has happened in the wake of industrialisation. But unemployment and underemployment was not so appalling there, as in India. In Europe and America there is individual liberty, there are ample jobs and opportunities. There is no concentration of economic and political power. There is population control.

Our economists, bureaucrats and social activists, and even the politicians, know well the state of affairs of Depressed Class people. We all know the fate of the village Leather Industry, the ruination of Khadi and Handloom Industry which employed millions of Dalits. But today in small and big cities these crafts have been taken over by the upper caste people due to money factor and treated no more impure work. The mechanized farming and introduction of improved tools have forced the landless Dalit labour and hereditary class of weavers, leather workers and other artisans to migrate from the villages. The rapid industrial growth and concentration of economic power in the hands of upper castes in a modern society have totally ruined the decentralised village economic structure, which was giving gainful employment to the skilled Dalit craftsmen. Industrialisation has caused complete ruination of the village industries. This is happening in India for the last five-six decades. The change of jobs have not abolished caste system and untouchability.

We are the largest Democracy, rather most successful, in the world. The contribution of the Depressed Classes in making the democratic system a grand success is well known. Politicians do exploit and then forget and neglect them after taking their precious votes. In an old civilization like India, the democratic system and the socio-economic disparities cannot go together for long, that too in modern times. Social scientists believe that, there would have been a bloody revolution if reservations had constitutionally not been granted. Concessions and job reservations have not benefited all, but only a few persons and families have got better opportunities. Since the administration and implementation of reservation policy was in the hands of caste Hindus, and they were not honest in implementing the reservations, that is why ST/SC representation is very poor even after 56 years of Independence. There is still more to be done. But who is going to do? This should be a matter of great concern to everybody. It is all in the nation's wider interest.

In the contemporary social pressures and problems, the education system needs total overhauling. For Dalits, the backward poors, education should have been free with certain packages. Even special institutions, special courses and special examination boards have not been created for them.

What is needed is that all our democratic organizations, educational institutions, scientific and social research centres are empowered to suggest ways and means to bring social change. A firm determination and a National Policy can contribute much in this regard.

In the new Millennium, it is important to make an analytical study, and document the past and present problems faced by India's Dalits. It is a big challenge before the state, the society and the elite.

The general feeling of the planners besides technocrats and scientists is 'that the mass education and advancement of Science and Technology alone can solve the problems of hunger, poverty, illiteracy and ignorance, superstition, deprivation and unemployment of a vast resource running to waste in a country, inhabited by the majority of degraded, downtrodden, exploited and crushed people, who are still not fully aware of their basic human rights.'

In our media and intellectual circle, this view is often expressed that the Plan Schemes have proved to be a hoax so far Dalits are concerned. There is a lot of paper work at the implementation level almost misleading and confusing, full of jugglery of statistics and quite unbelievable figures, if a close and deep study is made. Former Prime Minister Rajiv Gandhi said that out of every one Rupee spent only fifteen paise reach the grassroots for the developmental activities.

There are a large number of residential houses built for the Dalits in villages and urban areas that too only on paper. If somewhere, some honest officer has constructed such dwelling units, these have been found unfit for human living. Similarly there are thousands of improved handlooms and Janata Dhoties distributed and crores of rupees spent on Khadi. But to whom the benefits have gone? There are coaching centres, computer training institutes, formal education schemes, youth camps, awakening programmes. But many of them do not exist. The money is distributed between NGOs and the concerned official machinery and their agents.

The corrupt and influential people grab developmental money. They are not questioned seriously as they are in power, as they are the elected people in social life. It seems the dream of establishing an egalitarian society is still a mirage. Who is responsible for these ills? There are hardly effective watchdog committees to supervise and control such developmental activities. We got the levers of power from the colonial hands the Imperial System. But we have forgotten to create our own system. We have only followed the colonial pattern. There are State and National Level Commissions, but full of tired and retired people who are hardly aware of the problems of the crushed and uprooted classes.

Mostly in big cities, untouchability is not to be found in practice but seen every where. The Dalits are still visibly neglected and discriminated. They can be identified from their very look. They reside mostly in city slums, J.J. clusters and shanty huts. For the newcomers pavements places near garbages, railway lines, government parks are the safest available places for dwelling. It is happening in all big and medium sized cities. It is a big problem. Promises of proper housings are repeated in manifestoes, but very little comes out. The root cause of emerging slum culture is uprooting of our traditional village crafts due to mechanization of agriculture and industrial activities. Formerly the Dalits were not paid for their labour. They were bonded or forced labour of the Zamindars, the situation has changed now.

Our MIT trained economists and planning managers hardly think about the Dalit masses. So also our foreign trained technocrats. Even the root cause of migration from rural sector, has not been fully surveyed and studied. When Economics of Poverty of a limited area can won a Noble Prize, why nobody is touching this topic? Our JNU brand economists and leftist thinkers have hardly any interest in the Dalit and poor masses except obtaining degrees and joining Bureaucracy. What they have done to overcome the poverty?

Politicians create and patronize slums. Civil engineers

and contractors pocket money. Police take bribe from the squatters, and ultimately in the cycle of rehabilitation and planning for the poor, administration is forced to provide a chain of liquor shops to weaken the urge of revolt, or any possible social revolution. And in the final run, the area becomes a Potential Vote Bank, and the Dalits kept in good mood and misguided.

During the last four decades, country had faced political and social instability for various reasons. The popular slogans of Garibi hatao, Hum do hamare do coined by a certain political system have not yielded desired results. The elimination of poverty, establishment of equality and social justice is still a dream. We blamed British Rule for all our socio-economic ills, but Chaturvarna system, the untouchability, the caste inequality or caste distinctions, resulting in wide scale social backwardness and economic poverty was not at all created by the Englishmen. It was the creation of the Brahminical Order in league with the other dominating castes belonging to the feudal land lordism and the trading communities.

In services virtually, the caste system, the hateful behavioural pattern of caste Hindus, practice of untouchability, victimization and class hatred which look reduced and abolished have increased manyfold. Now the Dalits are being victimized and harassed not openly, but through other vicious discreet methods: with the help of the pen as they feel their present and future prospects are being ruined. Even in day-today working, they are being mentally tortured. Instead in the name of general and routine checking, they are subject to close watch. They are often allotted rough and undignified work. Bad postings have become a new form of victimization. Promotions, overseas scholarships have become a tough matter. For younger Generation efforts should be made to provide them higher education and job opportunities. But that is not being alone. These days, unless somebody enjoys patronage of elected representatives and brings pressure, he can easily be finished. Therefore, one has to be alert at every stage.

Preferential treatment has created a psycho-fear amongst the caste Hindus. According to a Survey made, the Dalits have done commendable services, with total dedication and hard work wherever they have been posted. Their leadership role in the nation's life is quite appreciable.

Several contemporary Indian and western scholars have studied the current problems of the Dalits, but unfortunately they do not trace the past history of their sufferings, disabilities, miseries and misfortunes, which were man made and created by the Brahminic scriptures. The Brahminic socio-economic pattern from village to city level, needs overhauling. Depressed Classes require wider economic empowerment, social justice and equal treatment.

In this age of science and technology, one should not care for the Scriptures and Samhitas at all. Most of the writings are viced and prejudiced. They are all against humanity and natural justice. The positive way of doing things is to ignore and forget all about them. Our Constitution and Democratic system is our strength. It is strange we think of advanced science and technology and simultaneously believe in age-old superstitions and religious practices. Democracy, education and science arc our strength. Religion or faith is a right of every individual.

Under the provisions of the Constitution, abolition of untouchability is a Great victory of the Dalit ex-untouchables, as promoted and practiced by the caste Hindus for centuries. Virtually, isolation and segregation of a vast majority of people has ended, though in rural areas and specially in backward districts it is still alive, in one form or the other. The minds and hearts of the caste Hindus have not changed. Villages in Bihar, Eastern UP, Rajasthan, Gujarat and MP are still in the grip of untouchability.

The media, our social activists, scientists and social scientists can contribute in proving and restoring social justice to the Dalits. Dalit authors and journalists should also contribute, through their creative writings in this direction.

In the New Millennium, the future of the new generation

of the Dalits seems not so much bright. They are taking much interest in their higher education. Success depends on hard work and right type of education. Certainly, the youngsters have a scientific outlook, and keen interest in the advanced technology, computer skills and automation processes. In social sciences and humanities also, they take keen interest. They are eager to know their past, and are trying to brighten their present and future as well. They are doing well in All India Competitions, engineering, technology and medical sciences. They certainly need support and guidance. More patronage and jobs is the need of the hour.

Awareness and alertness among the Dalit intellectuals is increasing. They have risen in revolt for their rights, social equality and social justice. The demand for sharing in governance has increased. But where are the jobs? Placement of more and more Scheduled Castes boys and girls in services has become a problem.

As said earlier a National Level New Millennium Programme for social justice and economic betterment of the Dalits should be prepared and implemented by the Union Government, so early so better and permanent broad based mechanism created.

To repeat again in the sphere of education, the Dalits should be provided free and compulsory education in all disciplines upto university level, with full financial help and special coaching. Actually, they should be adopted by the educational institutions in good spirit-both the meritorious and average ones. They should be provided special coaching in science, technology, computer and higher management courses with a provision of a higher percentage of admissions.

Unrealistic ill planning should be stopped. Existing plans should be reviewed and analyzed. Our intellectuals and social activists of repute must be consulted and problems solved.

The proceedings of this National Seminar will go a long way in building a strong and prosperous nation, as well as in promoting emotional integration.

World Conference against Racism

UN sponsored World Conference Against Racism (WCAR) was held at Durban from August 31 to September 7, 2001 where some NGOs and individuals tried to internationalise the caste issue and the socio-economic problems of the Dalits. But it was not so easy attempting to end 4 to 5 thousand years old, religiously sanctioned and feudalistically backed caste discrimination against Dalits. Buddha was perhaps the foremost to voice concern about caste system nearly 2550 years ago. The condemnation of caste system and ending discrimination, was strongly raised in the Durban Conference before the representatives of the international community. The Dalit NGOs, social activists tried to make best use of the influence and goodwill of the Durban Conference, and tried to globalise the issue of raising their voice, through documents, papers and speeches and attracted the global concern on the beating of drums and dance together.

Asian Human Rights Commission in its statement said: "The World Conference against Racism, Racial Discrimination, Xenophobia and Related Intolerance (WCAR), held in Durban, South Africa has brought into sharp focus several extreme forms of discrimination. Among these is the issue of caste-more specifically, the issue of the Dalits or caste became a highly visible issue during the international debate on racial discrimination."

It became obvious during the conference that Indian diplomats, in their extreme activism to keep caste out of the final declaration of this world gathering and its work programme, not only brought the Indian government into high disrepute, but also brought down the moral standing of India before the eyes of the world. India also lost any possibility of claiming to be a world leader in the promotion and protection of human rights until it changes its public position on the caste issue. The international conscience, which is being awakened to one of the cruelest forms of discrimination after many centuries of neglect, is naturally questioning the Indian stand and is asking "What kind of nation is this?"

WCAR NGO Forum in its draft declaration in para 19 to 24 said that; (19) Caste is a historically entrenched form of discrimination based on descent and occupation that results in segregation of communities, including the stigmatisation of certain of these communities as 'untouchable,' allowing for flagrant violations of human rights and dignity of members of these communities, and making them, especially women, vulnerable to the most barbaric forms of violence. (20) Caste discrimination is a heinous crime against humanity which is based on a false ideological construction sanctioned by religion and culture which affects 260 million Dalits in South Asia, as well as others in the Asia Pacific and African regions at the personal, social and structural levels, irrespective of their religious affiliation. (21) 'Untouchability' is a manifestation of caste based discrimination that labels people as `polluted' or `impure', thereby denying them entry into places of religious worship, assigning them menial and degrading work such as cleaning toilets, skinning and disposal of dead animals, digging graves and sweeping. (22) Discriminatory practices based on caste-distinction, exclusion and restrictions deny Dalits, enjoyment of their economic, social, political, cultural and religious rights, exposing the victims to all forms of violence and manifests itself in the segregation of housing settlements and cemeteries, denial and access to common drinking water, restaurants, places of worship, tea stalls ('two- cup' system), restrictions on marriage and other insidious measures all of which inhibit their development as equals. (23) Caste discrimination and 'untouchability' practised against generations of Dalits for centuries together amounts to a massive and systemic generational genocide, resulting in the gradual destruction of their individual and collective identity, dignity and self-respect. (24) Any action or even any sign of an attempt to act by Dalits either individually or collectively assert their rights is met with extreme measures of violence such as burning or destruction of their homes, property and crops, social boycott, rape or gang rape of Dalit women and murder by dominant caste individuals or groups, police or the bureaucracy, and that in such instances the State often acts with impunity and in connivance with these perpetrators" (WCAR NGO Forum Draft Declaration, Part B, Draft Aug. 31, 2001).

Beating of Drums

It was a great day in the Dalit history when the delegation of 200 Dalits, wearing their badges and headstrapes with the words Cast away Caste and telling their histories, won the hearts of everyone. In their demonstrations, they sang: Down, Down, Casteism; Up, Up Humanism. Of their drums, an observer at a conference session said, 'It was the Dalits' drum that helped all victims here at Durban dance together.' These long-time sufferers of one of the worst forms of discrimination that humanity has known, stole the hearts of everyone and became the humanising factor at this conference, where a few powerful governments disgraced themselves by arrogantly walking away from the conference because they did not have their own way.

A little more should be said of the Dalits' drum, however. This was at one time called derogatorily the scavenger's drum. After days of working under the most savage conditions, these people, the poorest people of India used to create a short spell of humanity in their own ghetto by dancing to the tune of their drums. The drum, therefore, was the sound of the ghetto and the sound of people who were silenced through the cruelest of punishments and religious sanctions. This drum now has become the symbol of pride of a newly awakened people who proudly sing, We are Dalits! we are Dalits!

From Durban, Davinder Kumar reported: "Perhaps only a handful of the 240 million Dalits back home know they are the subject of a passionate debate thousands of miles away in the coastal city of Durban. Even fewer would know about the 250 activists dancing and beating drums for their cause. And, in all likelihood, none would know that the World Conference

Against Racism (WCAR) comprises mostly foreigners with little experience of India's grim realities."

Yet, all the song and dance and the relentless propaganda came a cropper, unable as Dalits activists were to secure the inclusion of caste as a form of racism at the United Nations Conference here. Their failure was in stark contrast to the euphoria the Dalit campaign had generated in the four days of the NGO forum preceding the Conference.

Till then, the Dalit campaign, spearheaded by the National Campaign on Dalit Human Rights (NCDHR) had raced ahead of almost every single group, barring those representing the Israelis and the Palestinians, in the feverish jostling for space and spotlight at the world forum. Generously distributing head bands that screamed Dalit rights are human rights and wearing black jackets asking people to cast out caste, their cultural troupe had the audience swinging to their drum beats and dancing steps.

But the fizz from the campaign went out after UN Secretary-General Kofi Annan snubbed the agitating Dalits at the NGO forum plenary, refusing to respond to the Republican Party of India leader statement instead of asking to question which was what all participants were supposed to do. One Gujarat, M.P. Pravin Rashtrapal said, 'Racism is rape'.

With enthusiastic activists dissipating their energy, the more serious task of lobbying for the Dalit cause was left to a battery of foreigners sympathetic to the cause. Among them were Rikke Nohrlind of the Denmark Church, Peter Prove of the Lutheran World Federation, Geneva, Tim Gill of the Asian Human Rights Commission and Walter Hahn of Bread for the World a Germany-based worldwide Christian citizen's movement.

The main purpose of bringing the caste based discrimination at WCAR was to highlight the Dalits human rights issue at the international forum.

Foreign delegates and the world media could be seen at the various fora discussing caste based discrimination in India.

And yet, despite the sympathy, the desired results eluded the Dalits, at the official level. That South Africa President Thabo Mbeki didn't mention caste in his inaugural speech at the NGO forum and Annan restricted discrimination to descent (and not work) are illustrative points.

The problem for Dalits began when Switzerland withdrew its support to Para 73 in the programme of action that talked about discrimination on the basis of work and descent and on which the Dalits had rested their case. Ironically, the Swiss had introduced this para. China also threw its weight behind the Indian government's stance that caste was an internal issue and outside the ambit of WCAR.

With such formidable support behind him, it wasn't surprising to find Minister of State for Foreign Affairs Omar Abdullah, who led the official Indian delegation, speak assertively at the WCAR plenary. Accepting that much needed to be done to eliminate caste discrimination from India, he went on to argue his government's case thus: "We are here to ensure that there is no state-sponsored, institutionalised discrimination against any individual citizen or groups of citizens. We are not here to engage in social engineering with member states."

Omar Abdullah, however, was criticised by writer Ruth Manorma who said that his understanding of caste is very poor. For the past 45 years the mechanism to safeguard the human rights of Dalits have performed abysmally. Now that the issue has been internationalised, we hope some countries will lay down terms for safeguarding the human rights of Dalits and provide resources to the Indian government.

Dalit activists felt it was the clout of the Indian government that derailed their campaign. "The Indian government put tremendous pressure to dissuade many countries from supporting us," says Paul Diwakar, an NCHDR member. "An international human rights mechanism is the only peaceful, democratic way to fight for the Dalit cause."

Ultimately, the Dalits failed at Durban because they lack

a powerful mass movement back home. In contrast, a handful of Israelis and Palestinians succeeded because they were backed by powerful mass movements. Beating drums at Durban is no achievement if we are silent on home grounds.'

Hidden Apartheid

Even before UN sponsored Durban Conference on Racism took place, Eric S. Margolis' wrote from New York (August 26, 2001) that both US and India besides several other nations of the world are trying to save themselves from being exposed on the problem of race and caste discrimination.

For decades, India loudly denounced discrimination against blacks in the US and South Africa. But hidden from the world's gaze, India, according to many human rights groups, continues to practice and condone the world's largest most pernicious system of institutionalized racism and discrimination, the caste system.

Of India's one billion people, 160 million are untouchables, or Dalit (meaning broken people). Untouchables are at the bottom of the Hindu caste system of segregation; light-skinned Brahmins at the top. In between are a myriad of castes and subcastes. Untouchables, India's poorest people are forced to perform society's most menial, degrading tasks.

Untouchables are barred from sections of villages inhabited by caste Hindu. A Wits unclean shadow must never fall upon that of a Brahmin, lest he he defiled. Dalits may not draw water from higher caste wells, nor touch food implements of their betters. They may not enter higher caste temples, nor own land. Their children sit in the back of classrooms or are simply denied schooling.

The ancient Hindu caste system dates back to 1500 BC when fair-skinned Aryan tribes invaded northern India. The newcomers conquered India's dark-skinned indigenous Dravidian inhabitants. Though occupation and rank originally determined caste, over centuries, caste came to be associated with skin colour. Even in overseas Indian communities, including Canada, caste still reigns. Marriage solicitations routinely request light-skinned boys or girls.

Fair-skinned Brahmins, 3.5% of the population, are India's ruling elite, holding 78% of judicial positions and half Parliament seats. In recent tests, Indian scientists discovered that high-caste Hindus, particularly Brahmins, are genetically closer to Europeans than they are to dark-skinned, Dravidian Indians. Caste became a rigid system whereby India's fair skinned ruling class kept lower and swarthier orders in their places as labourers, landless peasants, and servants exploiting them in the name of religion.

The Sikh religion and Islam both reject the Hindu caste system. Millions of low caste Indians found refuge from racial oppression as Sikhs, Muslims, and more recently, Christians. All three religions have been and remain subject to varying forms of persecution by India's Hindu majority.

Dalits are forced to clean public toilets and remove human faeces, usually with their hands. They sweep up after Indians defecate in the streets and move dead animals. According to an extensive report on caste by the respected Human Rights Watch, large numbers of Dalit women are routinely raped and forced to become sex slaves for Hindu priests and land owners. Of Indians estimated 40 million indentured labourers, a modern form of slavery, most are Dalit children, often sold into lifelong servitude by starving parents.

When Dalits try to defend themselves from abuse and exploitation, they are attacked by higher-caste gangs and local police. Their shanties are burnt and their women gang raped. Dalits, like Muslim Kashmiris, are frequently subjected to beatings, rape, torture and arson by India's brutal police, says Human Rights Watch. The recent case of India's famous Bandit Queen a Dalit woman who killed a score of higher caste men who had raped her, is but one dramatic example of the suffering inflicted by India's cruel caste system, which makes South Africa's former apartheid look benign by comparison.

Modern India's father, the great Mohandas Gandhi,

struggled against caste and called for liberation of Dalits. India outlawed discrimination against untouchables in the 1950s, and has enacted affirmative action programmes for Dalits in education, voting and government jobs. Nepal just followed suit this summer. India's President, a ceremonial post, was a Dalit, though most of its leaders, are high-caste.

But, unfortunately the voice of the Dalits was ignored at Durban and nothing fruitful came out officially. However, the world community for the first time was briefed by the NGOs and Dalit activists regarding the suffering of the caste discriminated Dalits.

Discrimination

At Durban while Government of India delegation tried to take the problem of the Dalits in a light mood, the Dalit and social activists from India were of the opinion that caste system is worst than slavery and discriminates. At every stage the Dalits are humiliated by the upper castes. From land to wealth, from service to status every thing is divided. India's 4000-5000 year old caste system, a pernicious practice discriminates nearly the one fourth of the total population may be around 25-30 crores. Nirmala George, Associated Press writer opines:

"The caste system was described in Hinduism's ancient sacred text, the Rig Veda, as a social order intended to maintain harmony in society. It divides people into four main castes, but there also are those outside the system, the `untouchables.' Who now call themselves `Dalits,' literally `broken people'. Though discrimination based on caste has been outlawed since India's constitution was adopted in 1950, the practice pervades society.

And while admitting efforts to end caste discrimination have not been implemented as rigorously as they should, the Indian government wants to keep the matter out of the international spotlight. The government sent an official delegation, including many Dalits, to the UN World Conference on Racism. But India also worked to keep caste discrimination off the conference agenda condemning "the caste system would equate casteism with racism, which makes India a racist country, which we are not", Omar Abdullah, India's Minister of State for Foreign Affairs, said in Durban.

Dipankar Gupta, a professor at Jawaharlal Nehru University, accused India of a double standard for not wanting caste to be discussed in Durban. He said:

"India is ready to discuss racism so long as it is in other countries, but not caste in its own backyard." Indian officials describe caste as an internal problem that can only be cured by implementing-and strengthening anti-discrimination laws.

Fight in Delhi

The Durban meet could not yield any fruitful results. However, for the first time Dalits, social activists, intellectuals and NGOs as well as non-Dalit supporters of the Dalit movement raised their voice and concern as well as grievances in an international forum. Rajindar Sachar says that it was not proper to fight against caste discrimination in Durban, but the battle should be fought in India.

He writes: "We have witnessed a series of seminars and consultations, not with a view to drawing up to programme how to eradicate discrimination against Dalits but whether caste be included as an item of agenda of discussion at the Conference against Racism, Racial Discrimination, and Related Intolerance (WCAR) being held at Durban. I find this an exercise in futility."

'Judged by any measure it is not even arguable that the worst of discrimination and deprivation is the usual lot of Dalits. This shameful attitude of Hindu society towards Dalits made Swami Vivekanand cry out in anguish, 'India's doom was sealed the every day it invented the word mlechlia wand stopped from communion with other 0 Indian' forget not that the lower classes, the cobbler, the sweeper, are the flesh and blood, thy brothers.'

But not withstanding all this, the evil of casteism has the

vicious habit of persisting. Dr. Lohia was, therefore insistent that sustained efforts be made to put Dalits into positions of power and warned of the damage the caste system had done to India, and how she may rid herself of it. This pain was also reflected in 1982 in judgment of the Delhi High Court, which justifying that in the platter of allotment of land by the government, priority be given to Dalits, which said: "Our social system has had it must be remembered, to live down centuries of caste exploitation and sub-human existence to which this large chunk of our population, i.e. Harijans were condemned."

Annan snubbed the agitating Dalit activists that caste-based discrimination should be included in the programme for action and declaration at the inter-Government conference. "We have come here to listen to each other and not to believe in this way. Let us have a serious-dialogue." said Annan to the protesting Dalit activists. The Secretary-General further told a packed plenary of about 5,000 NGO delegates and media persons that Prakash Ambedkar's was a statement and not a question that he had to answer. "Let us listen to each other and respect each other," a visibly annoyed. Annan admonished the Dal it protesters. Also present was UN Human Rights Commissioner, Mary Robinson.

Their campaign, because of the size of the delegation and its aggressive media publicity, attracted tremendous media attention, second only to groups representing the conflicting interests of Palestinians and Israelis. But all their efforts seem to get aborted. In contrast a rather peaceful group of Roma Gypsies, who migrated from northwest India to the Balkans centuries back, have garnered support from all quarters including a mention from Annan.

NCDHR convenor Martin Macwan, however, expressed satisfaction over what the movement has achieved. "We have succeeded in making the Dalit issue very visible in this world forum. So far, people the world over had little knowledge about the caste system in India. Our sustained campaign has succeeded in correcting that besides garnering support from various quarters. We'll try our best for representation of Dalits in all forums at the inter-government conference." The campaign, essentially, has a six point programme including implementation of land reforms, comprehensive legislation to ensure proper wages to labourers in the unorganised sector, eradication of manual scavenging and rehabilitation of the segment involved in this work.

Dalits made themselves to be Heard

Angry Dalit protesters shouted from the roof top in Durban. They danced in streets on drum beating and tried to internationalize the whole issue of caste discrimination at the third UN World Conference Against Racism (WCAR). The Dalits made themselves heard, this was the rare achievement for them. But unfortunately this world meet on Racism and caste based discrimination or any other form displayed little eagerness of the power blocs to find common ground. The rich and the poor, the powerful nations and the emerging Afro-Asiatic countries were not successful to evolve any formula to solve their problem.

India's Official Stand

Addressing the plenary, Omar said India was committed to combating and eliminating discrimination in all manifestations, "We are firmly of the view that the issue of caste is not an appropriate subject for discussion at this conference," he said. "We are here to ensure that there is no state-sponsored, institutionalised discrimination against any individual citizen or groups of citizens. We are not here to engage in social engineering within member states. It is neither legitimate nor feasible nor practical for his world conference or, for that matter, even the UN to legislate, let alone police, individual behaviour in our societies." The minister said the battle had to be fought within the respective societies to change thoughts, processes and attitudes.

Prakash Karat in Peoples Democracy, writes: the first World

Conference against Racism was held in 1978. It had categorically rejected the idea of racial discrimination based on the biological idea of race. It had strongly condemned the institutionalised racism represented by apartheid system in South Africa. The second World Conference against Racism focussed more on the remedy to the prolonged history of racism and slavery. Most of the African and Asian countries demanded a formal apology for slavery as well as appropriate reparations to be put on the agenda of the Conference. The United States was dead against this proposal as it defined slavery and colonialism as 'a crime against humanity'. While the US opted out of the conference, the European Union decided to stay on and find some agreed formulation. After protracted negotiations, the declaration acknowledges and records the massive human sufferings and the tragic plight of millions of men, women and children 'as a result of slavery, slave trade, trans-Atlantic slave trade, apartheid, colonialism and genocide.' On the question of reparation, the strong opposition from European countries led to an unsatisfactory compromise; the Conference recognised the need for programmes for economic assistance to the Africa and do deal with the problem of debt relief and poverty reduction. Alongwith this was tagged 'the promotion of foreign direct investment and market access.'

One of the most sordid and inhuman aspects of colonialism was the practice of slavery by the capitalist powers of Europe and the USA. Millions of Africans were captured and sold off as slaves. The slave trade from Africa to the America and the use of slave labour to produce the wealth and accumulate capital is one of the worst episodes of the early period of the capitalist system. Prior to that was also the horrific genocide inflicted upon the indigenous peoples of America by the white colonisers.

Bhopal Document

In the New Millennium another serious concern to Dalit problem was expressed at Bhopal.

Around 250 Dalit intellectuals, historians, economists, bureaucrats and sociologists etc., from all over the country participated in the Dalit Agenda meet at Bhopal on 12-13 January, 2002 to discuss and adopt a 'Bhopal Declaration" to delineate Independence and voicing their aspirations for the future.

The Conference unanimously adopted 'Bhopal Declaration' declaring belief in the ideal of Social Democracy and endorsing the ideals of civil society enshrined in the Constitution of India. Recalling Dr. Ambedkar's contribution who had struggled for the emancipation of his marginalised people and the constitutional rights attained for them, it was felt that the Dalits even after 56 years of independence denied basic human rights and suffer all forms of discriminations and exclusion from the main stream of owning trade, industry and commerce.

Document X-Rayed: In this lengthy document history of the Dalits have been traced and certain model of growth suggested for overall social transformation in the name of the Dalits and the Tribals. Some of our observations are as follows: The socio-economic and cultural problems of tribals, specially of Madhya Pradesh have been highlighted though briefly in this Agenda. There is mention that this Dalit Millennium document edited by a Dalit with moral support of Chandan Mitra of National Herald, was presented to the President of India. But it is still doubtful what transformation of society it has brought so far or in any way influenced the nation's planners and technocrats, economists and the educationists.

Data Available: A lot of statistical data is already available in Government publications on the socio-economic conditions, educational and job percentage as well as various forms of atrocities, hardships etc. If X-rayed this Document has no special message to the crying and dying, rather a totally crushed and decayed society, which has been prepared in haste. Some of our Marathi Dalit intellectuals and poets waste energy in abusing and branding God as mother-fucker. Some fanatically oppose Gandhi as Bania and traitor, some so called inspirers and intellectuals enjoy political support and backing from Gandhians as well as RSS bosses to gain power. There is a long history of such compromises. The name of Baba Saheb is being misused by well known Dalit and non-Dalit leaders who are power hungry. There is decline in employment, as compared to the growth of education, in Government and public sector. Our people have no agricultural land and our ancestral employment and income generating cottage industries, arts and crafts have already been snatched away or ruined. They thus, have a bleak future. The unemployment will increase among educated Dalits in large proportions in future. We hope our economists and sociologists will present a real picture of the horrible situation faced by these unfortunate people, instead of providing international comparisons and equating India's Dalits with Afro-American social systems.

Affirmative Action Programme

In no way, Bhopal Declaration or any such other status papers are historic, unless a National Plan Agenda is drafted and debated.

There is demand at the highest level that India should learn from the affirmative action programme in America and the question of diversities should be taken into consideration by private sector and big business houses in the country. The employment in private sector still exists for all sections of society, without consideration of caste and creed factor. It is doubtful how and in what manner reservation can be made in private business houses and enterprises, which already employ skilled and unskilled workers of poorer and weaker sections in one way or the other. Thus it is the most misleading thinking.

When Poona Pact was signed the nations top business magnates promised to help the poorest untouchables as their brethren. America has every soft corner for African-Negro population. In America Negro problem is purely a racial question, which is not so acute these days as was a century ago. However, in India caste discrimination is still continuing and the Dalits facing all sorts of socio-economic problems.

Extending reservations in private sector constitutionally will lead to conflict. However the rich can take care of the poor, the privileged class can think of the unprivileged and ignored sector.

A national debate perhaps will be useful in this regard as how the masters can come to the help of the servile class. We are afraid politicians wish to bargain through this slogan.

Dipankar Gupta has written a well documented paper:

'Extending Reservations: what the President really meant in Times of India dated February 5, 2002 which refers to the Presidents' Republic Day message to the nation for an affirmative action plan. He says:

"The President in his Republic Day message to the nation said all the right things, he remarked that India should learn from the affirmative action programme in America and that, in doing so, the question of diversities should not be neglected by private business houses and enterprises in this country."

While some hotheaded activists might be encouraged to believe that the President was all for extending the existing system of reservations in this country to areas outside the public sector, K.R. Narayanan actually wanted to communicate a much deeper thought, and, in large measure, succeeded in doing so. By recalling the American experience with affirmative action, our President wanted us to re-consider our worn out ways of looking at the reservation policy in India. Given his quiet sagacity and intellectual acumen, he put across his views in a manner that would not offend and yet would stir people to think on the fundamentals of a policy that has been nearly unquestioned for over five decades.

Why did the President refer to America in this connection? There are many good reasons for this. By linking America and the issue of reservations to the private sector, the President was obviously prodding us to open our minds to other experiences. While both America and India have publicly debated how to integrate and promote the lives and fates of those who have been historically abused for centuries, the two countries came to quite different policy formulations. Unlike India, there is no constitutional sanction or Supreme Court ruling that allows for affirmative action in America. The affirmative action policy is largely an executive document that expresses a normative concern for grater representation, and on occasions even promises rewards to those organisations that demonstrate a fair sprinkling of colours in their ranks. In other words, there is no such thing as a quota for blacks in the affirmative action policy in America. But by recalling the way Americans handle the issue of diversity, the President is opening up the terms of debate on reservations in India. Politically we find it very difficult critically to engage ourselves in this terrain, for any dissenting voice on this subject is seen as anti-dalit or anti-reservation. It is because of this that we make unwarranted concessions to the reservation mentally leading to quite serious social and political distortions, as with the Mandal recommendations.

Interestingly, it is not the President alone who is keen on re-opening the debate, though no doubt his sermon counts a great deal. The recently held conference in Bhopal on 'Charting a new course for Dalits' (which was referred to by the President in his Republic Day broadcast) openly acknowledges that the consensus on reservations has broken down. Like the protagonists of the American affirmative action programme, the Bhopal Document also realises the inadequacies of a nothing but-reservation approach and, in this light, advocates the importance of not just compulsory schooling, but quality education for dalit children. It is quality again that counts and not the objective fact of enrolling in a school. In America too greater degree of attention is now being paid to improving school level education for blacks and other disadvantaged minorities. This, Americans believe, is the key to the success of the affirmative action programme."

The need of the hour in the light of the Delhi University

Millennium meet, the protests at Durban Racial Conference, Bhopal Declaration, Dalit President's Republic Day Sermon is that the Government should frame a time bound action plan and declare its national policy on the lives and fates of these historically abused people.

Mere sharing in governance by few individuals and leaders and swallowing government favours by certain communities will not change the socio-economic conditions of the marginalised sections of society.

Bibliography

Ambedkar, B.R.: *Writings and Speeches of Babasaheb Ambedkar*, Mumbai, 1990.

Anderson, J.D.: *Peoples of India*, Cambridge, 1931.

Bahadur, K.P..: *Caste, Tribe and Culture of India*, Ess & Ess Publications, New Delhi, 1977.

Berreman, G.D.: *Hindus of the Himalayas*. California University Press, Berkeley, 1964.

Bhattacharya, J.N.: *Hindu Castes and Sects*. Kolkata, 1896.

Blunt, E.A.H.: *Caste in Northern India*.

Briggs, G.W.: *The Chamars*. Kolkata, 1920,

Campbell, J.M.: *Gazetteer of the Bombay Presidency* (in 27 Vols.) Mumbai, 1877-1904.

Chandhreek, K.L.: *Social Justice and Political Safeguards for Depressed Classes*.

Cline, E.A.: *Memorandum on the Prevailing Castes*. Census, General Report and Appendices, Allahabad, 1867.

Cole, B.L.: *Census of India, 1931*, Rajputana-Agency Report and Tables. Meerut, 1932.

Croke, W.: *The Tribes and Castes*, Kolkata, 1896.

Dutt, N.K.: *Origin and Growth of Caste in India*.

Freeman, J.M.: *Occupational Changes in an Urbanising Hindu Village*, Man in India Series, 1947.

Forbes, James: *Oriental Memoirs-narrative of 17 years Residence in India* (in 4 Vols.). London, 1813.

Gandotra, S.R.: *Scheduled Castes in Delhi*, Census of India, Monograph Series, Delhi Publications, 1976.

Ghurye, G.S.: *Caste and Race in India*. Mumbai, 1962.

Gondal, Ram Partap: *Changes in Customs and Practices among some Lower Agricultural Communities*, 1948.

Hassan, S.S.: *The Castes and Tribes of H.E.H. the Nizam Dominion*, Mumbai, 1920.

Hastings, James: *Encyclopaedia of Religion and Ethics*, New York, 1909.

Hermanns, M.: *Hinduism and Culture*. Mumbai, 1957.

Hutton, J.H.: *Caste in India*. Mumbai, 1951.

Iyer. L.K.A.: *Lectures on Ethnography*.

Iyer. L. K. A.: *Mysore Tribes and Castes*.

Jagjivan Ram: *Caste Challenge in India*.

Jatava, D.R.: *Evolution of Indian Social Thought*.

Jiloha, R. C.: *The Native Indian*.

Juergensmeyer, Mark: *Religion as Social Vision – The Movement Against Untouchability in 20th Century Punjab*. University of California Press, Berkeley, 1982.

Katiyar, T.S.: *Social Life in Rajasthan*. Allahabad, 1964.

Kaul, H.K.: *Census of India, 1911, Report*. Lahore, 1912.

Kitts, E.J.: *A Compendium of the Castes and Tribes, Found in India*. Mumbai, 1885.

Latham, R.G.: *Descriptive Ethnology (Europe, Africa and India)*, London.

Macfarlane, E.W.E.: *Blood Groups among Balahis Weaver, Bhils, Korkus and Mundas with a Note on Pardhi and Aboriginal Blood Types*. Journal of the Royal Asiatic Society of Bengal, 1941.

Maclagan, E.D.: *Census of India. 1891. Report*, Kolkata, 1982.

Mahyavanshi: *A Successful Story of a Scheduled Caste*. Mittal Publications, Delhi, 1987.

Majumdar, D.N.: *Caste and Communication in an Indian Village*, 1958.

Majumdar, R.C.: *The History and Culture of the Indian People: The Vedic Age*. London, 1952.

Majumdar. R. C.: *Ancient India*.

Many, S. K: *Cultural Heritage of India*.

Mead, P.J. and Macgregor, G.L.: *Census of India*, Mumbai, 1912.

Nag, N.G.: *Family and Marriage, Eastern Anthropologist*, 1960.

Nath, Trilok: *Politics of Depressed Classes*. Deputy Publications, Delhi.

Nehru, Jawaharlal: *Discovery of India.*

Palmer, R.: *A Little Tour in India.* London, 1931.

Parmar, Y.A.: *A Successful Story of Upward Mobility.* Man in India Series. 1982.

Prabhu P. H.: *Hindu Social Organisation.*

Radha Krishnan, Dr. S.: *Hindu View of Life.*

Ram, Nandu: *Dalit Movements in India: A Macro-Sociological Analysis.* In Nation Building in India, Radiant Publishers, New Delhi, 1999.

Ram, Nandu: *The Mobile Scheduled Castes – Rise of a New Middle Class.* Hindustan Publishing Corporation, Delhi, 1988.

Randhawa, M.S.: *Farmers of India,* 1959.

Rapson, E.J.: *The Cambridge History of India.*

Risley, H.H.: *The People of India,* 1908

Rose. H.A.: *A Glossary of the Tribes and Castes,* Lahore, 1911.

Russell, R. V.: *The Tribes and Castes of the Central Provinces.*

Saberwal, Satish: *Mobile Men: Limits to Social Change.* Vikas Publishing House, New Delhi, 1976.

Sen, Biswajit: *Caste, Class and leadership in a Himalayan District.* In Tribal Situation in India, Indian Institute of Advanced Study, Shimla, 1972,

Shasmal, K.C.: *The Role of Forest in the Development of a Regional Culture.* Bulletin of the Cultural Research Institute.

Smart, Emile: *Caste in India.*

Thapar, Romila: *Ancient Indian History.*

Thurston, E.: *Castes and Tribes of Southern India,* 1909.

Usuda, Masayuki: *Pushed Towards the Partition,* In H. Kotani (ed.) Cast System, Manohar, New Delhi.

Vashistha, V.K.: *Struggle of the Chamar Peasents for the Removal of Social Disabilities in a Feudal Estate, in Social Inequality in India.* Jaipur, 1995.

Walter, Yust and Others (eds.): *Encyclopaedia Britanica,* London, 2000.

Wheeler. J.T.: *Ancient Hindu India.*

Williams, H. Smith: *The Historian's History of the World,* London. 1980.

Wilson, Dr.: *Indian Caste*.
Wilson. Dr.: *Rig Veda*.
Wilson, Rev. J.: *History of the Suppression of Infanticide in Western India*, Mumbai. 1855.
Wolpert, Stanley: *A New History of India*.

References

Cultural Research Institute, Kolkata, Report.
PUCL Bulletin, Nov. 2001.
Rig Veda.
Untouchability and the Depressed, Manohar.

INDEX

Abolition of Untouchability, 191
Aborigines, 48
 and Hindu disinterest, 184
Ad-Dharma, 303
Adi-Dravida Mahajan Sabha, 296
Agricultural Occupations (SCs), 211
 work phases, 212-13
Akbarnama and caste system, 65
Al-Beruni's accounts, 58
All India SC Federation, 190
 disobedience campaign, 190-191
All India Harijan League-Lahore, 303
Ambedkar
 -and Dalits, 6,192, 273
 -and caste system, 47, 49
 -books by, 153
 -in cabinet, 191
 -Views:
 -Chaturvarnya, 153-55
 -Shudras, 156-57
 -Caste system, 161
 -religion change, 192-93
American society discrimination, 8
Animal sacrifice, 181
Annie Besant, 135
Annihilation of Caste (Ambedkar),188
Anti-Brahmin feelings, 271
Antya/Antyaja/Antyavasin, 175-76
Artisans class (Shudra), 2
Aryans, 16
 -invaders, 39
Aranyakas, 24
Aurobindo criticism of Gandhi, 141
Avoidance types of SC, 199

Babar's period, 64
Bahishkrit Hitkarimi Sabha, 295-96
Bahujan Samaj Party, 8
Basavacharya, 72-73
Beef-eating and untouchability, 179
Beliefṣ (SCs), 226
Bhagat Amin Chand, 303
Bhakti
 -concept, 78
 -cult, 65, 78
 -cult poets, 5
 -movement, 4-5
Bhopal Declaration (2002), 362
Bhopal Documents, 362-63
Birth Rituals (SCs), 230
Bomb incident on Gandhi (Poona) 145-46
Brahmanas, 23-24
Brahmins, 41
Brahmin-non Brahmin rift, 270-71
Brahmasutra, 76

Broken men vs. settled tribes
- -(Ambedkar), 175
- -and Buddhists, 178

Buddha attack on untouchability, 21
Buddhist period castes in, 44
Buddhism and Shudras, 55
Buddhism vs. Hinduism hatred, 178
Budget (home) SCs, 218-19

Calicut address by Gandhi, 1934
127-29
Carrying of dead animals (Hindus)
- -refusal, 284, 286

Caste
- -definition, 32-34
- -history, 37
- -test, 34
- -theories, 35-36

Caste System, 1-2, 17
- -earliest reference, 19
- -Ambedkar, 161-63
- -features, 165-67
- -object, 170
- -idea of, 18

Caste Panchayat, 203, 205
- -duty, 206
- -head of, 205

Census Reports (1910) on untouchables
171
Chaitanya, 80
Chalcolithic People, 14
Chamars (occupation), 216
Chandalas, 30, 58, 87
Chandragupta caste during , 42
Chaturvarnya and Ambedkar's views
153 .
- -and caste system Ambedkar, 161

Chawda tank case, 274, 290
Chinese pilgrims accounts, 53
Churchill Winston on Democracy, 263
Civil Disobedience Movement, 131
- -Nehru's revolt, 148

Clashes (Aryan/Dravidian), 17
Class System, 47
Class and Caste, 41
Colonial Rule and untouchables, 5
Colour and caste system, 47
Communal Award,1932, 186
Common Wells and Tanks discrimination prevalent, 251-53
Community certificates issue of , 322
Conflicts related to SCs, 240
causes, 240
Conference on untouchables
resolution, 281-82
Congress leaders and Gandhi
142,149-50
Congress sessions, 150
- -and Gandhi break-up, 151

Cooperative society SC related conflicts
241
Conversions (Hindu to Islam), 61
Cow killing, 181-82
Criminal tribes, 48
Criticism of caste system Ambedkar
171
Current scenario status SCs, 243

Dalit
- -intellectuals, 349
- -reformers, 7
- -NGOs, 8

Dalits in Durban
- -drum protest, 352

Dalit Movement in North India, 302
Dasyus, 38
Death Rituals (SCs), 232-33
Debts (SCs), 217
Deities worshipped by SCs, 223-25
Democracy
- -and Dalits, 263
- -Churchill on, 263
- -Will Durant on, 262-63

-and SC contribution, 344
Depressed Class Association, 294
Development Programmes, 334
Devadasi System, 64
Devotion concept of, 77
Dharma Shastras, 26
Divorce (SC) reasons, 203
DNA (Dalit National Agenda), 265
Dravidians, 1,14-15
Dress (SCs), 216
Drum protest, 352
Durant Will on Democracy, 263
Dwaita Philosophy, 71

Earthquake Bihar(1934) and Gandhi's
Harijan tour, 138
Economic conditions SCs, 217-18, 222
Educational achievements, 311-12
-indicators, 313
-strategy, 315
Education system, 344-45
Elaya Perumal Committee, 236
Epic Age, 27
Evolution of religion, 75-76

Fake claims of being SC, 322
Family Budget SCs, 218-19
Fast for Harijan uplift (Gandhi)
131, 187
Festivals (SCs), 227-38
Feudal landlordism, 2
Food of untouchables, 178, 284

Gandhi
-and Dalits, 6
-and Swarajya, 93
-and Harijan, 88
-reforms, 88-92
-religion of, 93
-criticism of, 131
-on Hindus, 96-97
-murder, 271
-cult and Ambedkar, 189
-retirement declaration, 149
-/Nehru differences, 149
Gandhi's Constructive
Programme (Schools), 101-102
Ghazni Mahmud, 58
Ghori Muhammad, 55
Ghosts belief (SC), 226
Gita, 27
Government measures to end
untouchability, 236
Graded inequality, 49
Guilds, 31
Grihya Sutras, 25

Harijans and Gandhi, 86
Harijan Boards criterion conditions
114-15
Harijan Day, 118
-organisation, 118-20
Harijan Leaders post-independence
304
Harijan Sevak Sangh, 88,103-104,116
question and answers (Gandhi)
105-111
-Gandhi's remarks on, 112
-manning of, 117
Harijan tours by Gandhi, 1933
135,137-38
-outcome, 147
Hidden Apartheid US/India, 355
Hill untouchables, 304
Hindi vs. English Language tussle
(Gandhi on), 112
Hindu caste system
rejection of, 356
Hindu-non Hindu caste comparison,
171-72
Hindu Shastras and untouchables, 126
Hindu Social Order move against, 274
-direct action, 280
Hinduism rejection Ambedkar, 188-89

History of Castes, 43
Hiuen Tsang's accounts, 52
Hotel entry by SCs (scenario), 247-51
Human Rights Denial (Hindus), 49

Impurities amongst untouchables, 124
Indian National Congress role, 262
Individuals as reformers, 261
India's stand at WCAR, 360
Indo-Aryan society
  and shudras, 160
  -vs. modern Hindu society, 160
Inequality, 48
Institution of castes, 81
Inter-dependence (caste), 209
Inter-caste relations (SCs)
  issues, 240
Inter-caste dining / House entry, 254
Interview (bias in) JNU, 318
Islamic Period
  caste system in, 4
Islam and caste system, 57
Itsing's accounts, 53
Izhavas/Illavas (Kerala), 299

Jagjivan Ram, 17
  and Dalit movement, 303
Jail (Gandhi), 132-34
Jajmani System, 209-10
Jatakas reference to Hindu Society, 2
Jayprakash Narayan, 144
Jedhe, Keshavrao, 270
Jeeta System (servitude), 254
Joking relations in SC, 198-99
Jyotiba Phule Movement, 266

Kabir, 62, 79
Kabir Panthi's Family Budget, 268
Kala Ram Temple entry, 280
Kalpa Sutras, 25
Kamble, Shivram Janba reform movement, 272
Kanaka Das, 79
Kanshi Ram, 8
Karma Theory, 26
Kinship Relations SCs, 197
Kshatriyas
  during Buddhist period, 44
  -Ambedkar on, 160

Laundry (discrimination), 253
Legislations related to SCs
  conflicts, 240
Linguistic competence of Hindus, 58
Literacy among SCs, 238
Living conditions
  SCs, 220
Loans (SCs), 217

Madhavacharya and Dwaita Philosophy, 71
Madhavan Nair
  Gandhi on, 129-30
Madras Provincial Backward Classes League, 297
Mahabharata, 27
Mahar Community
  rights, 176
Mahar Political movement, 292
Mahar Vatan Abolition Act, 272
Mahad directive for Chawda tank, 275-76
Mahad Satyagraha, 292
Manusmriti Burning, 280
Manu and castes, 22, 39, 43, 49
Marriage (SC), 199-200
  types, 200-201
Marriage among castes, 39
Media in SC uplift, 348
Medieval period untouchables, 51
Megasthenes accounts, 42
Mira Behn, 144